Native North American Biography

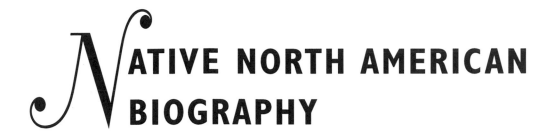

NATIVE NORTH AMERICAN BIOGRAPHY

Volume 2
J–Z

Edited by Sharon Malinowski
and Simon Glickman

U·X·L

An imprint of Gale Research,
An ITP Information/Reference Group Company

Changing the Way the World Learns

NEW YORK • LONDON • BONN • BOSTON • DETROIT
MADRID • MELBOURNE • MEXICO CITY • PARIS
SINGAPORE • TOKYO • TORONTO • WASHINGTON
ALBANY NY • BELMONT CA • CINCINNATI OH

NATIVE NORTH AMERICAN BIOGRAPHY

Sharon Malinowski and Simon Glickman, *Editors*

Staff

Sonia Benson, *U•X•L Developmental Editor*
Carol DeKane Nagel, *U•X•L Managing Editor*
Thomas L. Romig, *U•X•L Publisher*

Shanna P. Heilveil, *Production Associate*
Evi Seoud, *Assistant Production Manager*
Mary Beth Trimper, *Production Director*

Michelle DiMercurio, *Art Director*
Cynthia Baldwin, *Product Design Manager*

 ™ This book is printed on acid-free paper that meets the minimum requirements of American National Standard for Information Sciences—Permanence Paper for Printed Library Materials, ANSI Z39.48-1984.

ISBN 0-8103-9821-4 (Set)
ISBN 0-8103-9816-8 (Volume 1)
ISBN 0-8103-9817-6 (Volume 2)

Printed in the United States of America

I(T)P™   U•X•L is an imprint of Gale Research Inc.,
an International Thomson Publishing Company.
ITP logo is a trademark under license.

CONTENTS

CONTENTS

Volume 2: J-Z

ENTRIES BY
TRIBAL GROUPS/NATIONS

Abenaki
Alanis Obomsawin

Apache
Cochise (Chiricahua)
Geronimo (Bedonkohe Chiricahua)

Blackfeet
James Gladstone
Jamake Highwater

Cherokee
Louis W. Ballard
Elias Boudinot
Wilma Mankiller
John Rollin Ridge
Will Rogers
Sequoyah
Nancy Ward

Cheyenne
Ben Nighthorse Campbell (Northern)
Dull Knife (Northern)

Chippewa
Louise Erdrich
Pontiac

Choctaw
Phil Lucas

Comanche
LaDonna Harris
Quanah Parker
Sanapia

Cree
Harold Cardinal
Elijah Harper
Buffy Sainte-Marie

Creek
Mary Bosomworth
Chitto Harjo
Joy Harjo (Muscogee)
Will Sampson, Jr.

Dakota
Hank Adams
Charles A. Eastman (Santee)
John Trudell (Santee)
Rosebud Yellow Robe

Delaware
Delaware Prophet
Hanay Geiogamah

Dene
Ethel Blondin-Andrew

Duwamish
Seattle

Hopi
Frank C. Dukepoo
Ramona Sakiestewa

Huron
Deganawida

Inuit
William L. Hensley
Kenojuak
Peter Pitseolak

Kansa
Charles Curtis

Kiowa
Hanay Geiogamah
N. Scott Momaday

Kwakiutl
Mungo Martin

Lakota
Amos Bad Heart Bull (Oglala)
Black Elk (Oglala)
Mary Brave Bird
Crazy Horse (Oglala Brulé)
Tim Giago (Oglala)
Russell C. Means
Billy Mills (Oglala)
Leonard Peltier
Red Cloud (Oglala)
Sitting Bull (Hunkpapa)
Rosebud Yellow Robe (Brulé/Hunkpapa)

Lehmi
Sacagawea

Maidu
Frank Day

Menominee
Ada E. Deer

Métis
Tantoo Cardinal
Gabriel Dumont
Louis Riel

Micmac
Anna Mae Aquash

Modoc
Captain Jack
Michael Dorris

Mohawk
Joseph Brant
Molly Brant
Hiawatha
Emily Pauline Johnson
Robbie Robertson
Jay Silverheels
Kateri Tekakwitha

Nakota
Hank Adams (Assiniboine)
Gertrude Simmons Bonnin (Yankton)
Ella Cara Deloria (Yankton)
Vine Deloria, Jr. (Yankton)
Vine Deloria, Sr. (Yankton)

Navajo
Barboncito
Harrison Begay
Carl Nelson Gorman
R. C. Gorman
Manuelito
Peterson Zah

Nez Percé
Joseph

Nisqually
Billy Frank, Jr.

Numu (Northern Paiute)
Sarah Winnemucca
Wovoka

Ojibway (Ojibwa)
Dennis J. Banks (Anishinabe)
Clyde Bellecourt
Norval Morrisseau
Leonard Peltier

Omaha
Susan La Flesche Picotte

Oneida
Graham Greene

Onondoga
Hiawatha

Osage
Charles Curtis
Maria Tallchief

Ottawa
Pontiac

Pequot
William Apess

Pima
Ira Hayes

Powhatan-Renapé
Pocahontas
Powhatan

Pueblo
Paula Gunn Allen (Laguna)
Frank C. Dukepoo (Laguna)
Maria Martinez (Tewa/San Ildefonso)
Nora Naranjo-Morse (Tewa)
Leslie Marmon Silko (Laguna)

Quapaw
Louis W. Ballard

Salishan
Sherman Alexie
(Spokane/Coeur d'Alene)
Dan George (Squamish)
Seattle (Suquamish)

Sauk and Fox
Black Hawk
Jim Thorpe

Seminole
Betty Mae Tiger Jumper

Seneca
Handsome Lake
Ely S. Parker

Shawnee
Tecumseh

Shoshone
Sacagawea

Sioux
Paula Gunn Allen
Louis W. Ballard

Wampanoag
Massasoit
Squanto

Wanapam
Smohalla

Washo
Datsolalee

Yahi
Ishi

Yakima
David Sohappy, Sr.

READER'S GUIDE

Native North American Biography profiles 112 Native North Americans from the United States and Canada, both living and deceased, who are notable in their achievements in fields ranging from civil rights to sports, politics and tribal leadership to literature, entertainment to religion, science to military. The entries focus on the political, social, or historic environment in which these individuals have lived, as well as on their childhoods, family backgrounds, education, and the achievements and contributions for which they are known. A black-and-white portrait accompanies most entries, and a list of sources for further reading or research is provided at the end of each entry. Cross references to other profiles in these volumes are noted in bold letters within the text. The volumes are arranged alphabetically and conclude with an index listing all individuals by field of endeavor.

Related reference sources:

Native North American Almanac features a comprehensive range of historical and current information on the life and culture of the Native peoples of the United States and Canada. Organized into 24 subject chapters, including major culture areas, activism, and religion, the volumes contain more than two hundred black-and-white photographs and maps and a cumulative subject index.

Native North American Chronology explores significant social, political, economic, cultural, and educational milestones in the history of the Native peoples of the United States and Canada. Arranged by year and then by month and day where applicable, the chronology spans from prehistory to modern times and contains more than 70 illustrations and maps, extensive cross references, and a cumulative subject index.

Native North American Voices presents full or excerpted speeches, sermons, orations, poems, testimony, and other notable spoken works of Native Americans. Each entry is accompanied by an introduction and boxes explaining terms and events to which the speech refers. The volume contains pertinent black-and-white illustrations and a cumulative subject index.

Comments and Suggestions

We welcome your comments on *Native North American Biography* as well as your suggestions for people to be featured in future editions. Please write: Editors, *Native North American Biography,* U•X•L, 835 Penobscot Bldg., Detroit, Michigan 48226-4094; call toll-free: 1-800-877-4253; or fax: 313-961-6348.

PICTURE CREDITS

The photographs and illustrations appearing in *Native North American Biography* were received from the following sources:

Cover: Sitting Bull: **The Bettmann Archive;** Louise Erdrich: **Photograph by Michael Dorris;** Graham Greene: **© Barry King 1992/Gamma-Liaison.**

UPI/Bettman: pp. 1, 22, 35, 144, 150, 227, 246, 248, 251, 254, 277, 309, 321, 367, 372, 395; **Photograph by Tama Rothchild, Courtesy of Paula Gunn Allen:** p. 6; **The Granger Collection, New York:** pp. 19, 43, 62, 87, 131, 208, 236, 266, 284, 288, 296, 301, 304, 330, 340, 355, 360, 384, 388; **Mike Okoniewski/The Image Works:** p. 24; **AP/Wide World Photos:** pp. 26, 92, 112, 118, 156, 210, 239, 352, 378; **The Philbrook Museum of Art, Tulsa, OK:** pp. 32, 83; **Western Historical Manuscript Collection:** p. 39; **The Bettmann Archive:** pp. 45, 182, 231, 243, 270, 311, 315, 345, 358; **Bruguier Collection:** p. 49; **Archive Photos:** pp. 54, 74, 124; **Courtesy of Library of Congress:** pp. 58, 146, 264, 317, 333, 342, 364; **Reproduced by permission of Richard Erdoes:** pp. 67, 68; **Reuters/Bettmann:** p. 70; **Canapress Photo Service:** pp. 78, 176; **Photograph by Brian Willer, Toronto, Canada:** p. 80; **© M. Bernsau/The Image Works:** p. 89; **© 1994 Walter Bigbee:** pp. 100, 173, 178; **Photograph by Felix Farrar, Courtesy of Frank Dukepoo:** p. 121; **Courtesy of the Royal Ontario Museum:** p. 127; **Photograph by Michael Dorris:** p. 135; **Courtesy of Hanay Geiogamah:** p. 142; **Courtesy of R. C. Gorman Navajo Gallery, Taos, NM:** pp. 159, 160, 161; **© Barry King 1992/ Gamma-Liaison:** p. 163; **Courtesy of New York State Library:** p. 166; **Archives and Manuscripts Division of the Oklahoma Historical Society:** p. 168; **National Archives of Canada/Neg. No. C85125;** p. 204; **McCord Museum of Canadian History. All Rights Reserved:** pp. 213, 281, 282; **Reproduced by permission of West Baffin Eskimo Cooperative Ltd.:** p. 215; **Archives and Special Collections on Women in Medicine, Medical College of Pennsylvania:** p. 217; **Courtesy of Phil Lucas Productions, Inc.:** p. 222; **The *Toronto Star*/J. Goode:** p. 257; **Glenbow Archives, Calgary, Canada, NA-1039-1;** p. 258; **Photograph by Mary Fredenburgh, Courtesy of Nora Naranjo-Morse:** p. 260; **Photograph by Rafy, Courtesy of National Film Board of Canada:** p. 262; **Archive Photos/American Stock:** p. 294; **Glenbow Archives, Calgary, Canada:** p. 306; **© Copyright 1975. The Saul Zaentz Company. All Rights Reserved:** p. 325; **The Image Works:** p. 331; **Photograph by Robyn McDaniels:** p. 334.

Emily Pauline Johnson

Mohawk author and performer
Born March 10, 1861, Chiefswood,
Ontario, Canada
Died March 7, 1913, Vancouver,
British Columbia, Canada

Emily Pauline Johnson stressed the shared heritage of Canadians, while keeping Native culture and history a central theme.

Emily Pauline Johnson was the first Native Canadian (and the first Canadian author) to have her face and name on a postage stamp. She is remembered for her contributions to First Nations literature—as work by Native Canadians is called—and for her support of the works of Native women writers. Johnson descended from the well-known Brant and Johnson families of the Mohawk Nation. Her distant relative **Joseph Brant** (see entry), also known as Thayendanegea ("He Who Places Two Bets"), had been a firm ally of the British during the French and Indian War (a series of wars over colonial territory from 1689 to 1763) and the American Revolution (1775 to 1783). Joseph's sister, **Molly Brant** (also known as Degonwadonti; see entry), had married William Johnson, a British trader and superintendent of Indian affairs for the Crown. She became a diplomat and liaison for her people and the English Canadians.

Johnson was born March 10, 1861, in Chiefswood, Ontario, not far from Brantford and close to the Six Nations (Iroquois) Indian Reserve. Her father, Henry Martin Johnson (Onwanonsyshon), was a Mohawk chief whose full name is sometimes reported as George Martin Henry Johnson. Her mother was Emily S. Howells, an Englishwoman and an aunt of the American writer William Dean Howells. As a youngster, Johnson loved to read. She particularly enjoyed the classics of British literature, and, as was the custom for Victorian women of her day, she paid close attention to the Romantic (literary and artistic movement stressing nature, art, and imagination) writers of the nineteenth century as well as to English playwright and poet William Shakespeare. She tried her hand at writing early on, but doubted her own talent. Along with her shyness, this lack of confidence prevented her from revealing much of her early work to others. Educated at home until she was ready to enter Brantford College in her midteens, she also lacked experience reciting, or reading aloud, her creations in front of an audience.

Begins writing career

When Johnson entered college in her teens, she began to win praise from teachers for her poetry. She took drama classes and branched out into theatrical performance, appearing in plays and learning to develop a charisma (forceful presence) that captivated her listeners. In the mid-1870s, Johnson sent a single poem to the Brantford newspaper, hoping it might be published. Although she wanted a writing career, she had not as yet had any of her efforts reviewed for publication. With modest dreams, she mailed off the poem and was delighted to receive a very favorable review from the newspaper's edi-

Emily Pauline Johnson

tor. However, he suggested she set her sights higher, even for a first effort, and advised her to send it to poetry journals or a better-known magazine.

When magazines such as *Harper's Weekly* and the *Athenaeum* published her poems, Johnson was invigorated. Her confidence growing, she was determined to begin public readings in order to interpret her work for her audiences. Her local readings led to an invitation to present her poetry at a Canadian literature forum (formal discussion) in Toronto. The 1892 event was sponsored by the Young Liberals Club of Toronto, and the highlight of the evening was Johnson's reading of her poem "A Cry from an Indian Wife." The poem tells the story of the Northwest Rebellion, in which the Métis (a large Canadian culture group of mixed European and Indian descent) fought Canadian troops in order to secure their claims to land and self-government, but were defeated and displaced from their land in 1885. Johnson's reading of her work was enhanced by the visual impact of the traditional clothing she wore. The combination of Johnson's message—that Canada was still Indian land and had been taken unfairly—with the stunning drama of her recitation stole the show.

National sensation

Soon, Johnson was a national sensation. As word spread, eager audiences lined up for her full evening performances, and she tailored several new works for dramatic reading, the most popular of which was "The Song My Paddle Sings." Her performances focused on Native themes and political rights but were presented in the lilting style of Victorian recitation. Johnson's familiar form arose out of her love of British literature and the popular style of the day, making it understandable to most audiences. In 1885, however, just as her professional career blossomed, Johnson's beloved father died. To be closer to her newly famous daughter, Emily Howells Johnson moved into Brantford, and the two supported each other in their shared grief.

Songs of the Great Dominion, Johnson's first book-length collection, appeared in 1889. Soon she was on a poetry recital tour of Canada, and word of her talent spread to the United States and England. She was invited to London in 1894 and fulfilled her girlhood dream of meeting famous British authors. Wherever she went, Johnson's readings were well attended and her public praises grew. John Lane Publishers of London contracted to print her next poetry collection. *White Wampum* appeared in 1895, again to critical success. On the strength of the new volume, she returned to Canada for a triumphal tour, which included several U.S. cities.

Gains wide popularity with the public

Throughout the 1890s, Emily Pauline Johnson traveled and read her poems, wearing her now-famous Mohawk clothing. Saloons were popular sites for dramatic readings in Canada, and through them working-class Canadians and rural residents in the northern and western ports of the country were able to hear her poetry. By refusing to confine her tours to large halls in major cities or to places where only cultured intellectuals would go, she endeared herself to the common folk of Canada. Her 1903 volume, *Canadian Born,* was a reflection of this growing interest; Johnson stressed the shared heritage of Canadians, while keeping Native culture and history a central theme. Although she still loved having contact with her audiences, Johnson tired of the continual travel, and her health began to suffer.

Johnson later scaled back her touring to focus more on writing. She recorded the traditional stories she had collected from many First Nations in her years of travel. Settling far from her Mohawk homeland, she now made her home in Vancouver, where traditional tales of British Columbia Natives captured her heart. In 1911, she offered *Legends of Vancouver,* telling and interpreting tribal stories she had learned from Chief Joe Capilano. Collections of tribal stories formed the basis of much academic writing on Native people, but her clear, informed commentary aimed at a general reading audience was innovative. Many observers have since noted that the writing of fiction and nonfiction alike by Native women is "preservative"— that these writers preserve traditional stories and customs by weaving them into their narratives, creating a "printed museum."

Meanwhile, Johnson's fiction was developing new themes. She continued to write about Native characters, usually women, but she also began to include the experiences of white pioneer women (especially from the prairie provinces of Alberta, Saskatchewan, and Manitoba) and their similarity to Native women in their struggles to survive. She also began to focus more sharply on the difficult position of the Métis, the large mixed-blood segment of Canada's population. The Métis were often interpreters for both Indian and non-Indian interests, and Johnson saw her work as an author and performer as the natural outgrowth of this role. She dramatically explored the difficulty many Métis had in finding their identity in Canadian society. In this, she was an early explorer of what would become an important trend in modern Native writing—the theme of belonging to two cultures and not quite fitting in to either one.

Range of writing styles

While 1912's *Flint and Feather* was a collection of Johnson's then-familiar Indian-themed poetry, her 1913 prose work, *The Moccasin Maker,* introduced her new interests in pioneer women and the Métis. Critically acclaimed and widely popular, the work put Johnson in a ground-breaking position. Women were then generally believed to be incapable of writing long works of prose. That a Native woman could accomplish this feat was almost unthinkable to some. In fact, before Johnson's *The Moccasin Maker,* the only widely read fiction written by a Native woman had been the works of Sarah Callahan (a Creek author). Johnson's contemporary, the Okanogan writer Humishuma (also known as Chrystal Quintasket, or Mourning Dove), wrote a short novel, *Cogewea, the Half-Blood,* which sold more copies than Johnson's book. But Johnson is considered the more influential Native woman author because of her range of writing styles and the success of her poetic performances.

Johnson suffered from cancer for some time, and she lost the battle on March 7, 1913, just three days before her fifty-third birthday. She died in her home in Vancouver and was honored by her adopted hometown when she was buried in Stanley Park. Johnson's last book, *The Shagganappi,* was published after her death and her work continued to sell briskly for several years. *Legends of Vancouver* was reprinted in 1922, and a revised *Flint and Feather: The Complete Poems of Pauline Johnson* appeared in 1972.

Johnson has often been called the unofficial poet laureate of Canada. The country issued a commemorative five-cent postage stamp in 1961, coinciding with the hundredth anniversary of her birth. Its design shows Johnson in profile in Victorian clothes in the foreground; behind her there appears a traditionally clad woman with arms spread skyward in a dramatic gesture like those of her public performances.

Further Reading

American Indian Women: A Research Guide, edited by Gretchen M. Bataille and Kathleen Sands, New York: Garland Publishing, 1991.

Johnson, Emily Pauline, *Canadian Born,* Toronto: George N. Morang, 1903.

Johnson, Emily Pauline, *Flint and Feather,* Toronto: Musson Book Company, 1912.

Johnson, Emily Pauline, *Flint and Feather: The Complete Poems of Pauline Johnson,* Ontario: Don Mills, 1972.

Johnson, Emily Pauline, *The Legends of Vancouver,* 1911; reprinted, Toronto: McClelland and Stewart, 1922.

Johnson, Emily Pauline, *The Moccasin Maker,* Toronto: William Briggs, 1913.

Johnson, Emily Pauline, *The Shagganappi,* Toronto: William Briggs, 1913.

Johnson, Emily Pauline, *Songs of the Great Dominion,* 1889.

Johnson, Emily Pauline, *The White Wampum,* London: John Lane Publishers, 1895.

Native North American Almanac, edited by Duane Champagne, Detroit: Gale, 1994.

That's What She Said, edited by Rayna Green, Bloomington: Indiana University Press, 1984.

Joseph

Nez Percé tribal leader
Born c. 1840, Wallowa Valley,
    northeastern Oregon
Died September 21, 1904, Colville Reservation,
    Nespelem, Washington
Also known as Chief Joseph, Joseph the
    Younger, and Hin-mah-too-Yah-lat-kekt
    ("Thunder Rolling in the Mountains")

"Hear me, my chiefs, I am tired; my heart is sick and sad. From where the sun now stands, I will fight no more forever."

Chief Joseph was the leader the Nez Percé uprising of 1877, when the tribe arose in response to loss of their land through a fraudulent treaty agreement. The Nez Percé had tried for years to avoid conflict with the encroaching white settlers who were taking over their lands. Joseph, in particular, resisted war, and tried to use diplomacy to stop the invasion of his people's homelands. For many years, writers have depicted Chief Joseph as a fierce warrior who outwitted U.S. generals, a misconception created by the writings General O. O. Howard, his pursuer. Only recently have historians more clearly defined Joseph's role as that of an orator, diplomat, and statesman. An inspiration to his people, he remains a symbol of the tragedy suffered by nineteenth-century Native Americans.

Joseph was born in Wallowa Valley, Oregon, in about 1840. He was the son of Old Chief Joseph of the Wallowas, a half-Cayuga and half-Nez Percé who married a Nez Percé woman. Young Joseph had two brothers, one of whom died, and Ollokot (Frog), who became an accomplished hunter and warrior and the person in whom Joseph confided most. When he reached manhood, Joseph was very striking in appearance. About six feet in height, he was powerfully built, with strong features and a regal bearing. He married three times during his lifetime and fathered a set of twins.

The Nez Percé lived in the Wallowa Valley, a mountainous region on the boundaries of Idaho, Oregon, and Washington. Warfare had been a way of life for them and their neighboring tribes for centuries. They were traditional enemies of the Shoshone, Bannock, and Paiute tribes of the Great Basin region to their south and east. They were given the name of Nez Percé ("piercenose") by the French because some of the tribal members decorated their noses with shells or pendants. They herded animals, lived off wild plants, and fished for salmon in the mountain rivers. When the horse was introduced into their culture, they began hunting for buffalo and traveling farther for trade. They met white men for the first time when the famous explorers Lewis and Clark passed through their territory and befriended them. After this, the Nez Percé increased their contact with white settlers.

In the 1830s religious missionaries came to the Pacific Northwest region. Old Joseph was given a Christian wedding just before the birth of Joseph in 1840. A missionary named the baby Ephraim and gave him training as a Christian. But Joseph was also named Hin-mah-too-Yah-lat-kekt ("Thunder Rolling in the Mountains") and learned traditional tribal lore from his family.

Joseph

Discovery of gold

Joseph lived his early years in the quiet of the Wallowa and Imnaha valleys of northeastern Oregon. In 1860, however, the discovery of gold attracted thousands of adventurers into neighboring Idaho. Increased interest in the area among whites meant that Indians there began to lose their lands. A split in the tribe occurred in 1863 when those bands who had become Christians signed a treaty reducing Nez Percé lands by seven million acres. Since this agreement deprived many bands of their traditional homelands, they refused to sign. For this reason they became known as the nontreaty Nez Percé. In protest, Old Chief Joseph tore his copy of the treaty to shreds, destroyed his New Testament, and continued to oppose white settlement until his death in 1871.

Although it turned out that the Wallowa Valley had no gold in it, whites still wanted its grassy meadows. Finally, officials ordered the nontreaty bands to occupy unallotted lands—areas the government had not already parceled out to individual families—inside the boundaries of the reservation. If the nontreaty Indians did not obey this order, they said, force would be used against them. On May 14, 1877, General O. O. Howard gave the nontreaty Nez Percés 30 days to comply with the order.

On June 13, trouble began a few miles from the reservation border. Three young men decided to avenge earlier grievances with white settlers and led a two-day raid in which 21 whites were killed. The nontreaty bands were forced to flee. On June 17, 1877, Captain David Perry, two companies of the First Cavalry, and 12 civilian volunteers fought the Nez Percés in the Battle of White Bird Canyon. The whites suffered a resounding defeat, losing 33 soldiers. The Nez Percés, meanwhile, did not lose any warriors. In this battle and all those that followed, Joseph fought like any other warrior, leaving military strategy to others.

"I will fight no more forever"

During the next four months, the Nez Percés fled more than 1,000 miles over the Bitterroot Mountains, through what would become Yellowstone National Park, and across Montana. Of the 700 who began the journey, only 155 were able-bodied warriors. At Clearwater, Big Hole, and Canyon Creek, they fought troops with great success, only to suffer defeat at Bear Paw Mountain, just a few miles from Canada, where they could have taken refuge.

On October 5, after some of the Nez Percés escaped, the 414 who remained surrendered to General Nelson A. Miles. This marked the end of what the famous Civil War general William T. Sherman called one of the most extraordinary Indian wars in history. Joseph's poignant surrender speech ended with the oft-quoted lines, "Hear me, my chiefs, I am tired; my heart is sick and sad. From where the sun now stands, I will fight no more forever."

The Nez Percé prisoners were eventually sent to Indian Territory in present-day Oklahoma. In 1884, officials permitted Joseph and 150 of his band to live on Colville Reservation in Washington. The Nez Percé leader spent his remaining years there urging the young to pursue education and speaking out against gambling and alcohol abuse. The agency physician attributed his death on September 21, 1904, to a broken heart. An inspiration to his people, he remains a symbol of the tragedy suffered by nineteenth-century Native Americans.

Further Reading

Josephy, Alvin, *The Nez Percé Indians and the Opening of the Northwest,* New Haven, CT: Yale University Press, 1965.

McDermott, John D., *Forlorn Hope: The Battle of White Bird Canyon and the Beginning of the Nez Percé War,* Boise: Idaho State Historical Society, 1978.

McWhorter, Lucullus, *Hear Me My Chiefs!: Nez Percé History and Legend,* Caldwell Printers, 1952.

Native North American Almanac, edited by Duane Champagne, Detroit: Gale, 1994.

Betty Mae Tiger Jumper

Seminole nurse, tribal leader, journalist, and storyteller
Born 1923, Indiantown, Florida

Although her grandmother was opposed to the children's going to school or learning to read, Jumper found a comic book at a church and became determined to go to school.

B etty Mae Tiger Jumper is a woman of "firsts." She was the first Seminole woman to graduate from high school, the first to become a nurse, the first elected to the Seminole Tribal Council, and the first to lead it. As an administrator and storyteller, she has worked for much of her life to communicate and preserve Seminole cultural traditions.

Jumper was born in 1923 in Indiantown, a small village in the Florida Everglades. Her mother, Ada Tiger, was a full-blood Seminole woman who spoke little English and followed the "old ways"; her father was a white man. As Jumper related at a 1988 conference, "half-breed" children at that time were thrown into the Everglades immediately after birth. But her grandfather, a Baptist, would not allow angry relatives to kill either Betty Mae or her younger brother, Howard. The children grew up in very traditional surroundings, and their father's culture was not part of their early years.

Betty Mae Tiger Jumper

Determination to go to school

In order to keep cultural assimilation—or blending in—to a minimum, the Seminoles avoided contact with mainstream U.S. culture. When a land boom in southern Florida caused many whites to move to the area, the Seminoles (and the related Miccosukees) found it harder to remain isolated. Although her grandmother was opposed to the children's going to school or learning to read, Jumper found a comic book at a church and became determined to go to school.

She attended a day school operated near Indiantown (on the eastern shore of Lake Okeechobee) until it closed in 1936. She then convinced her family to let her and her brother, Howard, go to an Indian boarding school nearly 1,000 miles away in Cherokee, North Carolina. The youngsters found the colder, more seasonal climate of the Smoky Mountains a drastic change from that of the tropical Everglades, but their close friendship with the four other Seminoles at the school helped ease their homesickness. It was not long before the teachers at Cherokee saw how determined Jumper was to learn, and she made great strides in her years at the school. She and her cousin were the first Seminoles to graduate from high school.

After her graduation in 1945, Jumper moved to Oklahoma to study nursing at the Kiowa Indian Hospital. She finished a year-long course in public health nursing and then returned to Florida and married Moses Jumper, a friend from the Cherokee school. Howard Tiger also met his future spouse, a young Cherokee woman named Winifred, at the Cherokee school; they later married and moved to Florida to live with the Tiger family.

Like the well-known Navajo public-health worker Annie Dodge Wauneka, Jumper tirelessly used her nursing skills to eradicate disease and improve health on Indian reservations. Throughout the 1950s, she traveled to the reservations at Dania (in Hollywood, Florida), Big Cypress, and Brighton, speaking with tribal members in the Muskogee/Creek and Miccosukee/Hitchiti languages.

The Seminole Tribe of Florida was established by a document called a charter in 1957. At that time, the termination policy of the Bureau of Indian Affairs—by which the government took away Native groups' right of self-government and placed them under the jurisdiction of the states—threatened the Seminole tribe's status as a recognized Indian nation. The Seminole charter, however, was followed a couple of years later by the charter of the Miccosukee Tribe of Florida, Inc., establishing the tribe as a political entity. In their first formal tribal election, the Seminoles chose Jumper as one of their representatives. After her term expired in 1959, she became a member of the board of directors of the tribe. She remained a board member until 1963, helping direct the economic activities of the Seminoles.

Elected to lead Seminole Tribal Council

Throughout the 1960s, Jumper worked in tribal administration. Between 1963 and 1967, she held the position of secretary-treasurer and vice-chair. She made headlines throughout the Native American world in 1967, when she was elected chair of the tribe, the first Seminole woman so designated. She strove to improve social, educational, and housing conditions for the Seminoles, moving them toward economic self-sufficiency.

She also worked to incorporate the Seminole people into a regional network of tribes called the United Southeastern Tribes, now known as the United Southern and Eastern Tribes (USET), of which Jumper was a founding signatory (one who signs a document). In 1968 the leaders of the Seminoles, Cherokees, Choctaws, and several other federally recognized tribes signed the group's Declaration of Unity. For her work, Jumper was honored as one of the "Top Indian Women of 1970" and awarded an invitation to attend that year's national seminar for American Indian women. At about the same time, the Nixon administration recognized her with an appointment to the National Congress of Indian Opportunity.

Communications and folklife

After serving her people for nearly a decade in a political capacity, Jumper took another path after she left office in 1971. She assumed the post of director of operations for Seminole Communications, the publisher of the *Seminole Tribune,* a biweekly newspaper detailing local and national Indian news and serving as the Seminole nation's official publication. Jumper's work with the organization is only one of the ways in which she has served her people by using modern communication tools.

In 1980, the Seminole Print Shop published Jumper's history of Christianity among the Seminoles, . . . *and with the Wagon Came God's Word.* She frequently speaks at Indian church conferences, often working with a singing group that includes family members. Jumper also lectures widely on Seminole history and culture, tribal administration, Indian education, health care, and economic development.

Although she is known throughout the country, Jumper focuses her efforts in Florida. A regular at the Folklore and Folklife Festival in Brooksville each summer, she also appears at cultural events at colleges across the state, sometimes with her son, Moses Jumper, Jr. (one of her three children), who is himself a poet and author. In the early 1990s, Jumper and the Seminole tribe produced a video portraying several traditional stories, with Jumper in the role of the storyteller/title character "The Corn Woman," for whom the video is named.

Honors bestowed on Jumper in the 1990s have included a Woman of the Year award sponsored by the Jewish War Veterans of the U.S. Ladies Auxiliary of Florida and a Folklife Heritage Award from the Florida Department of State's Bureau of Florida Folklife Programs in May 1994. The *Seminole Tribune* noted that the latter award featured an inscription lauding Betty Mae Tiger Jumper's "outstanding contributions to the folklife of Florida, through her telling of Seminole traditional stories and her folk-cultural advocacy."

Further Reading

Jumper, Betty Mae Tiger, ... *and with the Wagon Came God's Word,* Hollywood, FL: Seminole Tribe of Florida Print Shop, 1980.

Native American Women, edited by Gretchen M. Bataille, New York: Garland Publishing, 1993.

Native North American Almanac, edited by Duane Champagne, Detroit: Gale, 1994.

Wickman, P. R., "State Awards Highest Folklife Honor to Tribune Editor, Tribal Leader, Betty Mae Jumper," *Seminole Tribune,* June 10, 1994, p. 1.

Kenojuak

Inuit artist
Born October 3, 1927, south Baffin Island, Northwest Territory

Kenojuak "is voicing the Inuit tradition in which making and decorating things is simply a part of daily life, and at the same time putting herself in the Western tradition of 'art for art's sake.'"—Charlotte Townsend Gault in Maclean's

Kenojuak (Ashevak) is generally regarded as Canada's foremost Inuit artist. Since her first print appeared in a 1959 collection, she has established an international reputation; her work has been featured in exhibitions throughout Canada, the United States, and Europe. Although most widely renowned for her prints, two of which have appeared on Canadian postage stamps, Kenojuak has worked in a variety of two- and three-dimensional media, including sewing, sculptures, copperplate engravings, paintings, and drawings. She was among the first group of Canadians to receive the prestigious Order of Canada Medal of Service, an award honoring achievement in all fields of Canadian life. Elected into the Royal Canadian Academy in 1974, Kenojuak has also been awarded numerous commissions, including the mural for the 1970 World's Fair.

On October 3, 1927, in south Baffin Island, Northwest Territory, Ushuakjuk, an Inuit hunter and fur trader, and his wife Seelaki named their newborn daughter Kenojuak, after the infant's deceased maternal grandfather. By participating in this Inuit naming tradition, the parents believed that all of the love and respect that had been given to the deceased during his lifetime would now be bestowed upon their daughter.

Although remembered by Kenojuak as a kind and benevolent man, her father caused conflict within the Ikerrasak camp and was murdered by its other members in 1933. After his death, Kenojuak went to live with her grandmother, Koweesa, who taught her the sewing skills that would resurface in her first works of art years later. While learning to repair sealskins being readied for trade at the Hudson's Bay Company, Kenojuak also devoted many of her childhood hours to chasing small birds, which would later serve as the subjects for many of her prints.

When Kenojuak was 19, her mother and stepfather, Takpaugni, arranged for her to marry Johnniebo, a local Inuit hunter. A spirited young woman, Kenojuak initially resisted the marriage, throwing rocks at her new husband whenever he approached her. In time, however, she came to regard him as a kind, gentle man, whom she loved a great deal. Years later, he developed his own artistic talents and sometimes collaborated with his wife on large projects. During the first few years of her marriage, Kenojuak gave birth to three children: two daughters, Jamasie and Mary, who died in childhood of food poisoning, and a son, Qiqituk, whom another family adopted at birth—a common Inuit custom.

In 1950, the first nurse arrived in the North, providing the Inuit people with their first access to modern medical care. After testing positive for tuberculosis, Kenojuak was sent to the Parc Savard Hospital in Quebec City, where she stayed from early 1952 to the summer of 1955, narrowly escaping death several times. While recovering, she learned to make dolls and do beadwork in the hospital crafts program; her work caught the attention of James Houston, an early promoter of Eskimo art.

Kenojuak

Launches career as an artist

Upon returning to her family, Kenojuak officially launched her career as an artist, selling her sealskin and beaded crafts through a program started by Houston's wife, Alma. She also began carving, selling her work primarily through the Hudson's Bay Company. At the encouragement of Houston, who provided her with supplies, she tried her hand at drawing. After destroy-

ing her first effort, she gained enough confidence in her abilities to show her drawings to the promoter, who praised her work and urged her to continue. In 1958 her first print, *Rabbit Eating Seaweed,* was produced from a design on one of her sealskin bags at a Cape Dorset print shop. Shortly thereafter, several of her original drawings were reproduced as prints, making her work accessible to a wider audience.

Encouraged by the income their art work might generate, Kenojuak and several other Inuit of Cape Dorset, under Houston's guidance, formed the West Baffin Eskimo Cooperative in 1959. The organization, in which the Inuit could purchase shares, served as a *senlavik*—"a place where one works"—for aspiring Inuit artists. Several of the early drawings, including a stencil by Kenojuak, were collected that same year and displayed in an exhibit in Stratford, Ontario. Viewing the Eskimo art for the first time, the southern audience responded favorably, providing the artists of West Baffin with an incentive to continue their work.

Fame spreads following documentary

By 1962, Kenojuak's art had gained enough recognition to be featured in a National Film Board production, *Eskimo Artist—Kenojuak,* which showed the artist at work and provided a detailed account of the printmaking process. The documentary, which took three months to film, also attempted to show Kenojuak and her family participating in the traditional ways of Eskimo life.

While the film-making process was tiresome and artificial, the money she earned from it enabled Johnniebo to purchase his own canoe and achieve his independence as a hunter. This was an added benefit to the family, which by this time had added a daughter, Aggeo, and an adopted son, Ashevak. Kenojuak's financial success, however, was not always admired within her own community. The fact that she was a woman in her early thirties earning significantly more money than anyone in the camp angered many of the men, but it did not prevent her from continuing her work.

As more of her prints were released to the public in subsequent Cape Dorset print collections, Kenojuak's fame spread throughout Canada. In 1967 she was honored with the Order of Canada Medal of Service from Governor General Roland Michener and had her work featured in the National Gallery of Canada. Three years later, her famous work *The Enchanted Owl* was reproduced on a six-cent Canadian postage stamp. Full-size printed versions of the work would sell for as much as $14,500 several years later, further demonstrating the strength of her reputation. With the help of Johnniebo, she painted a mural for the 1970 World's Fair in Osaka, Japan. By 1972, two years after her husband's death, she had been selected for membership in the Royal Canadian Academy and her work had been exhibited in several European countries, as well as throughout Canada and the United States.

Experiments go beyond traditional art

Despite her considerable fame, Kenojuak has never thought of herself exclusively as an artist, but rather has considered her artistic career to be only one facet of her life. "I don't put any aspects of my experience first as the main thing," she stated in Jean Blodgett's *Kenojuak,* a book-length study of her work. Kenojuak's unwillingness to view herself primarily as an artist is consistent with the traditional Inuit culture; living conditions demanded that men and women develop competence in a wide range of skills in order

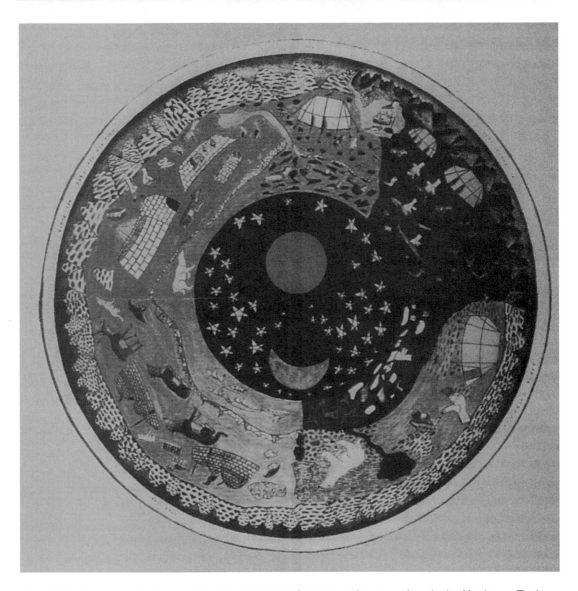

Kenojuak's stone lithograph, *Nunavut,* commemorates the proposed new province in the Northwest Territories. Nunavut ("Our Land" in Inukitut) will have an Inuit majority.

to survive. What is conventionally considered to be a work of art is valued by the Eskimo people primarily for its usefulness: as a ritual item, as a piece of clothing, or as a source of income. As Kenojuak told Blodgett, "The main reason why I create things is because of my children, my family."

While Kenojuak has placed her work within the Inuit tradition of functional art to some degree, she has also expressed the desire to simply create something beautiful. As she told Blodgett, "I try to make things which satisfy my eye, which satisfy my sense of form and color." Consequently, the subject matter of Kenojuak's work seldom reflects any mythological meaning or portrays scenes from Inuit life. She chooses her subjects instead for their inherent beauty and their adaptability to the print medium. As Charlotte Townsend Gault concluded in *Maclean's*, "She is voicing the Inuit tradition in which making and decorating things is simply a part of daily life, and at the same time putting herself in the Western tradition of 'art for art's sake.'"

With these two artistic approaches combined in her work, Kenojuak has created an original style that many have sought to duplicate. What has continued to set her work apart from her imitators, however, is her continual experimentation with form and color. While working within the familiar Inuit patterns of birds and animals, Kenojuak has developed unique systems of color by adding, superimposing, altering, and embellishing designs. According to critics, experimentation like this is what makes her work unique.

Although Kenojuak has achieved more financial success than any Inuit artist before her, she has remained firmly within the culture of the Inuit people. While she has replaced her traditional igloo with a modern frame house, she has not given up her love for the outdoors; she still travels with her third husband, Joanassie Igiu, and six children to some of her old campsite areas to hunt and fish during the summer, living off the land as she did as a child. While family obligations have limited the amount of time she devotes to her work, she has not given up drawing and carving. "I continue to do so primarily for the future these works of art will guarantee for my children," she noted in *Kenojuak*. "When I am dead, I am sure there will still be people discussing my art."

Further Reading

Blodgett, Jean, *Kenojuak*, Toronto: Firefly Books, 1985.

Gault, Charlotte Townsend, "Master of Decoration and Delight: Inuit Artist Kenojuak's One-Woman Show Has Been 20 Years Coming," *Maclean's*, April 20, 1981, p. 62.

Katz, Jane B., *This Song Remembers: Self-Portraits of Native Americans in the Arts*, Boston: Houghton Mifflin, 1980.

Native North American Almanac, edited by Duane Champagne, Detroit: Gale, 1994.

Susan La Flesche Picotte

Omaha physician and community leader
Born June 17, 1865
Died 1915

"I know that I shall be unpopular for a while with my people, because they will misconstrue my efforts, but this is nothing, just so I can help them for their own good."

S usan La Flesche Picotte was the first Native American woman to become a licensed physician. She served her community tirelessly in this capacity, and in others as well—as a missionary, as their representative in the East and in the nation's capital, and as a politically active supporter of temperance (moderate use or nonuse of alcohol). La Flesche Picotte was born June 17, 1865. She was the daughter of Joseph La Flesche (Insta Maza, or "Iron Eye"), who was half Omaha and half European and had become a chief of the Omahas in 1853. Her part-Iowa mother was Mary Gale (Hinnungsnun, or "One Woman"). Her half-brother, Francis La Flesche, was a noted ethnologist (a person who studies characteristics of groups of people) and interpreter.

Both La Flesche Picotte's parents worked closely with Presbyterian missionaries in the region. The Omaha tribe was considered by missionaries to be exemplary of what other tribes could become. The federal government had already begun allotment—or dividing up into individual farms—of Omaha tribal lands by the 1870s, a process that did not get started among many tribes until the next century, and conflicted with the traditional values of many Native peoples.

La Flesche Picotte grew up in a frame house on a plot of land owned by her father. Her family was Christian, influential, and respected and emphasized the importance of education. She attended Protestant missionary schools until she was 13, when she followed in the footsteps of her sister, Susette La Flesche Tibbles, and went off to the Elizabeth Institute, a finishing school for young women in New Jersey. In 1882 she returned to teach at a mission school on the reservation.

Education and the Connecticut Indian Association

In 1884 La Flesche Picotte enrolled at Hampton Normal and Agricultural Institute. Hampton had been founded with the goal of

Susan La Flesche Picotte

educating freed slaves but was experimenting at the time with Indian education as well. During her tenure at Hampton, she came into contact with the Connecticut Indian Association, which had been founded in Hartford in 1881 and was a branch of the nationwide Women's National Indian Association founded in Philadelphia in 1879. This group was one of many Protestant women's organizations of the late nineteenth century dedicated to improving the welfare and morality of Native Americans according to the standards and values of middle-class Protestants.

La Flesche Picotte's Presbyterian background provided her with the qualities that would make her an ideal representative of a "progressive" Indian—that is, one eager to embrace change for her people along European American lines. In 1886 she graduated from Hampton and gave a speech, reprinted in *Relations of Rescue,* which demonstrates the nature of her sense of mission: "From the outset the work of an Indian girl is plain before her.... We who are educated have to be pioneers of Indian civilization. We have to prepare our people to live in the white man's way, to use the white man's books, and to use his laws if you will only give them to us." She went on to underscore her religious beliefs, saying, "The shores of success can only be reached by crossing the bridge of faith."

The Connecticut Indian Association was interested in training "native missionaries" who would promote the development of Christian life-styles among their own people. La Flesche Picotte seemed a perfect candidate, so they agreed to fund her medical training at the Woman's Medical College at Philadelphia, Pennsylvania. She began study there in October 1886, a few months after finishing at Hampton. Throughout medical school she corresponded with her friend Sara Kinney, the president of the Connecticut Indian Association, assuring her that her professional goals were linked to her desire to return to Nebraska and help her people. When not busy studying, she demonstrated her interest in work with her community by speaking to church groups and visiting the Lincoln School for Indian children near Philadelphia. Yet despite these time-consuming activities, she graduated at the top of her class in 1889.

Soon after graduation La Flesche Picotte departed on a speaking tour to association branches in Connecticut, which added greatly to the group's membership rolls. Then she returned to Nebraska, as promised, and won a government appointment as physician for the Omaha Agency. Since she was the first Native American woman to become a physician, this was the first such post to be occupied by a Native American woman, and among the first to be filled by any Native American. In 1893 she resigned in order to care for her ailing mother.

Marriage and temperance

La Flesche Picotte herself was suffering from ill health at this time, too. The break from medical practice afforded her the time not only to convalesce and to care for her mother, but also to marry. She had promised her sponsors at the Connecticut Indian Association, who took an active interest in her personal life, that she would delay marriage until she had practiced medicine for a few years. She kept this promise and in 1894 wed a Yankton Sioux, Henry Picotte, who had gained popularity among the Omaha as a good storyteller.

Henry Picotte also had a reputation as a heavy drinker, which may be the reason her family opposed the marriage. The La Flesche family already had ties with the Picottes, because Henry's brother Charles had married Susan's sister Marguerite six years earlier. Susan and Henry Picotte settled at Bancroft, Nebraska, and had two sons, Caryl and Pierre. La Flesche Picotte found time for active involvement in the Presbyterian church at Bancroft.

Despite her marriage to a man who was fond of drinking, La Flesche Picotte herself was a teetotaler (nondrinker) and was developing a strong dedication to temperance. This probably caused some tension in her marriage, and it certainly created rifts between her and her tribe. Members of the Omaha tribe had been granted citizenship much earlier than other Indians (citizenship was not granted to all Indians until 1924), and citizenship included the right to buy alcohol—a right that previously had been restricted.

After the Omahas gained citizenship, there was no more government supervision of the sale of alcohol on the reservation and tribal police no longer enforced laws prohibiting use of alcohol. La Flesche Picotte viewed the increase in drinking on the reservation with concern. According to *Relations of Rescue,* in 1914 she looked back on this time and wrote, "Intemperance increased ... men, women, and children drank; men and women died from alcoholism, and little children were seen reeling on the streets of the town; drunken brawls in which men were killed occurred, and no person's life was considered safe." The drinking affected her in direct personal ways as well. She worried not only about her husband's drinking, but about her brother's. She became directly involved in the lives of women who were abused by drunken husbands.

La Flesche Picotte's vocal and active opposition to the sale and drinking of alcohol on the reservation caused controversy and was resented by other progressive, Indians educated by whites, who found her attitude condescending. They saw no reason Indians were less qualified than whites to

exercise the right to use alcohol. La Flesche Picotte considered such legalistic (law-related) arguments out of place in the midst of what she considered a dire social crisis.

She made the division between herself and members of her community even greater by supporting white politicians who, for reasons different from her own, supported prohibition of the sale of liquor to Indians. She boasted of her influence in the banning of alcohol sale in the newest reservation town of Walthill, Nebraska, by the Bureau of Indian Affairs, a federal office that was not much admired by most Indians. While many Omaha leaders were enraged by the brutal treatment of Indians arrested for drunkenness by white officials, she defended the arrests.

This kind of controversy was not new to Susan, as her father had also long been an advocate of temperance. In *Relations of Rescue,* she explained her feelings about the resentment held for her by many of her tribespeople: "I know that I shall be unpopular for a while with my people, because they will misconstrue my efforts, but this is nothing, just so I can help them for their own good."

Final years and new directions

After her husband died in 1905 of an illness that may have been related to alcoholism, La Flesche Picotte was appointed by the Presbyterian Board of Home Missions as missionary to the Omaha. In the years following, the anger members of her tribe felt toward her was overcome by her positive work on their behalf. One of her activities was to improve public health by pressing for modern health and cleanliness standards among the Omaha. In 1913 she realized a lifelong goal when a hospital for the Omaha opened at her new home in Walthill, Nebraska. But she served her tribespeople in other ways as well. In 1910 she headed a tribal delegation to Washington, D.C., to discuss issues of citizenship and competency—an unclear and often abused legal requirement for Indian citizenship—with the secretary of the interior.

In the years after her husband's death, La Flesche Picotte began to distrust the role of the government in supervising tribal life, a role she had not questioned before. Part of her change in attitude resulted from the difficulty she had in taking control of the inheritance left by her husband for their two sons. Government officials insisted that the inheritance should be controlled by a distant relative of Henry's who drank heavily, had only visited the children once, and lived in another state.

Only after submitting references from white friends did she gain the right to supervise the funds. This encounter with government bureaucracy angered her and fueled a major turnaround in the way she viewed the relationship between Indians and the Bureau of Indian Affairs. She had once likened her tribe to "little children, without father or mother." Now, she felt, "This condition of being treated as children we want to have nothing to do with ... the majority of the Omahas are as competent as the same number of white people."

Shortly before her death in 1915, La Flesche Picotte demonstrated her newfound distance from former white mentors (women like Sara Kinney and anthropologist Alice Cunningham Fletcher) by giving her support to a new Native American religious movement that worried Protestant missionaries: the peyote religion, a protemperance Christian group that later became known as the American Indian or Native American church.

Susan La Flesche Picotte became a great deal more than the first Native American woman physician. She was a symbol for many minority groups who sought greater control over their own affairs in the nineteenth century. She was a shining light not only for the Indian rights movement, but for the women's movement as well. She was ahead of her time as a Native American activist because she was among the earliest Indian leaders to look beyond the interests of her own tribe and address the broad issues facing Native Americans in general. She never failed to speak her mind in the face of criticism either from fellow tribespeople or from white supporters. Her courage, in concert with a physician's compassion, made her a unique and effective leader for her people.

Further Reading

Native American Women, edited by Gretchen M. Bataille, New York: Garland Publishing, 1993.

Pascoe, Peggy, *Relations of Rescue: The Search for Female Moral Authority in the American West, 1874-1939,* Oxford: Oxford University Press, 1990.

Phil Lucas

Choctaw film producer, director, writer, and actor
Born January 15, 1942, Phoenix, Arizona

"I clearly remember sitting, at the age of 12, in a darkened theater on a Saturday afternoon watching the larger than life images of the movie Stage Coach. *I suddenly found myself spontaneously cheering for the cavalry along with the rest of the audience. As the realization of what I was doing hit, I was devastated."*

Native American film producer, director, and writer Phil Lucas creates realistic images of his people to combat the stereotypes American movies have fostered for many years. Working mainly through documentary films, he has used his medium to bridge the gap in understanding between non-Indians and Indians, as well as to address other social problems of the contemporary world. Lucas has been tireless in his efforts to get Native messages out to movie and television audiences. He has formed his own movie production company, acted, written, directed, and found money to fund many Native American projects

Lucas was born in 1942 in Phoenix, Arizona, the son of Charles W. and Sally Lucas. His father was a Tennessee-born Choctaw and Crow Indian who had been sent across country by the government to attend Phoenix Indian School, where he eventually decided to make his home. He worked as the athletic equipment manager at Phoenix Community College.

Lucas grew up in Phoenix and attended North Phoenix High School. While he was in high school he formed a folk band, and he wrote and sang many of the songs the group played. Lucas spent a year at Phoenix Community College, but for seven years after that he traveled around the United States playing guitar and singing folk music. It was the early 1960s, and Lucas found himself at the center of a new social movement and meeting an exciting array of musicians and entertainers. But by 1963 Lucas realized his serious drinking problem was destroying him. He gave up both alcohol and his singing career and returned to Arizona in 1966 to attended Mesa Community College for a year. From there he went to Bellingham, Washington, to work on a bachelor of science degree in visual communication, which he completed in 1970 at Western Washington University. In addition to doing his own studies, he taught a class on the basics of black and white photography. His immediate goal was to work in advertising.

Since advancing to the account executive level at advertising agencies in the United States typically takes several years, after college Lucas decided to move to Honduras, where he opened an agency with friends. After a couple of years he found that he disliked the advertising business, and sold his interest in the agency. He began doing freelance photography while still in Central America and received an assignment on the Caribbean Coast of Nicaragua. There he became closely acquainted with some Misquito Indians, who helped him navigate the jungle to take pictures. While Lucas was in Nicaragua, the earthquake of 1972 hit, killing 10,000 people. Lucas was trapped for several hours in a collapsed building, and sur-

Phil Lucas

vived the chaos that followed without serious injury, but his experiences in Nicaragua changed his perspective.

When he returned home to Phoenix, Lucas decided to return to his first love: filmmaking. Although he had planned to take a more lucrative, mainstream job in film production, in January 1974 he began work at the United Indians of All Tribes Foundation in Seattle, Washington, where he created a media center, trained Native Americans in the fundamentals of movie-making, and began to create films. One of his first productions for the foundation, *An Act of Self Determination,* was funded by the Bureau of Indian Affairs (BIA) in 1974 to explain its policy. According to an interviewer for *Online* magazine, Lucas chose to work for the Indian foundation because "the tribal ties were stronger than Phil initially imagined. Growing up Indian, within a white culture, created feelings of always being on the outside, never really belonging. Phil's time in Nicaragua with the Mosquito Indians was a living example of the possibility of strong community and cultural ties. Money wasn't the issue on his job decision. The desire to *belong,* to be part of his tribe, and give something back was."

Shaping American thought

Since Europeans first came in contact with Indians, white people have recorded images of the Native people in America, first in drawings, then in paintings and photographs, and finally in moving pictures, beginning in 1894 with Thomas Edison's kinetoscope films. In accounts ranging from silent films to made-for-television movies, Indians were portrayed as either murderous savages or simple-minded, occasionally noble primitives. Although films were sometimes made on location at reservations around the country to give them authenticity (genuineness), white men typically wrote the scripts, directed the action, and even played the roles of the Indians. As a result, perceptions held by the writers, directors, and even actors determined what the American public saw on the screen and thus came to assume about Indians.

The films did not show the immense diversity that existed among the hundreds of different Native American cultures. Nor did they examine the moral conflict created by the invasion of the European culture, or the devastation that resulted when European Americans took land, split up families, and destroyed whole villages. A prime example of Hollywood's portrayal of Indians was the 1939 Oscar-winning western *Stage Coach,* starring John Wayne. In that film, **Geron-**

imo (see entry) supposedly has broken out of the reservation and is dashing across Arizona and New Mexico killing, raping, and burning anyone and anything in his path. When the stage coach on which Wayne is riding is attacked by the "savage Apaches," Wayne fends off the attack until the cavalry arrives to save the day.

"I clearly remember sitting, at the age of 12, in a darkened theater on a Saturday afternoon watching the larger than life images of the movie *Stage Coach*," Lucas wrote in an introduction to his "Images of Indians" film series. "I suddenly found myself spontaneously cheering for the cavalry along with the rest of the audience. As the realization of what I was doing hit, I was devastated." Lucas then realized that film had the power to influence and manipulate not only white people's thoughts, feelings, and opinions, but also Native Americans' ideas about themselves. He claimed that on that day, his idea for "Images of Indians" was born.

In 1979, Lucas began the long process of making his youthful idea into a reality. It resulted in a five-part series for the Public Broadcasting Service (PBS), which he wrote, coproduced, and codirected. The programs examined the distortions, misrepresentations, and stereotypes (oversimplified portrayals) of Indians that Hollywood filmmakers perpetuated in films and on television. It also questioned the impact those images have had on the self-esteem and self-image of Native Americans. In an interview with Catherine A. Clay, Lucas explained his primary goal as a filmmaker: "The underlying issue is how to get non-Indians to look at us as human beings ... even to get Indians, who often lack self-esteem, to see themselves as human beings." The "Images of Indians" series won a special achievement award for documentary film in 1980 from the American Indian Film Institute, and in 1981 won the Prix Italia Award.

Forms independent film production company

In 1980, Lucas decided it was time to strike out on his own, and he formed the Phil Lucas Production Company, of which he is president. He not only produced many of his early films, but also wrote and directed them. Much of his work reflects his desire to bridge the gap of understanding between the white world and Native Americans, while also dispelling derogatory myths. In 1989 he applied his multiple talents to the television program *Beyond Hunting and Fishing,* which documents the economic successes of British Columbian Indians. In the same year he produced a 15-part series, *Native Indians: Images of Reality,* for the Canadian Knowledge Network. That series and its 11-part sequel of the following year examine Indians' lives from an Indian perspective.

Broken Chain, which Lucas coproduced in 1993 for Turner Network Television, is a historical drama that looks at the relations of the Iroquois Confederacy (an alliance formed in about 1570 by the Seneca, Onondagan, Cayuga, Mohawk, and Oneida people) to the Americans and the British during the American Revolution. It features the Native American actors Wes Studi, Floyd Westerman, and **Graham Greene** (see entry), as well as the English actor Pierce Brosnan. Among other things, the film emphasizes the contributions the Iroquois Confederacy made to democracy and the influence the Constitution of the Five Nations had on the American Constitution.

Addresses social crises facing Indians

Although making films to help non-Indians better understand Native Americans has been part of his focus, Lucas also uses the medium to address other matters of concern to Indian communities. In 1985 and 1986, he produced, directed, and wrote a two-part documentary, *The Honor of All,* about the Alkali Lake band's successful rehabilitation from alcoholism, and how they combined modern treatment methods with traditional Native beliefs to achieve this goal. The film also aired on PBS and was selected in 1988 for an INPUT Award.

Lucas produced and directed *Lookin' Good* for the U.S. Department of Education in 1988; this two-part series discussed drug and alcohol prevention for junior high school students. The series was distributed to all the major public schools in the country and to schools at U.S. military bases. His 1990 documentary *I'm Not Afraid of Me* profiled a young mother and daughter infected with the acquired immunodeficiency syndrome (AIDS) virus, and he later made a music video featuring a song written by the mother. His 1992 film *Healing the Nation* focused on the efforts of the Nuu-Chan-Nulth Nation to end the sexual abuse cycle in families within their community.

A new form of storytelling

Storytelling is a respected tradition among Native Americans, and film has provided a new medium for passing along tribal lore to young people who may be more interested in Saturday morning cartoons than in elders' reminiscences about the past. Lucas, who does not see himself as a storyteller, nonetheless uses his skills to convey some vital Native American historical and moral lessons. In 1982, he wrote, directed, and produced *Nez Percé: Portrait of a People* for the National Park Service. Two years later, he wrote, directed, and produced *The Great Wolf and Little Mouse Sister* and *Walking with Grandfather* as pilot programs for PBS. Those two films won the 1984 award for best animated short subject from the American Indian Film Institute. *Walking with Grandfather,* which brought to life some traditional Native American children's stories, was expanded into a six-part series in 1988 and aired on PBS.

Lucas also wrote, directed, and produced for television *Voyage of Rediscovery,* which tells the story of a troubled British Columbian Indian youth whose family consents to his exile from his village for eight months by a judge. The boy is sent to an island, where he learns to survive in the traditional manner of his people. As a result of his experiences, the boy later helps revive the making of oceangoing canoes once used by the Native people of the West Coast.

Sometimes for fun or when in a bind, Lucas also has appeared in front of the camera. He has acted in roles in the CBS television series *Northern Exposure* twice, first as an accountant and then as an Indian. He also has been a technical and cultural content adviser for that acclaimed series, as well as for the action program *MacGyver.* In 1992, the actor scheduled to play an Iroquois sachem ("chief") in Lucas's movie *Broken Chain* became ill with a kidney infection shortly before filming began and was unable to work. Since producers are responsible overall for obtaining the actors, and the director and crew thought he fit the role, Lucas filled in as the sachem.

In 1995, Lucas finished filming a four-part series coproduced by PBS, ABC Television Australia, TV-New Zealand, and TV Ontario, called *Storytellers of the Pacific.* The series is about the native peoples of the Pacific Rim and how colonization of their homelands affected them.

Producers have the responsibility of finding the money to cover the costs of their productions. That has not been an easy task for Native American producers wanting to make films from Indians' point of view. It is especially difficult when the production is a documentary instead of a potential blockbuster drama or comedy. Lucas stays busy tracking down government agencies, tribal groups, and other organizations willing to invest the capital needed for his productions. He has succeeded in finding funds for the more than 60 films and television programs he has to his credit. His efforts at presenting a more realistic view of the diverse Native American population and their history have enlightened and won the respect of North American audiences.

Further Reading

"An American Portrait: Phil Lucas—Writer, Producer, Director," *Online,* publication of American Production Services, May, 1995, pp. 4-9.

Hirschfelder, Arlene, and Martha Kreipe de Montaño, *Native American Almanac,* New York: Prentice Hall, 1993.

Native North American Almanac, edited by Duane Champagne, Detroit: Gale, 1994.

Weatherford, Elizabeth, "Starting Fire with Gunpowder," *Film Comment,* May-June 1992, pp. 64-67.

Wilma Mankiller

Cherokee tribal leader
Born November 1945, Tahlequah, Oklahoma

"I wept tears that came from deep within the Cherokee part of me. They were tears from my history, from my tribe's past. They were Cherokee tears."

W ilma Pearl Mankiller was both the first woman deputy chief and the first woman principal chief of the Cherokee Nation of Oklahoma. She overcame many personal hardships and returned home to Mankiller Flats, Oklahoma, to establish herself as a political powerhouse working for the betterment of all people.

Mankiller was born at Tahlequah, the capitol of the Cherokee Nation, in November 1945, and lived at Mankiller Flats until she was ten years old. Her father, Charlie Mankiller, was a Cherokee, and her mother, Irene Mankiller, was of Dutch-Irish descent. Mankiller grew up with four sisters and six brothers.

Trail of Tears

Wilma Mankiller's story is profoundly interwoven with the history of the Cherokee. Once the Cherokee lived in Tennessee and across the South. By the early 1800s white settlers were pushing them out of their native lands. Some left willingly and established new bases in Arkansas, only to be moved later to Indian Territory (now Oklahoma). Some refused to leave and hid out in the forests of the South, later forming an Eastern Cherokee nation. In the 1830s two-thirds of the Cherokee Nation were finally rounded up and forced to travel, mostly by foot, on a march now called the Trail of Tears. Those who survived the difficult march were placed on a reservation in Indian Territory. Once there, they were again neglected or mistreated by the government and by white settlers. In Oklahoma, as in the Southeast, there were Cherokees who tried to adopt white ways. The result was a mix of some Indians who kept to Cherokee customs and others who joined economically and socially with whites. The confusion that resulted would greatly affect Mankiller's early life.

Mankiller's great-grandfather was one of the over 16,000 Cherokees, Choctaws, Creeks, Chickasaws, Seminoles, and African slaves who struggled along the Trail of Tears to Oklahoma. It was a journey filled with suffering and danger, and there was little comfort at its end. The government had adopted a policy of allotment, which worked against tribal bonds by changing the way Native American groups owned land. Granting plots of land to individual Indians, the government encouraged them to try the white way of personal landownership. Mankiller's grandfather was allotted 160 acres in eastern Oklahoma, at a place called Mankiller Flats. This land eventually became the homestead of Charlie Mankiller, Wilma's father, who eked out a living as a subsistence farmer.

The Mankillers were very poor in Oklahoma, but generally happy. The land was not rich, but it was pleasant. Charlie and Irene were devoted to each other and to their children, and evenings were spent telling stories

of Cherokee history. Wilma attended Rocky Mountain Elementary School and there, for the first time, she confronted hostility from white people.

In the 1950s Congress decided it would be better if Native Americans were not concentrated into one area, and began to encourage—with offers of help—individuals and families to relocate to cities around the country, where they would be forced to adopt white ways. At this time, especially due to a recent drought, Mankiller's father found it difficult to maintain his family with any semblance of dignity in Oklahoma. Although they did not want to move to California, Charlie Mankiller thought he could make a better life for them there and accepted a government offer to relocate. But promises faltered, money did not arrive, and there was often no employment available, so their life did not improve after their arrival in San Francisco.

The children were homesick even before they started for California. As Mankiller recalled in her autobiography, "I experienced my own Trail of Tears when I was a young girl. No one pointed a gun at me or at members of my family. No show of force was used. It was not necessary. Nevertheless, the United States government through the Bureau of Indian Affairs, was again trying to settle the 'Indian problem' by removal. I learned through this ordeal about the fear and anguish that occur when you give up your home, your community, and everything you have ever known to move far away to a strange place. I cried for days, not unlike the children who had stumbled down the Trail of Tears so many years before. I wept tears that came from deep within the

Cherokee part of me. They were tears from my history, from my tribe's past. They were Cherokee tears."

In California, cringing at the laughter that always followed the school roll call when the teacher said "Mankiller," she finished high school. Her family began to spend hours at the San Francisco Indian Center and their frequent moves brought Wilma into frequent contact with people of different ethnic backgrounds. Mankiller's father became a longshoreman, and soon was busy as a union organizer and a social activist. Wilma Mankiller went on to pursue a higher education. In the 1960s she attended Skyline Junior College in San Bruno, then San Francisco State College. At San Francisco State she met and married Hector Hugo Olaya de Bardi. Their first daughter, Felicia, was born in 1964 and their second, Gina, two years later. In college, Mankiller was introduced to some of the Native American activists who would soon occupy and reclaim Alcatraz Island for the Native American people.

Alcatraz occupation fuels political awakening

The "invasion" of Alcatraz—the former site of a maximum-security prison—by Native Americans quickly became a focal point for many Native people, Mankiller included. The point of the action was to protest conditions on Indian reservations. The occupiers "claimed" Alcatraz, using the 1868 Treaty of Fort Laramie which held that if land acquired from the Indians was not in use, its ownership reverted, or went back, to them. After small activist groups were removed twice from the island, 89 Indians moved in with food, water, and sleeping bags. Man-

Wilma Mankiller

killer's brothers and sisters joined in the occupation and stayed on the island, but because she had young children, Mankiller stayed at home to raise money for supplies for the occupiers. Stirred by the bold move onto Alcatraz by San Francisco State student Mohawk Richard Oakes, along with his "All Tribes" group, Mankiller realized that her mission in life was to serve her people.

She yearned for independence, something that caused a conflict with her marriage. "Once I began to become more independent, more active with school and in the community, it became increasingly difficult to keep my marriage together. Before that, Hugo had viewed me as someone he had rescued from a very bad life," she noted in her autobiography. Hugo also was conservative politically, while Mankiller was becoming more active in civil rights and antiwar issues. In 1974 the couple divorced, and Mankiller became a single head of the household. She took her daughters to Oklahoma, got a job with the Cherokee Nation writing proposals for grants to improve Cherokee life, and built a house on the old Mankiller land.

Endures personal tragedies and health problems

In 1960, Mankiller's brother Bob was badly burned in a fire. Not wanting to be an added burden to the survival of the family, he had traveled north to pick apples in Washington State. In the chill of early morning, he mistakenly started a fire with gasoline instead of kerosene, and his wooden shack exploded in flames. Bob survived for only six days. He had been Mankiller's role model for a "care free" spirit.

In 1971, Mankiller's father died from a kidney disease in San Francisco. His passing, she recalled in her autobiography, "tore through my spirit like a blade of lightning." The family took Charlie Mankiller home to Oklahoma for burial, then Mankiller returned to California. It was not long before she too had kidney problems, inherited from her father. Her early kidney problems could be treated, though later she had to have surgery and eventually, in 1990, needed a transplant. Her brother Donald became her "hero" by donating one of his kidneys so that she could live.

In 1976, after Mankiller had returned to Oklahoma for good, she found time to pursue higher education. She enrolled in graduate courses at the University of Arkansas, Fayetteville, which required her to drive a great distance every day. She was returning home one morning when an automobile approached her on a blind curve and, from seemingly nowhere, another automobile attempted to pass it. She swerved to miss the approaching automobile, but failed. The vehicles collided.

Mankiller was seriously injured, and many thought she would not survive. The driver of the other automobile did not. It turned out to be Sherry Morris, Mankiller's best friend. It was terribly difficult, both physically and emotionally, but Mankiller recovered. Shortly after this accident, she came down with myasthenia gravis, a muscle disease. Again her life was threatened, but her will to live and her determination to mend her body with the power of her mind prevailed.

Rebuilding

When she recovered from the auto accident, Mankiller returned to her job with the Cherokee Nation. In 1981 she developed a proposal to help the small community of Bell, Oklahoma. It was to be a model that other communities could follow as they rebuilt Cherokee settlements. Mankiller had become convinced that Native Americans should become independent and self-reliant.

Mankiller secured the money to rebuild or repair several of the houses in the small community and to supply these houses with a reliable water source. She directed the rebuilding and the construction of pipeline to bring in water. The nearest steady source of water was 16 miles away, and yet the men, women, and children of the tiny village of Bell managed to lay the 16 miles of pipe. Completing this task in 1981, Mankiller gained a reputation for effectiveness among the Cherokee. Chief Ross Swimmer, the elected head of the Cherokee Nation, was impressed by her work.

Becomes Principal Chief of the Cherokee Nation

In 1983 Ross Swimmer asked Mankiller to be his Deputy Chief in the election, and she accepted. They won the election and took office on August 14, 1983. On December 5, 1985, Swimmer was nominated to head the Bureau of Indian Affairs in Washington, D.C., and Mankiller was sworn in as Principal Chief. She was reelected in 1987 and again in 1991 by her people.

During the Bell community project, Mankiller had worked with a quiet but powerful Cherokee named Charlie Soap. The two found that they had many common interests, and their friendship grew. In 1986 they married, and Charlie Soap became a major advisor and supporter of Chief Mankiller.

As Principal Chief, Mankiller planned immediately to involve the Cherokee people in their own community improvements. She carried on Swimmer's policy of developing industries and served as head of a corporation that included a motel, an electronics manufacturing plant, and a bank. She raised $20 million for new construction in Cherokee communities and $8 million to found a Cherokee job training center. There are now schools for Cherokee children that teach the Cherokee language and customs, knowledge that Mankiller believes builds pride among the people.

One of Mankiller's great achievements was her 1987 effort to reunite the Cherokee Nation. The small group of Cherokee who had hidden from authorities in 1830 eventually settled on a reservation in Tennessee. They were the Eastern Cherokee, and Eastern and Western Cherokee had remained divided through the years. In 1987 Mankiller called and presided over a conference of all Cherokee, taking a first step toward reuniting the whole Cherokee Nation.

Power is returning to the Western Cherokee people, who number more than 175,000. Mankiller has proved an inspirational leader who empowers people to independence. The key to Cherokee success, says Mankiller, is that the Cherokee never give up.

Further Reading

Mankiller, Wilma, and Michael Wallis, *Mankiller: A Chief and Her People,* New York: St. Martin's Press, 1993.

Native North American Almanac, edited by Duane Champagne, Detroit: Gale, 1993.

Waldman, Carl, *Atlas of the North American Indian,* New York: Facts on File, 1985.

Manuelito

Navajo tribal leader
Born c. 1818, southeastern Utah
Died 1894
Also known as Hastin Ch'ilhajinii/Childhajin
("The Man of the Black Weeds"),
Hashkeh Naabah ("The Angry Warrior"),
Little Manuel, and Pistol Bullet

"My God and my mother live in the West, and I will not leave them. It is a tradition of my people that we must never cross the three rivers—the Grande, the San Juan, the Colorado. Nor could I leave the Chuska Mountains. I was born there. I shall remain. I have nothing to lose but my life, and that they can come and take whenever they please, but I will not move. I have never done any wrong to the Americans or the Mexicans. I have never robbed. If I am killed, innocent blood will be shed."

Manuelito was a tribal leader who led his warriors in the Navajo wars of 1863 to 1866. He and his followers were the last to surrender after a scorched-earth campaign (the burning of lands and villages to make homelands uninhabitable) by U.S. Colonel Kit Carson that was intended to force the Navajo to relocate to a reservation. As a tribal leader, Manuelito was a source of support and encouragement for his people during their days in confinement. He pleaded with the government to return the Navajo to their homeland, and he led them back from exile in 1868. There he was selected to be the head of tribal police. In his later years he advocated education, hoping to improve the Navajo condition of life in the changing world.

Manuelito was born a member of the To'Tsohnii ("Big Water") clan in 1818, in southeastern Utah, probably near Bears' Ear Peak. He was a powerful warrior who rose to prominence among his people during years of attacks and raids against Mexicans, U.S. Army troops, and neighboring Indian tribes. In 1855, he became headman of his tribe, succeeding Zarcillas Largas ("Long Earrings") who resigned because of his inability to control his warriors. Manuelito had two wives; the first was the daughter of Narbona, the great Navajo leader, and the second a Mexican woman named Juana.

The Navajo lived in the southwest, in what are now the states of Utah, Colorado, Arizona, and New Mexico. Their territory was bordered by four mountains, which they considered sacred. They believed they could only be happy if they stayed within the confines of those boundaries. They called themselves Dineh or Diné, which means "the people." ("Navajo" was a name given to them by the Spanish.) They survived by raising sheep, hunting wild game, growing wheat, corn, melons, and peaches, and gathering wild piñon nuts and berries.

Navajo territory had been claimed by many nations, including the Spanish, the Mexicans, and the Americans, for many years. Under the Treaty of Guadalupe Hidalgo—which was signed in 1848, marking the end of the Mexican-American War—Mexico handed over to the United States the present-day states of Texas, New Mexico, Arizona, Colorado, Utah, Nevada, and California. All Mexicans who were living in that

Manuelito

region became U.S. citizens automatically, but the Indians did not. The U.S. Government considered itself responsible for the protection of its citizens in the territory from the Indians and instructed the Navajos to stop all raids against Americans and Mexicans.

The government moves in

In 1855, Fort Defiance was built in Canyon de Chelly, in the heart of Navajo country. The same year the Navajos signed a treaty decreasing the size of their territory to 7,000 square miles, of which only 125 square miles were suitable for cultivation. The Navajo leaders found it too difficult to keep their people from raiding neighboring Indian or American settlements, and clashes between the Indians and the settlers continued.

In 1858, the pasture land around Fort Defiance became a point of contention when the new post commander, Major William T. H. Brooks, decided that he wanted to use the land as grazing ground for the army's horses. Brooks ordered Manuelito to move his livestock or they would be killed. Manuelito, whose father and grandfather before him had used the land to graze their livestock, refused to give it up. Under Brooks' orders, the army shot and killed 60 of Manuelito's horses and over 100 of his sheep.

The Navajos were outraged by the slaughter of their leader's livestock and retaliated by killing a slave who belonged to Major Brooks. Brooks ordered the killer to be found and turned in, and the army began to harass the Indians. Manuelito attempted to settle the matter, but assaults against the Navajos continued. After several weeks of fighting, the Navajo chiefs went to the fort to sign a peace treaty promising to remain on their land.

In 1860, many of the troops began to leave the fort to join the Civil War. With the strength of the army decreased, the Indians saw an opportunity to attack the fort and run the intruders out of their country. The headmen held a council to discuss their plans. Navajo leaders Manuelito, **Barboncito,** and Herrero Grande were in favor of the attack. Ganado Mucho, another headman, opposed the plan. The Navajos invited other tribes of the region, including the Utes, Apaches, and Pueblos, to join them in war.

On April 30, 1860, between one and two thousand warriors stormed the fort. But the army had been warned of the impending attack and had cannons and guns ready when the Indians arrived. The warriors made an impressive show against the well-armed troops, but were driven back. Many warriors were killed, and the rest retreated to their stronghold in the Chuska Mountain canyons. Colonel Edward R. S. Canby pursued them, but the Indians eluded him in the many hiding places of Canyon de Chelly.

The government stepped up its efforts to control the rebelling Indians. On June 23, 1863, General James H. Carleton sent a message from Fort Wingate to the Navajo headmen, demanding that they turn themselves in by July 20 or face the possibility of war if they did not. Carleton wanted to convince the Navajo that they could no longer resist the power of the U.S. government. He believed that they had no choice but to give up their land and relocate to a new home beyond the Rio Grande.

The deadline passed but the Navajo refused to surrender. Carleton then recruited Colonel Christopher "Kit" Carson to help him to persuade the Indians to leave their homeland. Carson began a scorched-earth campaign to drive the Navajos out. He and his troops confiscated as much of the Indians' crops and livestock as they could use for their own purposes and destroyed the rest. Fields of crops were burned, hogans (Navajo dwellings) were destroyed, and livestock was slaughtered.

With nothing left to eat but wild berries and piñon nuts, some of the Indians moved on to join other tribes. Manuelito and his band, however, went down into the Grand Canyon. Kit Carson and his men went back to Fort Defiance to wait for the winter, when the Indians would be forced by starvation to surrender. The Indians who stayed struggled to survive as best they could on whatever wild foods they could gather in the Chuska Mountains. Many died of starvation or froze to death during the winter, yet they still refused to surrender. It was not until February 1864 that thousands of weak, sick, and hungry Indians began to turn themselves in at Fort Defiance.

The Long Walk

On March 6, 1864, the soldiers at the fort formed the 2,500 refugees into a long line and started them on a long trek past the borders of their homeland to the reservation of Bosque Redondo near Fort Sumner. This was the "Long Walk", a part of Navajo history still remembered with great sorrow and bitterness. Many people died or were killed on that journey. The army had not supplied enough food, but the Indians were forced to continue marching onward in spite of hunger and cold. Those who were too sick, weak, or old to keep up were killed or left behind.

By the time the group reached the Rio Grande the spring melt had flooded the river, making it very treacherous to cross. The Indians tried to get across any way they could but many were swept away and drowned. At the end of their ordeal they arrived at the wasteland that was to be their new home, the Bosque Redondo reservation. This place that Carleton had promised would be a "garden of Eden" was nothing but a desolate, barren flatland with no means of support for the Indians. Carleton had not provided enough food or supplies for the large number of new inhabitants in the remote reservation, nor had he considered how difficult it would be for the exiles to become self-supporting as farmers on such a worthless piece of land.

Delgadito, Herrero Grande, Armijo, and Barboncito had all surrendered with their bands by September 1864. Manuelito and his followers, however, held out longer than any of the others. Carleton sent Herrero Grande and five other Navajo headmen to find Manuelito and give him a message. He was advised to turn himself in peaceably or be hunted down and killed. Dee Brown records Manuelito's response in the book *Bury My Heart at Wounded Knee*: "My God and my mother live in the West, and I will not leave them. It is a tradition of my people that we must never cross the three rivers—the Grande, the San Juan, the Colorado. Nor could I leave the Chuska Mountains. I was born there. I shall remain. I have nothing to lose but my life, and that they can come and take whenever they please, but I will not move. I have never done any wrong to the Americans or the Mexicans. I have never robbed. If I am killed, innocent blood will be shed." Herrero Grande went back to Carleton alone.

In September 1866, however, Manuelito and 23 of his still surviving people were forced by hunger to surrender at Fort Wingate. He then joined the others at Bosque Redondo. The conditions at the reservation continued to worsen as each year the crops failed. About 2000 Navajos died at Bosque Redondo of disease or starvation. The terrible conditions that the Indians faced, as well as their continued longing to return home, increased anger and unrest among them.

In the late 1860s Manuelito traveled to Washington, D.C., to petition on behalf of his people for a return to their homeland. On May 28, 1868, General William T. Sherman and General Samuel F. Tappen called a council with the Navajo headmen Manuelito, Barboncito, Delgadito, Herrero Grande, Armijo, Largo, and Torivo. Manuelito pleaded for his people to be allowed to return to the Chuska mountains. General Sherman offered them land in Indian Territory (now Oklahoma) instead. After much debate it was finally decided that the Navajos would be allowed to return home. They were happy to agree to any terms just to be in their beloved lands again.

The new treaty was signed June 1, 1868, at Fort Sumner. The Navajo promised never to fight again and to remain on the 5,500 square mile reservation in their former homeland that the treaty provided for them. The U.S. government promised to provide sheep, goats, farm tools, and a yearly clothing allowance, as well as schools for their children.

Home from exile

In the early morning hours on June 18, 1868, more than 7,000 Navajo people began their six week journey home from exile. Manuelito was one of two men in charge of leading the people safely home. Once they were back in their familiar environment the Navajo began to rebuild their lives. The area of land that was allotted to them was much less than what they had been accustomed to before their forced evacuation. They were no longer free to roam between the four sacred mountains that had previously been their boundaries. The U.S. government was slow to follow through with their promises, and the Indians had many setbacks with their crops.

To maintain some sense of order, the people were divided into groups with appointed leaders. Barboncito was appointed head chief; Manuelito and Ganado Mucho served as subchiefs. All three of them urged their people to live peacefully on the reservation and work hard to rebuild their herds and fields. Slowly the Navajo people began to recover and prosper. In 1870, Barboncito died and Ganado Mucho became head chief, while Manuelito became second-in-command. A Navajo police force, led by Manuelito, was established in 1872 to guard the reservation. He lived in an area the people called the "place dark with plants," which is now called Manuelito Springs. He was a popular leader, and his hogan was always full of his followers.

Even though Manuelito still commanded the respect of his people, the pressures of the reservation made living difficult. After traders brought whiskey to the reservation, Manuelito began to drink; his last years were spent in and out of prison for drunkenness. Even so, he continued to represent his tribe. In 1875 he traveled again to Washington, D.C., to discuss with President Ulysses S.

Grant his concerns about the construction of the railroad through Navajo grazing lands.

Before his death in the winter of 1893, Manuelito traveled to the World's Fair in Chicago, where he was once again impressed by the white man's accomplishments. His counsel to his people is recorded by Marie Mitchell in her book, *The Navajo Peace Treaty, 1868.* On his return home he advised his people for the last time: "The white men have many things we Navajo need but we cannot get them unless we change our ways. My children, education is the ladder to all our needs. Tell our people to take it."

Further Reading

Brown, Dee, *Bury My Heart at Wounded Knee,* New York: Holt, 1970.

Loh, Jules, *Lords of the Earth: A History of the Navajo Indians,* New York: Crowell-Collier Press, 1971.

Mitchell, Marie, *The Navajo Peace Treaty, 1868,* Mason & Lipscomb, 1973.

Navajo Stories of the Long Walk Period, Tsaile, AZ: Navajo Community College Press, 1973.

Wood, Leigh Hope, *The Navajo Indians,* New York: Chelsea House, 1991.

Maria Martinez

Tewa San Ildefonso Pueblo potter
Born c. 1887, San Ildefonso Pueblo, New Mexico
Died 1980

"I just thank God because it's not only for me; it's for all the people. I said to my god, the Great Spirit, my Mother Earth gave me this luck. So I'm not going to keep it. I take care of our people."

Maria Montoya Martinez is one of the best known American Indian artists of all time. Together with her husband, Julian Martinez, she introduced new stylistic approaches and sweeping changes in pottery-making techniques that gave rise to a widespread revival of this Native American art form. For Martinez success was not an individual gain; she used her talent and skills—and even her signature—to further the economic conditions of her pueblo and to educate her people in the arts.

Martinez was the second daughter born to Tomas and Reyecita Peña Montoya in the San Ildefonso Pueblo, about 20 miles northwest of Santa Fe, New Mexico. Guided by her aunt, Nicolasa Peña Montoya, a respected potter, Martinez made her first pottery as a child of seven or eight. She attended the government school in her pueblo and then was selected by the council to attend St. Catherine's Indian School in Santa Fe. She considered becoming a school teacher, but her marriage to Julian Martinez directed her interests toward family life and pottery making.

Maria Martinez with her son, Popovi Da

The couple shared artistic talents and an openness to innovation, which fueled their successful pottery-making career for over 40 years. Martinez produced, shaped, and polished vessels. Julian decorated and helped fire them in ovens called kilns to make them solid. Martinez continued her work for more than 30 years after her husband died in 1943.

Beginnings

Martinez and her husband Julian spent their honeymoon at the St. Louis World's Fair in 1904, demonstrating Pueblo pottery-making techniques and dancing. By then pottery in the pueblo had mostly been replaced by cheap, machine-made items. In 1907 Julian began working at the Pajarito Plateau excavations (archaeological digs) of prehistoric Pueblo sites. Edgar Hewett, director of the project, asked him to copy pottery and wall designs and to try to duplicate a potsherd, or pottery fragment, found at the site. Through constant experimentation with a variety of clays, polishings, and firings, Martinez and her husband were able to recreate the ancient pottery. It was thinner, harder, and more highly polished than pottery made in their pueblo.

In 1911, the Museum of New Mexico in Santa Fe allowed Martinez and her husband—who worked there as a janitor from 1909 to 1912—to demonstrate their craft at the museum and to sell directly to the public. By 1915 Martinez had learned to create large pottery and was acknowledged as the master potter of San Ildefonso, excelling in both classical and modern forms. Julian's decorative designs worked in harmony with the shapes and surfaces. He kept a notebook of designs and rarely repeated decorative drawings except for his famous *avanyu,* a mythical water serpent, and his feathers, adapted from the prehistoric Mimbres feather designs. By 1919 the couple had developed a black-on-black vessel.

Value of work increases

Encouraged by the Museum of New Mexico, and Kenneth M. Chapman, who purchased the best examples of their black pottery, the couple saw the value of their work increase steadily. Demand from the public led them to create large amounts of dinnerware and housewares. Their black-on-black pottery was known throughout the United States and in many museums worldwide. A critic of their work at the Museum of New Mexico in 1920 compared it to "the best of the Orient or the Occident, ancient or modern."

In 1923, in response to the demand from collectors, Martinez began to sign her pottery on a regular basis. She even put her name on works by other potters. By signing other artists' work, she did not wish to claim credit, but to share the fame and profits she enjoyed with her community. It was clear that pottery with Martinez's signature would sell at a good price. As her fame and success grew, other Pueblo natives wanted to learn her craft. Eager to help others, Martinez held pottery classes at San Ildefonso and at the Indian School in Santa Fe.

Achieves national and international acclaim

Throughout her lifetime Martinez received hundreds of awards and commendations, both national and international. Her first award came at the Santa Fe Indian Market in 1922 for pottery she created with other family members. In 1934, when Martinez was awarded a bronze medal for Indian Achievement by the Indian Fire Council, she became the first Native American woman to receive the nation's most prestigious emblem of recognition for Native Americans. In 1954 she was given the Craftsmanship Medal, the nation's highest honor for craftsmanship. Martinez received several honorary degrees, and four invitations to the White House. Many of her awards recognized not only her superior craftsmanship, but her leadership in reviving a nearly extinct ancient craft and in developing and preserving it for her people.

Martinez and Julian had four children, Adam, Juan, Tony, and Philip. A daughter died in infancy. After Julian's death in 1943, Martinez collaborated with her daughter-in-law, Santana Martinez, Adam's wife. In 1956 her son, artist Tony Martinez, who then used his Indian name Popovi Da, became her partner. Many experts felt that working with her son enabled Martinez to express the highest level of her creativity.

After her death, the family tradition of pottery making was carried on by Maria's grandchildren, great-grandchildren, and great-great-grandchildren. Her grandson Tony Da and great-granddaughter Barbara Gonzales are the most famous of her descendants. The younger potters, like Martinez, extended the boundaries of their craft, creating new styles while maintaining the family tradition of excellence.

Martinez's efforts transformed San Ildefonso from an economically poor farming community into one of the Pueblo Indian arts and crafts centers in the Southwest. A gifted, generous woman of great humility, she told her biographer, Richard Spivey, "I just thank God because it's not only for me; it's for all the people. I said to my god, the Great Spirit, my Mother Earth gave me this luck. So I'm not going to keep it. I take care of our people." Her legacy lives on in the generations of potters she inspired and in the timeless art she created.

Further Reading

Dittert, Alfred E., Jr., and Fred Plog, *Generations in Clay: Pueblo Pottery of the American Southwest,* Flagstaff, AZ: Northland Publishing, 1980.

Native American Women, edited by Gretchen M. Bataille, New York: Garland Publishing, 1993.

Native North American Almanac, edited by Duane Champagne, Detroit: Gale, 1994.

Peterson, Susan, *Maria Martinez: Five Generations of Potters,* Washington, DC: Smithsonian Institution Press, 1978.

Spivey, Richard L., *Maria,* Flagstaff, AZ: Northland Press, 1979.

Mungo Martin

Kwakiutl tribal leader and artist
Born c. 1879, Fort Ruport, British Columbia, Canada
Died August 16, 1962, off the Victoria, British Columbia coast

"Perhaps no Canadian Indian did more than Chief Martin to secure recognition and honor for the culture of his people."
—Frederica De Laguna, American Anthropologist

Mungo Martin was the third highest chief of the Kwakiutl—or Kwagiulth/Kwakwaka'wakw, as they are also known—and an internationally known artist and craftsman highly regarded for his original carvings and restorations of totem poles. At a time when the Canadian government attempted to ban important forms of Native American art and language, Martin was instrumental in the survival of tribal traditions. By 1952, the political climate for Native Americans had improved and the Provincial Government of British Columbia commissioned (hired) him to display his work at Thunderbird Park, Victoria, enabling him to preserve numerous Native totem poles. Among his most famous original creations are a 127-foot pole—the tallest in the world—located in Victoria's Beacon Hill Park and a 100-foot totem commissioned by Queen Elizabeth to stand in Windsor Great Park as a celebration of the British Columbian provincial centennial in 1958. For his many contributions to Canada's

Mungo Martin (right) with brother Dave Martin

artistic, cultural, and intellectual life, Martin was posthumously (after his death) awarded a Canada Council medal in 1962, the first Native American to receive the prestigious honor.

Martin, who was born in Fort Ruport, British Columbia, was the son of Yanuk-walas ("No one leaves the house without a gift"), a prominent Kwakiutl, and Sarah Finlay, the daughter of a Hudson's Bay Company employee and a Kwakiutl woman. Martin estimated his date of birth—sometime in the spring of 1879—from the great Seattle fire of 1889, which he remembered witnessing as a boy of nine or ten during a trip south to pick hops with his family. As a baby, Martin was symbolically given artistic skills through a ritual in which four hairs of his eyebrows were plucked to form a paintbrush. He was then placed into a wooden box drum, which was beaten to give him musical gifts. While he was still a young child, Martin's father died, and his mother married Charlie James, a noted carver who instructed Martin in the art forms of the Kwakiutl.

Defies laws to preserve culture

In the early years of the twentieth century the Canadian government passed laws forbidding many forms of Native American cultural expression, including totem poles. Despite these laws, Martin continued carving pieces in the tradition of his ancestors, openly defying the laws of the state while many others abandoned their art. In addition to painting and carving, Martin sought to preserve the language and folklore of the Kwakiutl, tape-recording numerous traditional songs and stories. These cultural artifacts have made their way into such museums as Alert Bay, British Columbia's U'mista Cultural Centre. Representatives of Alert Bay told the *Seattle Times,* "Without Mungo Martin, many artistic features of the Kwakwaka'wakw, and much cultural knowledge, would have been lost forever." In the words of the *Seattle Times* art critic Deloris Ament, Martin "represents the slender thread that carried tribal traditions from the past into the present."

Martin's artistic talents were presented in the 1991 U'mista Cultural Centre display, the first international traveling museum exhibit of its importance ever arranged by a Canadian Native cultural center or museum. The exhibit, entitled "Mungo Martin: A Slender Thread," presented more than 40 of his works, including masts, rattles, model totem poles, and other carvings, as well as 30 carvings by other Native artists who worked under his teaching. One of the most stunning achievements in the collection, according to Ament, was a Chief Shakes Killer Whale hat, an elaborate crest carving made with alder, human hair, and abalone shell that serves as the "royal crown" of the Nanyaayi clan of the Stikene Tlingit.

Teacher of future generations

In addition to leaving an artistic legacy of his own, Martin went to great lengths to pass on his skills to future generations and preserve the disrupted culture of his tribe. During the last ten years of his life, a period in which he was no longer encumbered by laws against native art, Martin restored many of the old poles that stood in the park of the Royal British Columbia Museum in Victoria and, while there, instructed novice (beginning) artists in the traditional Kwakiutl carving style. One of his best students was his son-in-law, Henry Hunt, who became a famous carver himself, carrying on the restoration work of his stepfather at the museum and passing on his skills to two of his own sons, Tony and Richard Hunt, and a cousin, Calvin Hunt, all of whom are recognized as notable artists in their own right.

Mungo Martin drowned on August 16, 1962, while on a fishing trip off the Victoria coast. He was 83 years old. His funeral was testimony to the strength of his art and tribal leadership. After a day-long Kwakiutl mourning service authenticated by Martin's ritual art and his own tape-recordings of tribal songs, he was buried at sea by the Canadian Navy with every flag in port dropped to half-mast, an honor unprecedented for a Native American. As Frederica De Laguna of *American Anthropologist* magazine concluded after attending the day's events, "Perhaps no Canadian Indian did more than Chief Martin to secure recognition and honor for the culture of his people."

Further Reading

Ament, Deloris Tarzan, "Burke Show Displays Tribal Art," *Seattle Times,* December 15, 1991.

De Laguna, Frederica, "Mungo Martin, 1879-1962," *American Anthropologist,* August 1963, pp. 894-896.

New York Times (obituary), August 18, 1962, p. 19.

Massasoit

Wampanoag tribal leader
Born c. 1600, near present-day Bristol, Rhode Island
Died 1661
Also known as Great Chief, Massassoit, Ousamequin, Woosamequin, and Yellow Feather

Caught between his traditional enemies to the west and the English on the coast to the east, Massasoit may have had little choice other than to throw in his lot with the newcomers.

Massasoit is best known as a Native American leader who worked hard to maintain friendly relations with English settlers. He is also believed to have taken part in what has become known as the first Thanksgiving, even though no real record of the event exists and the feast has more or less turned into a fable over the years. While it is true that Massasoit strove for good relations with the Europeans, his story is more complicated—and full of hardship—than generations of schoolbooks have led Americans to believe.

Massasoit and the Pilgrims

From his home village in Pokanoket, near present-day Bristol, Rhode Island, Massasoit ruled the Wampanoag and a number of related tribes in southeastern New England. Some months after the Pilgrims (early English settlers who wished to freely practice their own form of Christianity) arrived in

Plymouth, Massachusetts, in 1620, the Indian leader appeared in their new colony and offered friendship. After some negotiations, the chief signed a peace treaty with the English, which promised that the Indians and English would not make war on each other and that they would defend each other from outside attacks. It was a treaty and a friendship that Massasoit would honor for the next 40 years.

Over the decades, the two groups exchanged friendly visits. When Massasoit became ill, Plymouth sent people on the two-day trek through the forest to Pokanoket to help cure their ally. On several occasions, Massasoit or his fellow Wampanoags probably saved the colonists from slaughter by warning them of possible attacks by warring tribes. When Roger Williams, a renegade religious thinker who left behind the conservative beliefs of his native England, appeared cold and starving at Massasoit's door, the chief took in the desperate man and made him welcome. In fact, the two men were reported to have become close friends, and Massasoit probably influenced Williams's understanding and favorable view of New England's Indians' lives and right to territory

Little is known about Massasoit except that he was physically strong and, when conversing with the settlers, was "grave of countenance and spare of speech"—in other words, he was serious and chose his words carefully. In March 1621 the great chief first appeared at the head of 60 warriors on a hill overlooking tiny Plymouth. His face was painted red and he wore a thick necklace of white beads, the sign of his authority. His image struck fear into the little band of Europeans huddled below, although he was about to bestow much-needed assistance and goodwill.

Despite his authority, Massasoit was in a difficult situation. Disease had recently swept through the tribe, ravaging his people. For this reason his number of warriors had greatly decreased, and his enemies in other tribes wanted to take advantage of this fact. To the west, across Rhode Island's Narragansett Bay, roved the powerful Narragansett tribe, eager to slaughter Massasoit and the Wampanoags. To the east, the English, whatever their troubles, were rumored to have valuable trade goods and strange, new, fire-breathing weapons. Caught between his traditional enemies to the west and the English on the coast to the east, Massasoit may have had little choice other than to throw in his lot with the newcomers. After all, they might be able to help.

Pilgrims waste away

As to the situation of the English, when the ship known as the *Mayflower* sailed back to England in the winter of 1620, it left behind a group of men, women, and children almost totally unprepared to deal with life in a wild land. As they shivered in their brush huts against the New England cold, they felt surrounded by a "howling wilderness," an endless forest they imagined to be full of bloodthirsty savages, wolves, maybe even devils. The new settlers didn't know how to hunt, fish, plant, or build adequate shelters. They had few supplies to carry them through to spring.

In such terrible conditions, staying alive became the foremost issue. One by one they died of malnutrition, disease, and gnawing

Treaty with Massasoit, engraved from a drawing by Palo Alto Pierce

hunger. Only half of them survived that first winter, and those who remained were weakened and confused, with little hope for the future. It seemed they would soon all be gone, dying thousands of miles from home on this wild, foreign shore, their bones dragged into the forest by the fierce animals.

When Massasoit and his 60 warriors stepped out of the wilderness and stood on the hilltop fearsomely looking down on Plymouth, the few able-bodied colonists who were left scrambled for their guns. But the settlers slowly realized they were not confronting enemies capable of killing off the remainder of the weakened settlers but friendly human beings who would give them food in exchange for baubles and, on top of that, help protect them against marauding tribes. Massasoit seemed to be a blessing sent from Heaven.

Massasoit and Squanto

Years before, in 1614, an English sea captain had kidnapped a number of Indians—in the area where the Plymouth colonists would later land—and sold them as slaves in Spain. Through a fantastic turn of events, **Squanto** (see entry)—who was also known as Tisquantum—was bought out of slavery by some monks. He made his way to England and from there was able to return to his homeland. When he arrived, however, he was horrified to find his home village abandoned, ravaged by disease. Tribeless, he joined Massasoit's people. When the Pilgrims arrived a year later, Squanto stepped out of the forest to greet them in English, and helped them survive their harsh conditions. Squanto's friendship helped ease the way for the friendship of the far more powerful Massasoit.

Not all relations between Europeans and Indians had been so congenial. European contact with the Indians in the New England area had gone on for decades before the colonists set foot on Plymouth Rock, and it often was not kindly. Kidnappings and other violence took place between the sea captains and fishermen touching the New England shore and the Indians they met. The Europeans also carried diseases, among them smallpox, typhus,

and measles. Lacking immunity, whole Indian villages were killed by these sicknesses. Understandably, most of the Indians, even those who had not yet seen white men, thought they were hostile, dishonest bearers of deadly illnesses. Indian societies already were in turmoil when the colonists came, and in light of this, Massasoit's friendship was the exception to the general rule.

Pressures of the European invasion

Despite earnest efforts at goodwill, such as Massasoit's, the situation was bound to get worse. New colonists starting other settlements cared nothing about an old, carefully nurtured friendship. Having lived with little or no land of their own in Europe, they had not pulled up stakes and risked the dangerous, months-long voyage to be restrained upon their arrival. What they wanted was land of their own, land that seemed theirs for the taking. All that stood in their way were the Native peoples, who fought back more strongly as the pressures of the invasion increased.

In the face of these building pressures and loss of land to the new colonists, Massasoit kept mending his good relations with the whites. The chief of the Wampanoags has been seen by some as one who exchanged his people's birthright (natural rights) for the trade goods, renown, and personal power he gained against the enemy Narragansetts.

In any case, Massasoit took a minority position by linking his fortunes to the English. As pressures against the Indians mounted, many of them decided to unite and either drive out the invaders or die in the attempt. Massasoit, too, began to deeply resent the encroachment of English settlers on Wampanoag land toward the end of his life. It would be his son Philip, fourteen years after his death, who would angrily lead what is known as King Philip's War (1675-76), which involved several tribes and all the New England colonies and was the bloodiest Indian-white conflict in the history of New England.

Further Reading

Biographical Dictionary of Indians of the Americas, volume 1, Newport Beach, CA: American Indian Publishers, 1991.

Native North American Almanac, edited by Duane Champagne, Detroit: Gale, 1994.

Weeks, Alvin Gardner, *Massasoit of the Wampanoags,* Fall River, MA: privately printed, 1919.

Wood, Norman B., *Lives of Famous Indian Chiefs,* Aurora, CA: American Indian Historical Publishing Company, 1906.

Russell C. Means

Lakota activist
Born November 10, 1939, Pine Ridge
Reservation, South Dakota

"I am not a 'leader.' I am an Oglala Lakota patriot. That's all I want or need to be. And I am very comfortable with who I am."

R ussell C. Means has been an outspoken Indian rights activist for more than two decades. He has organized numerous protests against the U.S. government's treatment of Native Americans and has been a major figure in the American Indian Movement (AIM). Means is probably best known for leading a 71-day takeover of Wounded Knee, South Dakota, which drew national attention to Indian rights issues in the early 1970s. The head of the American Indian Anti-Defamation League since 1988, Means continues to fight for the unique identity and independence of Native Americans.

Russell Charles Means was born November 10, 1939, on the Pine Ridge Reservation in South Dakota. He is the oldest son of Harold ("Hank") Means, a mixed-blood Oglala Sioux, and Theodora (Feather) Means, a full-blood Yankton Sioux. (Means prefers the traditional tribal name *Lakota* to the term *Sioux,* which he considers a negative white word.) He attended the U.S. government's Bureau of Indian Affairs (BIA) school on the reservation and later public schools in Vallejo, California.

During his high school years, Means transferred from the racially mixed Vallejo School to the almost all-white San Leandro High School, where he was bullied by other students because he was an Indian. Not knowing how to deal with such cruelty, Means at first fought back and then retreated into drugs and delinquency. After barely graduating from high school, he worked at various jobs and attended five colleges without graduating. He spent much of the 1960s drifting throughout the West, working as a cowboy and a day laborer and at an advertising firm. In 1969 he moved from a position on the Rosebud Sioux tribal council on the Rosebud Reservation in south-central South Dakota to the post of director at the government-funded American Indian Center in Cleveland, Ohio.

Russell C. Means

Protests Thanksgiving Day

In Cleveland, Means met **Dennis J. Banks** (see entry), who had helped set up the new, militant (aggressive or combative) Indian civil rights group known as the American Indian Movement. Inspired by Banks and his movement, Means set up AIM's second chapter in Cleveland. He quickly became a national media figure representing protesting Indians when, on Thanksgiving Day in 1970, he and a small group of others confronted whites dressed up as "Pilgrims" on the *Mayflower II* in Plymouth, Massachusetts. The whites were celebrating the arrival of the English in America, and AIM argued that Thanksgiving was a phony story that covered up centuries of abuse of Native Americans by whites. Dressed in combination western and Indian style, Means became an effective symbol for AIM. Well-spoken and powerful, he inspired local Indian people while his fiery statements riled non-Indians.

That same year, Means participated in a prayer vigil on Mount Rushmore—South Dakota's monument to former U.S. presidents—to symbolize Lakota claims to Black Hills land. His next protest was to file a $9 million lawsuit against the Cleveland Indians baseball team for using Chief Wahoo as a mascot, asserting in the suit that the symbol insulted Native Americans. This action angered many Cleveland baseball fans and led to Means's decision to resign his position at the Cleveland Center in 1972. He returned to South Dakota and continued working to draw attention to Indian rights.

In February 1972, Means led 1,300 angry Indians into the small town of Gordon, Nebraska, to protest the suspicious death of Raymond Yellow Thunder. The demonstration convinced town authorities to conduct a second autopsy (examination of a body after death) which eventually led to the indictment of two white townsmen for manslaughter. The Indian protest gained further success when the city council suspended a police officer accused of molesting jailed Indian women and then organized a multiracial human rights council. Violence against Indians increased all over the country that summer, leading to further defensiveness among local Indian people. Many Native Americans felt they needed to arm themselves against murderous attacks.

At the annual Rosebud Sun Dance celebration, Means helped plan a mass demonstration to occur in Washington, D.C., during the week of the 1972 presidential election. He urged a march to demand a federal law that would make it a crime to kill an Indian, even if the law had to be added as an amendment to the Endangered Species Act, which protected animals with dwindling populations. A series of cross-country caravans called "The Trail of Broken Treaties"—named for the promises made to Indians by the government and never kept—reached Washington on November 2.

The protesters arrived to find that the adequate housing promised by the U.S. Department of the Interior was crowded and rodent-infested. Feeling that the government officials were pushy and didn't take the Indians seriously, Means then led the group to the Bureau of Indian Affairs. There they successfully seized the offices and renamed the building the Native American Embassy. On November 6 a U.S. District Court judge ordered that the group be forced out. Angry and frustrated, the Indians destroyed furniture and equipment and removed files they felt exploited Indian people. The next day they agreed to leave the building peaceably after government officials promised to investigate federal programs affecting Indians and to consider the issue of Indian self-government. The government also offered $66,000 to cover their travel expenses.

Occupies town of historic massacre

When Means returned to South Dakota, he learned that the president of the Oglala Tribal Council, Dick Wilson, had obtained a court order prohibiting members of AIM from attending public meetings on the Pine Ridge Reservation. Wilson, a conservative opposed to the extreme activities of AIM, received government support to increase his police force and had Means arrested twice for challenging the court order.

When a white man was charged with second-degree manslaughter instead of murder for the stabbing death of an Indian man, Means was among the leaders of a protest through the town of Custer, South Dakota, where court was held. He and nearly 80 others were arrested for rioting and arson. The conflict heated up as traditional leaders requested AIM's help in getting rid of the council president, Wilson, whom some viewed as a puppet of the U.S. government. On February 27, 1973, Means and a group of nearly 200 armed supporters occupied the community of Wounded Knee, the site of the 1890 massacre of some 350 Sioux men, women, and children by the U.S. military. Tensions mounted as heavily armed FBI agents and federal marshals surrounded the area.

More than a month later, Means agreed to fly to Washington, D.C., to negotiate an agreement to end the siege, but the government refused to negotiate until all arms were laid down. Means refused to surrender unconditionally and left the meeting. He was arrested and detained for the remainder of the siege when he announced his intention to return to Wounded Knee. On May 8, 1973, the remaining Indians surrendered when the government agreed to meet with tribal elders to begin an investigation into tribal government under Wilson, who had been accused of ignoring the tribal constitution, among other things. Highly publicized in the national

Means (center) and Dennis Banks (right) conferring with Rev. Ralph Abernathy and other AIM members at Wounded Knee, South Dakota, 1973

media, the ten-week siege became known as "Wounded Knee II" and won the sympathy and support of many non-Indians, including several Hollywood personalities.

Means ran against Wilson in the 1974 election for tribal council president. He was under federal indictment (charged with committing a crime against the national government) for actions during the Wounded Knee occupation and lost the election, receiving 1,530 votes to Wilson's 1,709, but claimed that his election results showed strong support for AIM causes on the reservation. His trial opened on February 12, 1974, and con-

tinued until September 16, when U.S. District Court Judge Fred Nichol dismissed the charges against Means and Banks and denounced the prosecution's handling of the case, which had included the use of information obtained from a member of Means's defense team by an informant paid by the Federal Bureau of Investigation (FBI).

When asked years later about the beneficial results of the Wounded Knee occupation, Means described watching three little Indian boys playing, one pretending to be Banks, one pretending to be Means, and the third refusing to be Wilson. Means felt that the protests influenced the development of a new sense of Indian identity: that "government" Indians were considered traitors.

During the Wounded Knee occupation, Means was shot by a BIA officer. In the following six years, he survived four other shootings and was stabbed while serving a term in a South Dakota prison. These attempts on his life sent a message to other Indian people that they were not safe from violent attacks. In 1975 Means was indicted for a murder in a barroom brawl. His lawyer, William Kunstler, who had been one of the defense attorneys during the Wounded Knee trial, argued that the government had created so much fear that Indians were armed in self-defense. The jury acquitted Means of the murder charge on August 6, 1976. He was convicted of riot charges relating to the 1973 Custer demonstration and served one month in jail. In November 1977, he served a term in a South Dakota state penitentiary for rioting.

Reclaims Indian land at Yellow Thunder Camp

Russell Means was also among the group who occupied federal land at Yellow Thunder Camp. In April 1981, a group of Dakota AIM and traditional Lakota people established a camp on federal land in Victoria Creek Canyon, about 12 miles southwest of Rapid City, South Dakota. Named in honor of Raymond Yellow Thunder, the man murdered in Gordon, Nebraska, in 1972, the camp was established as the first step in reclaiming the Black Hills land for Lakota use. When the U.S. Forest Service denied a use permit for the camp, Means acted as a lay—or nonprofessional—attorney in the

complaint against the Forest Service for violating the American Indian Freedom of Religion Act of 1978. In 1985, Judge Donald O'Brien ruled in favor of the Indian camp, but a higher court overturned the decision.

After the Yellow Thunder trial, Means became involved in Native rights issues in other countries, including supporting the cause of the Miskito Indians in the Central American country of Nicaragua. He has been associated politically with the Libertarian party, which believes in maximum individual freedom. In 1992 he became an actor, playing the role of Chingachgook in the movie *The Last of the Mohicans*. While on the set, Means served as a go-between during a labor dispute involving Indian extras (people who appear in crowd scenes in films) and the movie's producers. In an article in *Entertainment Weekly*, Means commented, "I have been asked whether my decision to act in *The Last of the Mohicans* means that I've abandoned my role as an activist. On the contrary, I see film as an extension of the path I've been on for the past 25 years—another avenue to eliminating racism."

In the spring of 1994, AIM's cofounder, **Clyde Bellecourt** (see entry), accused Means of selling out the AIM cause by accepting a $35,000 settlement from the 1972 suit against the Cleveland Indians baseball organization. Means, who left the American Indian Movement in 1988, responded that his current organization, the American Indian Anti-Defamation League, would be filing another lawsuit against the ball club since he never received any of the money.

Although Means generally avoids writing, considering it a European custom, he agreed to have his words published as a chapter in a book, *Marxism and Native Americans,* in order to communicate with a wider audience. He urged each American Indian to avoid accepting European ideas and customs and to follow traditional tribal values instead. He criticized the European intellectual traditions, including Christianity and capitalism, and said that Europeans had despiritualized, or taken the magic out of, the universe. He also warned that as a European tradition, Marxism—the philosophy of Karl Marx that communism is based on—is also no solution for American Indians' problems. He concluded: "I am not a 'leader.' I am an Oglala Lakota patriot. That's all I want or need to be. And I am very comfortable with who I am."

Further Reading

Deloria, Vine, Jr., *God Is Red: A Native View of Religion,* second edition, Golden, CO: North American Press, 1992.

Entertainment Weekly, October 23, 1992, pp. 34-37.

Marxism and Native Americans, edited by Ward Churchill, Boston: South End Press, 1983, pp. 19-33.

Matthiessen, Peter, *In the Spirit of Crazy Horse,* New York: Penguin Books, 1991.

Means, Russell, with Marvin J. Wolf, *Where White Men Fear to Tread: The Autobiography of Russell Means,* St. Martin's, 1995.

Native North American Almanac, edited by Duane Champagne, Detroit: Gale, 1994.

Paulson, T. Emogene, and Lloyd R. Moses, *Who's Who among the Sioux,* Vermillion: Institute of Indian Studies, University of South Dakota, 1988.

Billy Mills

Oglala Sioux athlete
Born 1938, Pine Ridge Reservation, South
    Dakota

"My Indianness kept me striving to take first and not settle for less in the last yards of the Olympic race."

Billy Mills was the first American to win a gold medal in a distance race in the Olympics. Against tremendous odds he set a world record during the 1964 Olympic Games in Tokyo, Japan, becoming an instant celebrity in the process. William M. Mills was born on the Pine Ridge Reservation in South Dakota in 1938. His mother died when he was seven and his father died six years later, leaving eight orphaned children. His father had boxed for a living, but after his death there was no one to support the family. As was often the custom, Billy was sent away to a Bureau of Indian Affairs boarding school.

He entered Haskell Indian School in Lawrence, Kansas. Taking after his father, he tried out for the boxing team. Although he was only five feet, two inches tall and weighed a mere 104 pounds, he joined the football team. He was attracted to the vigorous discipline of football and felt, at that time, that track was a "sissy" sport. But when he eventually turned to track, he discovered that it was extremely demanding. He soon began to develop physical endurance and strength through robust training. The physical and mental discipline it required, along with his natural abilities, helped him develop into a successful competitive runner. He won the Kansas State two-mile cross country championship three years in a row and took the state mile championship as a junior and senior. When he graduated from high school, the University of Kansas awarded him a full athletic scholarship.

In college, Mills often felt lonely and isolated. He had little contact with his scattered brothers and sisters, and no one took a special interest in him or his running. Despite the lack of attention that he received individually, Mills set a conference record of 31 minutes in his first 10,000-meter race and became the Big Eight cross-country champion during that time. His team won the National Track Championships two years in a row while he was a junior and senior. Still, he did not gain prominence or recognition as a runner.

After trying and failing to qualify for the Olympic team, he became discouraged, finishing poorly in races and occasionally dropping out of events. In an interview for *Contemporary American Indian Leaders,* he recalled this period: "I didn't realize then, but it was because of my attitude. I just didn't want to make the effort. I wasn't interested and because I wasn't, it was impossible for me to win. I blocked myself off from winning." Just before graduation, Billy married his college sweetheart; shortly thereafter, he accepted an officer commission from the U.S. Marine Corps.

Some of his fellow marines were aware of his extraordinary athletic talent, and one of them encouraged him to begin running again. He began training and won the interservice 10,000-meter race in Germany with a time of 30:08. Also, concentrating on the one-mile race, he got his time down to 4:06 minutes.

Billy Mills wins 10,000-meter race at 1964 Olympics

Astonishing victory at 1964 Olympic Games

The marines sent Mills to Tokyo, Japan, to compete in the Olympic Games in 1964. This was a unique opportunity for the young Sioux athlete. He entered the games as a complete unknown, with odds of 1,000 to 1 against him—no American had ever won a distance race in the Olympics. Just minutes before the race, the American coach was calculating the possibilities that any of his athletes would place in the race. Billy Mills's name was not even mentioned.

He began the race with silent determination, and by the last 300 meters he was actually leading the other 36 world-class track stars. Suddenly he was pushed by another runner and he stumbled, dropping 20 yards behind. In the next few seconds he charged ahead, capturing one of the major upsets in Olympic history. He won the race in 28:24.4, establishing a new Olympic record and winning the gold medal. "My Indianness kept me striving to take first and not settle for less in the last yards of the Olympic race," he said in his interview. "I thought of how our great chiefs kept on fighting when all of the odds were against them as they were against me. I couldn't let my people down."

The world was astonished at Mills's run and he became an instant international hero. Yet he remained modest and dignified. The president of the International Olympic Committee commended Mills for his ability to respond to pressure, saying never in 50 years had he seen a better reaction to such circumstances.

The honor of successfully representing the United States meant a lot to Mills, but his most cherished tributes came from his own Lakota people in the form of traditional gifts. He became a role model to generations of young people growing up in Pine Ridge. He traveled all over the world, speaking in over 51 countries. He always emphasized his tremendous desire to win as well as his Indianness. "I wanted to make a total effort, physically, mentally, and spiritually," he insisted. "Even if I lost, with this effort I believed that I would hold the greatest key to success."

His story was admired around the world, and a movie—*Running Brave*—was filmed about his early hardships, his determination, and his Olympic victory. An honored spokesperson for Indian athletes, Mills remarked: "[Other Indians] have ability far greater than mine, and if they are given the opportunity to explore and develop their talents, they can achieve any personal and educational goal they choose, especially if they make this total physical, mental and spiritual effort."

After the Olympics, further discouragement

After the Olympics, Billy Mills continued to train and to run, setting another record in the six-mile race. At this time he lived in California with his family and sold insurance for a living. He tried out for the 1968 Olympic Games, but because of a technicality regarding his application form, he was denied a place on the team. Several other Olympians voiced their objection, but he was not reinstated. He ran in the qualifying 5,000-meter trial, even though he was not a contestant for the team, finishing 13 seconds ahead of the fastest runner who qualified for the games.

For a time he felt bitter and discouraged. It seemed that politics had kept him out of the 1968 Olympics. Then, as he had so often, he put the bitterness behind him and went on with his life. "A man can change things," he explained in his interview. "A man has a lot to do with deciding his own destiny. I can do one of two things—go through life bickering and complaining about the raw deal I got, or go back into competition to see what I can do." He has devoted a great deal of his time to Indian causes, speaking out about the benefits of physical discipline and self-esteem. In 1977 he was named one of ten outstanding young men of the United States by the U.S. Junior Chamber of Commerce. In 1994 he published a book, *Wokini: A Lakota Journey to Happiness and Self-Understanding.*

Further Reading

Contemporary American Indian Leaders, edited by Marion E. Gridley, New York: Dodd, Mead & Company, 1972.

Mills, Billy, *Wokini: A Lakota Journey to Happiness and Self-Understanding,* New York: Crown, 1994.

Native North American Almanac, edited by Duane Champagne, Detroit: Gale, 1994.

N. Scott Momaday

Kiowa writer, poet, and educator
Born 1934, Lawton, Oklahoma
Also known as Tsoai-talee ("Rock Tree Boy")

"Some of my mother's memories have become my own. This is the real burden of the blood; this is immortality."

One of the most distinguished Native American authors writing today, N. Scott Momaday is chiefly known for novels and poetry collections that relate the oral legends (traditional tales and fables that have been passed on, generation to generation, through the spoken word) of his Kiowa heritage. His 1969 novel, *House Made of Dawn,* was the first novel by a Native American to win the Pulitzer Prize in fiction. The book played a key role in developing a widespread readership of Native American literature in the United States. Published in the late 1960s, when groups of non-native American youth were discovering and embracing many aspects of Native American traditions, *House Made of Dawn* influenced—and also brought attention to—other gifted Indian writers, including **Vine Deloria, Jr., Leslie Marmon Silko** (see entries), and James Welch.

Born in a Kiowa Indian hospital in Lawton, Oklahoma, on February 27, 1934, Navarre Scott Momaday was the only child of Kiowa artist Alfred Morris Momaday and teacher Mayme Natachee Scott Momaday. A descendant of early American pioneers, Momaday's mother derived her middle name from a Cherokee great-grandmother, Natachee. Momaday's father inherited the Kiowa family name "Mammedaty" from Momaday's grandfather. Momaday explains how his grandfather's name became a family name, in European rather than Kiowa tradition. "At that time," Momaday explains "people had but one name. [Mammedaty] was the name that was given to him as a child, and that was the only name he had. But during his lifetime the missionaries came in, and the Indians adopted the Christian tradition of the surname and the Christian name. And so my grandfather was given the name John, and he became known as John Mammedaty, and Mammedaty simply became the surname of his family. It was passed down. Some of my relatives in Oklahoma still use that spelling, but my father abbreviated it to Momaday."

Much of Momaday's writing is a collection of memories, but not all of his memories stem from personal experience. Momaday attributes many of his memories to his parents. "Some of my mother's memories have become my own. This is the real

Cultivates vivid early memories

Momaday remembers that the first notable event in his life occurred when he was just six months old and he accompanied his parents on a journey to the Black Hills in Wyoming to see Devil's Tower. Referred to in Kiowa as Tsoai ("Rock Tree"), Devil's Tower became the source of Momaday's Kiowa name, Tsoai-talee. The name was given to him by Pohd-lohk ("Old Wolf"), a Kiowa elder. Pohd-lohk had in his possession a ledger from the Supply Office at Fort Sill that depicted the history of the Kiowa people from 1833. Momaday would later derive a great deal of knowledge about the origin of his people from that book.

An only child, Momaday learned at an early age to give free reign to his imagination, or as he states, "to create my society in my mind." His mother encouraged him to learn English as his native language, and this sometimes made him feel uncertain about his cultural identity. Figures from European literature blended into his Indian surroundings. He writes that as a child he once perceived the shadow of Grendel, the monster in the Old English epic *Beowulf,* on the walls of Canyon de Chelly, an ancient Native American trade center and ceremonial town in Arizona. Similarly, he once believed he saw English novelist Charles Dickens's hero David Copperfield at a local trading post.

When he was 12, Momaday's family moved to the Pueblo village of Jemez in northern New Mexico. Momaday remembers "not being able to imagine a more beautiful or exotic place." Many details from his life there pop up in his later writings.

N. Scott Momaday

burden of the blood; this is immortality," he relates in *The Names: A Memoir.* Born of mixed blood, his mother began to identify with her Indian heritage around the age of 16. A beautiful girl, she called herself "Little Moon" while her cousins referred to her as "Queen of Sheba." Both names pleased her mightily. To pursue a degree and to learn more about her Indian heritage, Natachee attended the Haskell Institute, the Indian school at Lawrence, Kansas, in 1929. She passed on to her son her intense love of books, especially English literature.

Academic pursuits

Momaday enrolled at the University of New Mexico in 1952. He earned a bachelor's degree in political science in 1958. Taking a one-year break from his studies, he taught school on the Jicarilla Apache reservation before pursuing graduate studies in literature. During his years as an undergraduate student, Momaday distinguished himself as a writer and a public speaker, receiving the John Hay Whitney Fellowship in creative poetry writing and the Stanford Wilson Dissertation Fellowship at Stanford University.

While at Stanford, Momaday met famed scholar Yvor Winters, who later became a close friend and adviser. Momaday obtained his master's degree in 1960 and his Ph.D. three years later. In 1965 he published his first book, *The Complete Poems of Frederick Goddard Tuckerman,* which was based on his doctoral dissertation.

Following his graduate studies, Momaday became an assistant professor of English at the University of California at Santa Barbara (UCSB) in 1963. He remained at UCSB until 1969 except for spending the 1966 to 1967 academic year doing literary research at Harvard University. In 1969 he became professor of English at the University of California, Berkeley, where he taught creative writing and introduced a new curriculum (a set of courses specializing in a particular field) centered around American Indian literature and mythology.

The prize-winning novelist

Momaday's academic pursuits did not hinder his creative writing. In 1968 he published his influential novel, *House Made of Dawn.* The story follows the adventures of Abel, a Native American World War II veteran who attempts to balance his identity between Native and non-Native cultures. Unable to exist peacefully in either culture, Abel feels lost and returns to the reservation to try to heal himself. In 1969, *House Made of Dawn* was given one of literature's highest honors, the Pulitzer Prize for fiction.

Momaday's next novel, *The Way to Rainy Mountain* (1969), blends several Kiowa myths and legends. The book is a semi-fictional account of the tribe's migration from the Yellowstone region, where the Kiowa originated, to the plains, where they learned to domesticate horses and developed into a sophisticated society. Momaday retells the legend of how the Kiowas came into the world through a hollow log. When they entered it, he writes, "there was a woman whose body was swollen up with child, and she got stuck in the log. After that, no one could get through, and that is why the Kiowas are a small tribe in numbers." *The Way to Rainy Mountain* features illustrations by Momaday's father, Alfred. A reviewer for *Choice* magazine called it "a beautiful book—honest, unique, dignified, and told with a simplicity that approaches the purest poetry.... It is a book for all seasons, for all readers."

Momaday's reputation has grown and spread throughout the world. In 1979 he was awarded Italy's highest literary award, the Premio Lettario Internationale "Mondello." In 1990 he was selected as a keynote speaker before the Conference on Environment and Human Survival, the Global Forum, and the Supreme Soviet in Moscow. That same year he was asked to be a member of the Pulitzer Prize Jury in fiction. The father of four daughters, Momaday continues to write and teaches classes on oral tradition at the University of Arizona.

Further Reading

Choice, September 1969.

Momaday, N. Scott, *The Ancient Child,* New York: Doubleday, 1989.

Momaday, N. Scott, *Angle of Geese and Other Poems,* Boston: David R. Grodine, 1974.

Momaday, N. Scott, *The Gourd Dancer,* New York: Harper & Row, 1976.

Momaday, N. Scott, *House Made of Dawn,* New York: Harper & Row, 1968.

Momaday, N. Scott, *In the Presence of the Sun: A Gathering of Shields,* New York: St. Martin's Press, 1992.

Momaday, N. Scott, *The Names: A Memoir,* New York: Harper & Row, 1976.

Momaday, N. Scott, *The Way to Rainy Mountain,* Albuquerque: University of New Mexico Press, 1969.

New York Times Book Review, June 9, 1968.

Shubnell, Matthias, *N. Scott Momaday: The Cultural and Literary Background,* Norman: The University of Oklahoma Press, 1985.

Norval Morrisseau

Ojibway artist
Born March 14, 1932, near Beardsmore, Ontario, Canada
Also known as Copper Thunderbird

"My paintings are also icons; that is to say, they are images which help focus on spiritual powers, generated by traditional belief and wisdom."

Norval Morrisseau is considered the major figure of Canadian woodland Indian art and a major influence on the younger Cree and Ojibway artists today. Morrisseau was one of the first Native artists to break into the world of mainstream Canadian art with his pioneering pictographic (picture-writing) style. His acrylic paintings, silkscreen works, and pen-and-ink drawings have been exhibited in galleries in North America and Europe. His work has been influenced both by the rock paintings found along the northern shores of Lake Superior and by the birch bark scrolls of the Midewiwin, or Grand Medicine Society, a Native religious group. Awarded the prestigious Order of Canada in 1978, Morrisseau describes himself as a shaman (a priest who uses magic to cure the sick and control events) and an artist. In *The Art of Norval Morrisseau,* he wrote, "My paintings are also icons; that is to say, they are images which help focus on spiritual powers, generated by traditional belief and wisdom."

Norval Morrisseau

Norval Morrisseau was born on Sand Point Reserve, near Beardmore, Ontario, on March 14, 1932. The eldest of seven boys, Morrisseau, following the Native custom, was raised by his mother's parents, Moses (Potan) Nanakonagas, a shaman, and his wife, Vernique, on the shores of Lake Nipigon. The Native legends and spiritual teachings presented by Nanakonagas form the basis of Morrisseau's art. When the artist published *Legends of My People: The Great Ojibway* in 1965, he dedicated the book to his grandfather.

Tuberculosis changes life

As a child, Morrisseau earned only a fourth-grade education at an Indian residential school in Fort William (now Thunder Bay), Ontario, before returning home to the reserve. There, he struggled against poverty and isolation for many years. At age 19, he had tuberculosis (a severe and contagious lung ailment) and was sent to a sanatorium—a live-in, long-term care hospital—at Fort William. One of the doctors there encouraged Morrisseau to paint.

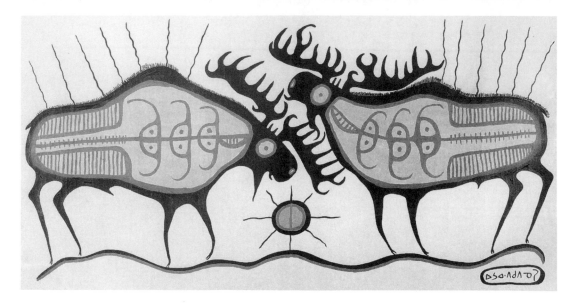

Two Bulls Fighting, by Morrisseau

The same year, Morrisseau began having visions that revealed to him that his role in life was to be a shaman-artist. It was also at the hospital that Morrisseau met his wife, Harriet Kakegamic, a Cree Indian. The couple had six children before the marriage dissolved. The artist traditionally signs his work with his native name, Copper Thunderbird, written in the Cree symbols his wife taught him.

In 1962, Jack Pollock, a Toronto artist and gallery owner, met Morrisseau when Pollock was teaching painting in northern Ontario. Pollock was so impressed with the vibrant imagery of Morrisseau's paintings that he organized a one-man show for the artist at the Pollock Gallery. Morrisseau's work sold out on the first day of the show. Although the artist's work was immediately popular with critics and collectors, some of

his fellow Ojibway felt the artist should not reveal the tribe's legends and beliefs to outsiders. Morrisseau defended his actions, telling of his desire to restore the pride of the once-great Ojibway people through the images in his art.

Survived alcoholism and health problems

In both his paintings and his life, Morrisseau has struggled to reconcile his Native religious beliefs with his Christian faith. The artist has always been a wanderer and a loner, moving restlessly across Canada, often living on the streets. In 1976, he adopted the Eckankar religion, with its belief in "soul travel," which in some ways resembles Native religious teachings.

Morrisseau's first brush with death occurred in 1972, when the artist suffered second-degree burns to more than one-third of his body in a Vancouver, British Columbia, hotel fire. Three years later, staying at a Catholic detoxification center, he painted *Lily of the Mohawk* and other works filled with Roman Catholic images (symbols and pictures that represent ideas). Morrisseau has continued to be plagued by health and alcohol-related problems. Each tragic experience in his life, however, has seemed to produce fresh ideas, which he translates into his art. The artist, now living on the coast of British Columbia and again exhibiting his work, remains one of Canada's most celebrated Native artists.

Further Reading

McLuhan, Elizabeth, and Tom Hill, *Norval Morrisseau and the Emergence of the Image Makers,* Toronto: Art Gallery of Ontario, 1984.

Morrisseau, Norval, *Legends of My People: The Great Ojibway,* edited by Selwyn Dewdney, Toronto: Ryerson Press, 1965.

Sinclair, Lister, and Jack Pollock, *The Art of Norval Morrisseau,* foreword by Norval Morrisseau, Toronto: Methuen, 1979.

Southcott, Beth, *The Sound of the Drum: The Sacred Art of the Anishnabec,* Erin, Ontario: Boston Mills Press, 1984.

Nora Naranjo-Morse

Tewa Pueblo poet and potter
Born 1953, Santa Clara Pueblo, Espanola, New Mexico

"Nora Naranjo-Morse reminds us that the Sky and the Earth are relatives of the artist and are part of each conception, as is the human family—most importantly the unforgettable character Pearlene, the wild thing in all of us."—Joy Harjo.

Nora Naranjo-Morse, an artist who works in clay, metal, and words, struggles, as she says, "in two worlds, between Pueblo tradition and modern values." Her work, though modern and unique, is nevertheless deeply rooted in Pueblo culture and traditions. Through her creations—which have appeared in exhibitions, audiovisuals, and a book combining poetry with pictures of her clay figures—she tries to make sense of those two worlds.

Ninth of ten children of Mitchell and Rose Naranjo of Santa Clara Pueblo, in Espanola, New Mexico, Naranjo-Morse was born into a family known for pottery making: her mother and sisters are potters. Converted to the Christian religion by Baptist missionaries, her father became a minister, setting the family apart from the Pueblo community and causing them to be viewed as different. He served first in Santa Clara and then at Taos, New Mexico, but eventually left the ministry. The family returned to

Nora Naranjo-Morse's *Pearlene Teaching Her Cousins Poker*

Santa Clara, but still felt alienated from the pueblo, and so Naranjo-Morse and other members of her family learned to pursue their dreams in their own ways.

After graduation from Taos High School in 1971, Naranjo-Morse left New Mexico and went on to travel extensively. She sorted mail in Washington, D.C., and sold firecrackers in South Dakota. She also rebelled against the church at this stage of her life. She finally returned to Santa Clara, reuniting with her family. In her poem, "Two Worlds," she asks, "Had I forgotten who I was, where I'd come from?" At the pueblo she married Greg Morse from Connecticut and became the mother of twins, Eliza and Zachary. In 1976, she began seriously working with clay; soon, in addition to making bowls, she began sculpting clay figures of animals and people, blending Pueblo traditions with her own images of the outside world.

In 1980, she graduated from College of Santa Fe with a degree in social welfare, but, already a recognized potter, she continued with her art career. Combining different kinds of clay, she made figures, often humorous and inspired by her personal experiences and observations as well as her culture. Sometimes Naranjo-Morse's figures achieve an identity that continues through a series of sculptures. One such figure is Pearlene, wearing tight, short skirts and purple "tennies." Pearlene, Naranjo-Morse explains in

Mud Woman: Poems from the Clay, "fluctuates between confusion and clarity, reverence and mischief, while searching for her niche in life." When someone offered to mass-produce Pearlene, Naranjo-Morse, struck with the horror of a multitude of identical, plastic Pearlenes, made one final Pearlene and went on to other things.

Participates in "a separate vision"

Besides displaying her work in galleries and Indian markets, Naranjo-Morse was part of a two-year project beginning in 1987 at the Museum of Northern Arizona in Flagstaff. Called "A Separate Vision," it sought to generate support and understanding for the works of Native American artists. As one of four artists in the project, Naranjo-Morse spent a month in residence at the museum gallery, displaying and practicing her art. She participated in the making of a videotape called *Separate Visions* and in an educational program for children and adults.

In 1989, she was one of seven poets in the annual Taos Poetry Circus, sponsored by Society of the Muse of the Southwest (SOMOS). Her book, *Mud Woman: Poems from the Clay,* juxtaposes poems and pictures of her clay sculptures. "This collection of poems and clay forms," she asserts in the book's preface, "documents a fifteen-year milestone of creating." According to the noted Native American poet Joy Harjo, "Nora Naranjo-Morse reminds us that the Sky and the Earth are relatives of the artist and are part of each conception, as is the human family—most importantly the unforgettable character Pearlene, the wild thing in all of us."

Speaking of her vision and her creative processes, Naranjo-Morse mentions *Gia* (mother) and *Nan chu Kweejo* (Clay Mother) as most responsible for her approach to art. From *Gia* she learned respect for the clay and the steps in making pottery, from the gathering, sieving, soaking, and draining of the clay, through hanging of pillowcases filled with clay in trees, to the shaping and firing of the clay. A prayer of thanks is offered to *Nan chu Kweejo* at the site of the clay gathering, a disordered area covered with branches and earth.

As her mother taught her, Naranjo-Morse has taught her children pottery making, and she encouraged them to help with the adobe house she and her husband, Greg, built. Her other projects include a series of masks and several works in bronze. She wants to be remembered, according to Linda Eaton, "as an artist who listened to the clay, who followed her art where it led, and had faith that it would take care of her."

Further Reading

Native American Women, edited by Gretchen M. Bataille, New York: Garland Publishing, 1993.

Eaton, Linda B., *A Separate Vision: Case Studies of Four Contemporary Indian Artists,* Flagstaff: Museum of Northern Arizona Press, 1990.

Naranjo-Morse, Nora, *A First Clay Gathering,* Modern Curriculum Press, 1994.

Naranjo-Morse, Nora, *Mud Woman: Poems from the Clay,* Flagstaff: University of Arizona Press, 1992.

Trimble, Stephen, "Brown Earth and Laughter: The Clay People of Nora Naranjo-Morse," *American Indian Art,* autumn 1987, pp. 58-65.

Alanis Obomsawin

Abenaki filmmaker and singer
Born 1932, Lebanon, New Hampshire

Alanis Obomsawin's involvement in humanitarian causes is especially reflected in her later films, which expose the systematic and often harsh oppression of Native Americans.

In addition to being an accomplished producer, director, and singer, Alanis Obomsawin is one of Canada's foremost documentary filmmakers on Native life, culture, and arts. Born in Lebanon, New Hampshire, in 1932, she grew up on the Odonak Reserva-

tion in Québec. In 1967 she began working with the National Film Board of Canada on her first film. Completed in 1971, *Christmas at Moose Factory* delves into Cree life as interpreted in the artwork of Native children.

Traditionally, many Native cultures are matrilineal—meaning that power descends through women—and thus emphasize women's activities and their direct influence on culture. Obomsawin's film, *Mother of Many Children* (1977) is a celebration of Native oral tradition, focusing on traditional women's use of language and storytelling in passing on culture. *Amisk,* made the same year, emphasizes Native music and dance.

Obomsawin is also an accomplished singer. Her singing debut took place at New York City's Town Hall in 1960. Afterward, Obomsawin traveled extensively through Canada, the United States, and Europe, performing at schools, universities, museums, prisons, and art centers. She has also appeared in folk festivals and various fund-raising events. Like her film work, her singing has focused on and been inspired by Native themes. In 1988 she released her first solo album, *Bush Lady,* which is a collection of songs she wrote in Abenaki, French, and English.

Used documentary to further humanitarian causes

Obomsawin's involvement in humanitarian causes is especially reflected in her later films, which expose the systematic and often harsh oppression of Native Americans. One such example is *Incident at Restigouche,* a 1984 documentary portraying the raid by Québec Province police on the Restigouche Reserve, a violent showdown over Native fishing activities. Her focus on such unjust actions sometimes has positive results. As a result of her bringing such governmental cruelty to the attention of the public, some Native American groups have, despite the extensive commercialization of fishing, gained subsistence (survival) fishing rights. Such is the case with Natives of Kodiak and the Aleutian Islands of Alaska.

Obomsawin created seven more films from 1986 to 1992, all illustrating governmental injustices to Indians. Produced in 1986, *Richard Cardinal: Cry from a Diary of a Métis Child* tells the true story of a Cree boy driven to suicide by the abuse and neglect of the child welfare system. *Poundmaker's Lodge: A Healing Place,* produced in 1987, focuses on a drug and alcohol center's attempts to rebuild the lives of Natives devastated by substance abuse. Homelessness, another dilemma faced by many Indians, is the topic of her 1988 film *No Address.*

In 1983 the Canadian government awarded Obomsawin its highest honor, the prestigious Order of Canada, for her ongoing commitment to indigenous (native) peoples. In addition to her 16 films and documentaries, she has directed and produced a number of different filmstrips, two vignettes, and two multimedia packages, *Manowan* and *L'ilawat.* She has also continued to pursue her singing career. Obomsawin resides in Montreal, Canada, where she is an active board member of the Native Women's Shelter and Canada Council's Native Advisory Committee.

Further Reading

Canadian Who's Who, edited by Kieren Simpson, Toronto: University of Toronto Press, 1993.

Native North American Almanac, edited by Duane Champagne, Detroit: Gale, 1994.

Ely S. Parker

Seneca tribal and military leader, government official, and engineer
Born 1828, Indian Falls, Tonawanda Indian Reservation, near Akron, New York
Died August 31, 1895, Fairfield, Connecticut
Also known as Ha-sa-no-an-da

Parker later reported that Confederate General Robert E. Lee was momentarily taken aback on seeing Parker in such a prominent position at the surrender. Apparently, Lee shook hands with Parker and said, "I am glad to see one real American here." Parker replied, "We are all Americans."

Ely Samuel Parker was the first Indian commissioner of Indian affairs. During the Civil War, Parker, who was a close friend and colleague of General—and later President—Ulysses S. Grant, served the Union and wrote the final copy of the Confederate army's surrender terms. As commissioner of Indian affairs, Parker's humanitarian policies soon made him some powerful enemies in Washington, but to much of the public his brief term demonstrated integrity and fair-mindedness.

Parker (Ha-sa-no-an-da) was born in 1828 at Indian Falls on the Tonawanda Indian Reservation, near Akron, New York, the second of six children of a distinguished Seneca family. His mother was Elizabeth Johnson (Ga-ont-gwut-ywus), a Seneca Indian and member of the wolf clan. Elizabeth may have descended from a white Quaker captive, Frances Slocum, but there is no way to

Ely S. Parker

edly, the Parker surname is derived from a Congregational missionary friend of Chief William Parker, Reverend Samuel Parker, the son of a Revolutionary War veteran who briefly served in western New York until 1812 when he become prominent in missionary activities in the West. According to at least one biography, William Parker, his two brothers, and Elizabeth Johnson, Ely's mother, had migrated to Tonawanda from the Allegany Reservation at the same time that Handsome Lake was driven from Allegany to Tonawanda.

Ely Parker received his early education at the Baptist boarding school associated with the mission church on the Tonawanda Reservation. Leaving the mission school when he was ten years old, Parker had a limited knowledge of English, being able to understand but not speak the language. He was taken to Canada for several years where he was taught to hunt and fish, but returned to the Tonawanda Reservation at the age of 12, resolved to learn English and to further his education. He eventually was assigned the job of interpreter for the school and the church.

Becomes intermediary with government delegations

Recognizing Parker's abilities in his early teens, the Seneca chiefs sent him to assist in numerous Seneca tribal delegations to Albany and Washington, D.C. He served as a translator and intermediary, accompanying his father and other Seneca chiefs on official trips. It was during one of these trips to Washington that Ely attended a dinner in the White House at the invitation of President James K. Polk. The experience of direct involvement in

know if this is true. Parker's maternal grandfather, Jimmy Johnson (So-So-Ha'-Wa), was a grandson of the Seneca prophet **Handsome Lake** (see entry), the founder of the Iroquois religion. Ely Parker's father was the Seneca Chief William Parker (Jo-no-es-do-wa); he was a veteran of the War of 1812 and a grandson of Disappearing Smoke (also known as Old King), a prominent figure in the early history of the Seneca.

Parker was also related in some way to many major figures in the history of the Iroquois, including the tribal leader Cornplanter, Governor Blacksnake, and the great orator Red Jacket. This family background was an influential factor in his later service to his people. Chief William Parker owned a large farm on the reservation and became a converted member of the newly formed missionary Baptist church. Ely reputedly received his first name from Ely Stone, one of the local founders of the mission. Suppos-

Seneca and Iroquois political and diplomatic affairs provided Parker with a valuable education that served him later in life.

Parker attended Yates Academy from 1843 to 1845 and Cayuga Academy from the fall of 1845 to 1846. He left school at the age of 18 to, once again, accompany a Seneca delegation to Washington. Parker's early role during this period was critical in the fight of the Tonawanda Seneca to regain the title to their reservation, which had been taken from them by the Buffalo Creek Treaty of 1832. The Tonawanda Reservation was not restored to the Seneca in the so-called "Compromise" Treaty of Buffalo Creek of 1842 and the Towanda Seneca had struggled with this issue for years. A portion of their former reservation was finally purchased in 1857.

During one of his visits to Albany in 1844, Parker met Lewis Henry Morgan, an ethnologist (someone who studies the races or groups of human beings in terms of where they came from, where they live, their social relations, and their characteristics as a group). Morgan's major interest was American Indian culture and particularly that of the Seneca. This meeting with the Seneca delegation provided the initial opportunity for Morgan to begin collecting data on the Seneca, with Parker serving as his interpreter. Their friendship was to last for the rest of their lives. Parker became the major source for the continuing anthropological data for Morgan's famous book, *League of the Ho-de-no-sau-nee, or Iroquois* (1851), which is considered to be the first and one of the finest ethnographies (descriptive works that systematically record the characteristics of human cultures) of an American Indian

group. Morgan acknowledged his great debt to Parker by dedicating the book to him while Parker was still a teenager.

Parker's value to the Seneca was formally recognized by his tribespeople and further enhanced in 1852 when he was designated to fill the vacant Seneca chief's wolf clan title of Do-ne-ho-ga-wa (Keeper of the Western Door), one of the major titles in the Iroquois Confederacy. This title had previously been held by the venerable Chief John Blacksmith, who died in 1851. At that time, Parker received the Red Jacket medal that had been given to Red Jacket by President George Washington in 1792 and was then inherited by Jimmy Johnson, Parker's grandfather. Parker retained his title and the medal for the remainder of his life.

Becomes engineer

Beginning in 1847, Parker wanted to become a lawyer and studied law in the offices of Angel & Rice in Ellicottville, New York, north of the Allegany Reservation. This firm had represented the Seneca Indians in several cases, and Parker had become acquainted with partner W. P. Angel when he served as sub-agent from 1846 to 1848 for the New York Indian Agency. Parker, however, was denied admittance to the bar in the State of New York on the basis of his race. Indians were not recognized as citizens of the United States until 1924.

Frustrated in his legal career, Parker turned his attention to the field of civil engineering and attended Rensselaer Polytechnic Institute. In this field he quickly became a recognized success, obtaining a number of important positions, beginning with work on

Parker (seated, far right) with General U. S. Grant and aides at Cold Harbor, Virginia, June 1864

the Genesee Valley Canal in 1849, and later on the Erie Canal. After a political difference of opinion, Parker left the Canal Office in Rochester in June 1855. He moved on to engineering positions in Norfolk, Detroit, and finally, in 1857, he accepted the position of superintendent of construction for a number of government projects in Galena, Illinois, where he resided for a number of years. It was here that Parker initially became acquainted with a store clerk and army veteran, Ulysses S. Grant. They established a life-long friendship.

Begins military career during Civil War

With the outbreak of the Civil War, Parker tried to obtain a release from his engineering responsibilities at Galena but did not receive one. He therefore resigned in 1862, and returned to the Tonawanda Reservation to obtain his father's approval to go to war. Once again, race proved to be an obstacle; he was unable to obtain an army commission from either the governor of New York or the Secretary of War. In fact, Secretary William H. Seward informed

Parker that the rebellion in the South would be suppressed by the whites, without the aid of Indians.

Eventually, in the early summer of 1863 Parker was commissioned as a captain of engineers of the Seventh Division, Twenty-seventh Corps. This assignment was due in part to his friendship with General Ulysses S. Grant, and later that year, on September 18, Parker became Grant's staff officer at Vicksburg. A year later, on August 30, 1864, Parker was advanced to lieutenant-colonel and became Grant's military secretary.

As Grant's military secretary, it was Parker who made draft corrections in the terms of the Confederacy's surrender at Appomattox Court House on April 9, 1865, and wrote the final official copies that ended the Civil War. Parker later reported that Confederate General Robert E. Lee was momentarily taken aback on seeing Parker in such a prominent position at the surrender. Apparently, Lee shook hands with Parker and said, "I am glad to see one real American here." Parker replied, "We are all Americans."

At the conclusion of the Civil War, Parker continued as Grant's military secretary. He was also commissioned a brigadier-general of volunteers at the date of surrender at Appomattox. In addition, two years later, on March 2, 1867, Parker's gallant and meritorious service was recognized through his appointment to first and second lieutenant in the cavalry of the Regular Army, and brevet appointments as captain, major, lieutenant-colonel, colonel, and brigadier-general, also in the Regular Army.

On Christmas day, 1867, with Ulysses S. Grant as best man, Parker married Minnie Orton Sackett of Washington, D.C., the step-daughter of a soldier who had died in the war. In 1878, Ely and Minnie had a daughter, Maud Theresa Parker.

Enters into troubled political career

Following his election to the presidency, Grant appointed Parker as Commissioner of Indian Affairs on April 13, 1869; he was the first American Indian to hold the office. He had long been a strong advocate for the assimilation (blending a group into mainstream culture through loss of tribal identification and self-government) of the American Indian. He had also been a supporter of Grant's Peace Policy, which was directed to the "improvement" of the American Indian. But Parker's term as commissioner troubled many powerful people. As commissioner he worked to rid the bureau of fraud and corruption and tried to establish new and more progressive interactions between government and Indian agencies. The major reform and restructuring of the Bureau of Indian Affairs that he tried to accomplish made him unpopular in some political quarters. In addition, his humanitarian and just treatment of western Indians created many influential political enemies in Washington.

Parker was tried by a committee of the House of Representatives in February 1871 on charges of defrauding the government. Most people believe that Parker was falsely accused, and he was completely exonerated of any misconduct. He nevertheless resigned from government service in July, feeling that the office of commissioner had been greatly reduced in authority and effectiveness.

Parker entered the stock market on Wall Street and made a fortune, which he eventually lost in settling a defaulted bond of his business partner. Other attempts at business opportunities also proved unsuccessful. Later, Parker served with the New York City Police Department. He died on August 31, 1895, at his home in Fairfield, Connecticut, where he was initially buried. In 1897, his remains were reinterred with those of Red Jacket and his ancestors in Forest Lawn Cemetery, in Buffalo, New York.

Further Reading

Armstrong, William H., *Warrior in Two Camps: Ely S. Parker, Union General and Seneca Chief,* Syracuse, NY: Syracuse University Press, 1978.

Morgan, Lewis Henry, *League of the Ho-de-no-sau-nee, or Iroquois,* Rochester, New York: Sage, 1851; reprinted, Corinth Books, 1962, 1990.

Olson, James C., *Red Cloud and the Sioux Problem,* Lincoln: University of Nebraska Press, 1965.

Parker, Arthur C., *The Life of General Ely S. Parker: Last Grand Sachem of the Iroquois and General Grant's Military Secretary,* Buffalo, NY: Buffalo Historical Society Publication, 1919.

Waltmann, Henry G., "Ely Samuel Parker, 1869-71," in *The Commissioners of Indian Affairs: 1824-1977,* edited by Robert M. Kvasnicka and Herman J. Viola, Lincoln: University of Nebraska Press, 1979, pp. 123-131.

Quanah Parker

Comanche tribal leader and rancher
Born c. 1852, Cedar Lake, Texas
Died February 25, 1911, Oklahoma

Parker's famous residence, the Star House, was more a mansion than a house. Two-storied with a double porch, its metal roof was decorated with prominent white stars and the interior was as sumptuous as the homes of wealthy non-Indians of the day. Some of Quanah's critics said he had built the Star House to lord over the more traditional leaders of the Comanche. Others said he needed the room for his seven wives and seven children.

Quanah Parker was a leader of the Comanche people during the difficult change from free-ranging life on the southern Plains to the settled ways of reservation life. Although he fought in one of the most fearless and powerful of the "renegade" groups and resisted relocation to reservations, once he had surrendered to the government in 1875, he settled well—and prosperously—into reservation life. A successful and wealthy cattle-rancher, Parker could be a shrewd negotiator with government agents and offered a strong voice in favor of formal education for Native children. Parker was viewed with some suspicion by his people for using his position as the principal chief of the Comanche to advance himself personally, yet he retained this position throughout his life and was viewed by many as a great and powerful leader.

Quanah ("Fragrant") was well-suited to help his people bridge the two worlds because of his own mixed ancestry. He was born to Peta Nocona, a Quahadi (Kwahado, Quahada) Comanche war leader, and Cynthia Ann Parker, a white woman who had been captured by the Comanche and raised as an Indian. When Cynthia's family home in Texas was attacked by the Comanche on May 19, 1836, several family members died in the raid, but nine-year-old Cynthia was one of those taken alive. She and her brother were adopted by the Comanche, but her brother apparently died soon after. Cynthia was renamed Preloch and was brought up in a traditional Quahadi village.

In her teens, Cynthia married Peta Nocona. About 1852 (some sources say as early as 1845), Quanah was born to them as their band camped at Cedar Lake, Texas. Approximately three years later, Quanah's sister Topsannah ("Prairie Flower") was born. As they grew up, major changes were taking place in Comanche life: whites settled on more and more land and free movement for Indians and the buffalo they hunted decreased.

Cynthia's family kept looking for her. Finally, in 1861, Texas Rangers recaptured Cynthia and brought her and Topsannah back to her relatives. Although she knew about her early years, Cynthia had become completely Comanche, and she mourned for her Indian family and friends. It is believed that Topsannah died in the mid-1860s, and Cynthia followed her to the grave in 1870.

Back amid the Quahadi, Quanah was trying to deal with the loss of his beloved mother and sister. The death of Peta Nocona in 1866 or 1867 was another crushing blow. Without his parents, Quanah had to depend on help from his other relatives. Meanwhile, other Quahadi made fun of him for his mixed ancestry. He was a striking figure, but taller and thinner than other Comanches, with lighter skin and grey eyes. Still, he felt completely Comanche in his beliefs and way of life.

The move to Indian Territory

In 1867, the Treaty of Medicine Lodge was signed. This treaty meant that the Comanche, Cheyenne, Riowa, Kiowa-Apache, and Arapaho had to move onto reservations in Indian Territory (later the state of Oklahoma). Most of the Comanche bands accepted the treaty, but the Quahadi fought against settlement the longest, refusing to obey the treaty. Seven years of fighting white settlers and frontier towns followed, and each Comanche attack led to a reprisal by the whites.

The final insult, the Quahadi felt, was the increasing presence of buffalo hunters, professionals hired to hunt the huge animals for the eastern market. These hunters threatened the survival of the Plains Indians, forcing them onto reservations to avoid starvation. In June 1875, a group of 700 allied tribes' warriors attacked a group of buffalo hunters at a fortification called Adobe Walls, in the Texas Panhandle.

After three days of bitter fighting, the Indian raiding force was turned back. After this, General Ranald Mackenzie chased the Quahadi for two years. Until recently, historians believed Quanah Parker led the Indians at Adobe Walls, became the war chief of the Quahadi during Mackenzie's pursuit, and reluctantly surrendered to reservation life as the last fierce war leader of the free

Quanah
Parker

Comanche. Recently, historians have shown that Quanah was too young to have been a war chief, but did fight at Adobe Walls.

The Quahadi surrendered to reservation settlement in 1875. Their leader at that time was probably Eschiti ("Coyote Droppings"), who had started the raid on Adobe Walls. A medicine man as well as a leader, Eschiti would see his influence decrease as Quanah Parker's increased. Early on, the U.S. government believed that as a mixed-blood Parker could be more easily converted to white ways and could then influence his people to change also. However, they had not taken into account that Parker's mixed ancestry was the reason many traditional Comanche refused to accept his leadership. The fact that he was being "created" as an Indian leader by white officials caused more trouble.

A chief emerges

These first years of settled life took quite a toll on the Quahadi. Not only was their old way of life dying, but many Indian people sickened and died as well. Perhaps this high death rate also explains why Quanah Parker had few rivals for power. In fact, his strongest opponent, Mowaway, who had been a war chief, gave up his position in 1878, clearing the way for Quanah to become the principal chief of the Comanche around Fort Sill.

Parker then moved quickly from the status of a "ration chief"—the recognized leader of a small band of reservation-dwellers who together count as one unit for the purpose of handing out rations—to a member of the Comanche Council. Throughout the late 1870s, however, the council functioned mainly to agree to whatever the government's Indian Agent decided.

The single major disagreement between the agency and the council in this period arose over the Indian Department's decision to consolidate the Wichita, Kiowa, Kiowa-Apache, and Comanche agencies and to move the headquarters from Fort Sill to the Washita River. This change would place the source of rations some 60 miles away from the Comanche settlements. With rations being handed out three times per week, most Comanche would be traveling constantly to or from the headquarters. Parker joined in with other, more traditional leaders in opposing this move. The growing anti-Quanah faction saw this as one of his last "loyal" acts. Already, Parker's giving in to the whites was earning him enemies.

Heading into the 1880s, Texas cattlemen were regularly driving cattle across Comanche lands on the way to Dodge City and Abilene, Kansas. The grasslands were lush and provided a last chance for cattle barons to fatten their stock before sale. At first, the Comanche ignored this trespassing, as the cattlemen also ignored the occasional poaching of a cow by the Indians. Eventually, though, the ranchers in the areas by Comanche land were putting their herds on Comanche grasslands on purpose. In 1881, the Comanche Council formally protested. Sensing that Quanah Parker was a man who could see both sides of the issue, the cattlemen agreed to pay him (and Eschiti) to ride with white "cattle police" keeping an eye on property lines. Later, Permansu (also known as "Comanche Jack") would join them.

Being on the cattlemen's payroll provided Quanah Parker with money, "surplus" cattle, and influence among the cattle barons. He started his own herd with gift cattle and a bull, courtesy of the king of the cattle barons, Charlie Goodnight. Parker set up his own ranch, where he would eventually build his famous residence, the Star House. More a mansion than a house, it was two-storied with a double porch. Its metal roof was decorated with prominent white stars, and the interior was as sumptuous as the homes of wealthy non-Indians of the day. Some of Quanah's critics said he had built the Star House to lord over the more traditional leaders of the Comanche. Others said he needed the room for his seven wives and seven children.

The Indian Agency was horrified that Quanah, a strong believer in formal education for his people and their participation in the developing money economy of Indian Territory, was an equally strong believer in polygamy—that is, the practice of having several wives at once—and in the Peyote Cult. This new religion, which involved the ritual use of a drug that came from a cactus, uplifted many Indians after the devastating changes of those years.

It is not certain when Quanah was introduced to the peyote rite (originally a religion of the native peoples of northern Mexican deserts), but he was well respected in the Comanche branch of the faith, becoming a "road man" (a ritual leader). The Ghost Dance—another new religious ritual designed to make the old Plains life come back—swept the Plains tribes during this time, and people from the Lakota to the Paiute danced themselves into trances, trying to make the buffalo return. But Parker rejected the movement. He remained true to his peyotism, but allowed the bringing in of Christian elements, perhaps out of respect for his mother.

"Progressive" in two worlds

In 1884, Quanah Parker made his first of 20 trips to Washington, D.C. He went to discuss allotment and the changes it would bring to the lease arrangements the Comanche had been able to work out with the cattle ranchers. The Comanche had made money by leasing grasslands they were not using themselves. But they were going to have to pay high taxes after allotment, the process of dividing tribally held land into individually owned plots. Despite several trips, Quanah was unable to hold off the allotment, but he did improve the deal for his people.

The anti-Quanah Parker faction on the reservation criticized Parker for trying to arrange a larger allotment for himself and a higher price-per-acre payment for the sale of surplus land. In the 1890s, the Indian Agent was issuing official "chief certificates," a sort of identification. Quanah was able to convince the agency that he should be issued the certificate for the principal chieftainship, which would make him his people's most powerful leader. After this, Eschiti was out of the picture completely, and Parker went so far as to have stationary printed with his name and the title of principal chief. All this impressed white men, but further angered the more traditional Comanche.

Starting in 1886, Parker had been a judge of the Court of Indian Affairs, but lost his position as the tribe made the final move toward allotment near the end of the century. The breakup of communally held lands and the resulting breakdown of age-old tribal traditions greatly angered many Comanche. They saw Quanah as the source of their problems. Quanah, meanwhile, courted a public image as a "progressive" Indian in the eyes of white America and became something of a national celebrity. Visitors to the Star House included Theodore Roosevelt and British Ambassador Lord Bryce. In fact, Quanah was one of the four Indian chiefs to ride in President Theodore Roosevelt's inaugural parade.

The circle is completed

In the first decade of the twentieth century, Quanah Parker's influence began to fade. Two of his wives left him, angered over what they saw as a self-important pursuit of multiple wives. Tonarcy was considered his principal wife, but among his others were Topay, Chony, Mahcheettowooky, and Aerwuthtakum. Since most of his wives were widows when he married them, Parker saw this arrangement as a way to take care of women who would otherwise have had to rely on relatives for their survival, due to their young ages. In the world of tribal politics, Quanah was also losing ground. Allotment had reduced his land base and therefore his personal fortune, and he would eventually resort to taking a paid position with the Indian Service as an "assistant farmer."

By the beginning of 1911, Quanah Parker was very ill. He had rheumatism and his heart was weakening. In February, after a long and tiring train ride, he took to his bed, suffering from heart trouble. On February 25, 1911, Quanah Parker died at the Star House, Tonarcy at his side. Despite criticism during his life from traditional Comanche, Quanah Parker was so revered that the pro-

cession to his resting place was said to be over a mile long. After a Christian service in a local church, Quanah was buried next to his mother's and sister's remains in Cache County, Oklahoma. Four years later, grave-robbers broke into his grave, taking the jewelry with which he had been buried. The Parkers ritually cleaned and then reburied him. Quanah Parker, Cynthia Ann, and Topsannah were all moved to Fort Sill Military Cemetery in 1957. The life of Quanah Parker is today seen as the extraordinary story of a person successfully living in two worlds and in between two eras.

Further Reading

Andrews, Ralph W., *Indian Leaders Who Helped Shape America, 1600-1900,* Seattle: Superior Publishers, 1971.

Dockstader, Frederick J., *Great North American Indians,* New York: Van Nostrand Reinhold, 1977.

Edmunds, R. David, *American Indian Leaders: Studies in Diversity,* Lincoln: University of Nebraska, 1980.

Hagan, William T., *Quanah Parker, Comanche Chief,* Norman: University of Oklahoma, 1993.

Leonard Peltier

Ojibway-Lakota activist
Born September 12, 1944, Grand Forks,
    North Dakota.

"In honesty, I wish I hadn't been at that camp, but I do not regret that I was one of those who stood up and helped to protect my people."

A leader in the American Indian Movement (AIM) in the early 1970s, Leonard Peltier is serving two consecutive life sentences at Leavenworth Prison in northeastern Kansas. He was convicted of killing two Federal Bureau of Investigation (FBI) agents in 1975 at the Pine Ridge Reservation in South Dakota. Peltier claims he is innocent of these killings, and many people consider him a political prisoner, that is, they believe he was jailed for his political activities rather than for the crimes of which he was convicted. With the support of a large and diverse group of individuals and organizations, Peltier works for his release from prison and for justice and improved conditions for all Native Americans. His supporters include hundreds of tribes, lawmakers in the United States and Canada, the human-rights organization Amnesty International, religious leaders such as South African Archbishop Desmond Tutu and the British Archbishop of Canterbury, Nobel Peace Prize winner Rigoberta Menchu, a Belgian princess, and a U.S. Court of Appeals judge.

Peltier was born in Grand Forks, North Dakota, in 1944. At that time, his large family worked in the potato fields, migrating from Turtle Mountain in north central North Dakota to the Red River Valley on the North Dakota-Minnesota border. Peltier's maternal grandmother was a full-blood Lakota Sioux. His father, Leo (who died in 1989), was three-quarters Ojibway, one-quarter French. Leo separated from Leonard's mother, Alvina Showers, when the boy was four. Peltier and his younger sister, Betty Ann, then went to live with his paternal grandparents, Alex and Mary Peltier.

Imprisoned for beliefs as teenager

Peltier moved with his grandparents to Montana to look for work in the logging camps and copper mines. After he experienced a racist incident in Butte, his grandparents returned with him and his sister to the reservation in North Dakota. Peltier attended Wahpeton Indian School, and then returned to the Turtle Mountain Reservation in North Dakota to live with his father. There, he became interested in traditional medicine and ceremonies. In 1958, Peltier participated in his first sun dance, a widespread purification ceremony, on Turtle Mountain. The ceremony was illegal at that time, and Peltier and other participants were jailed.

During the 1950s, the U.S. government began a policy known as "termination," which took away the reservations' power to make and enforce their own laws and placed them under the laws of the states. With reservations greatly weakened politically and economically, large numbers of Indians moved into cities. Tribal communities suffered and the desperate living conditions Peltier saw among the Ojibway affected him powerfully. As he told the authors of *It Did Happen Here,* "When I was a teenager, I heard an old Ojibwa woman, a relative of mine, get up and speak at an Indian meeting. She was pleading for food for her children. 'Are there no more warriors among our men,' she asked, 'who will stand up and fight for their starving children?' That day, I vowed I would help my people the rest of my life."

Becomes active in AIM

In 1959, Peltier's mother moved to the West Coast as part of the government's relocation program, and Peltier soon followed. In Oakland, California, he and his cousins Bob and Steve Robideau learned carpentry and machine work from the Robideaus' father. Peltier and Steve Robideau then worked as welders in shipyards in Portland, Oregon. By the age of 20, Peltier was part-owner of an auto body shop in Seattle, Washington. At this time, he became a more active advocate for Native American issues, participating in the local fishing rights fight. His first real political confrontation was the takeover of surplus Indian land at Fort Lawton outside Seattle in 1970.

After the Fort Lawton episode, Peltier began traveling the country with leaders of the relatively new American Indian Movement (AIM) such as **Dennis J. Banks** (see entry) and Vernon Bellecourt. AIM was an activist organization that used sit-ins and other forms of protest to draw attention to its struggle. In November 1972, Peltier went to Washington, D.C., with other AIM members as part of the Trail of Broken Treaties march. AIM leaders had alerted Washington officials that they would be in town to discuss treaty matters. When they got there, government officials did not provide the housing and food that they had been led to expect. In protest, members of the Trail of Broken Treaties barricaded themselves in Bureau of Indian Affairs (BIA) offices for a week.

AIM leaders had drafted a list of "20 points," which focused on Indian treaties, including the Fort Laramie Treaty of 1868. This treaty recognized Indian sovereignty (self-government, free from control of outsiders) and Indian land rights, including those of Peltier's people, the Sioux. Violations of this treaty had left the Oglala Sioux only a fraction of their original homeland. The government promised to consider the 20-point proposal but never did. Instead, after the incident at the BIA building, the FBI classified AIM as an "extremist organization" and added its leaders—including Peltier—to its list of "key extremists."

Troubles begin

Events quickly escalated for Peltier and other AIM members. In late November 1972, Peltier was beaten by two off-duty policemen in Milwaukee, Wisconsin. When they found a gun (which was broken) in Peltier's possession, they charged him with attempted murder. After he spent five months in jail, AIM raised bail for Peltier's release and he went underground. Instead of appearing at a pretrial hearing in July 1973, Peltier headed for the Dakotas.

Meanwhile, members of the Pine Ridge Reservation in southwestern South Dakota had begun experiencing conflicts under the tribal chairmanship of Richard "Dick" Wilson. Wilson had been elected under suspicious circumstances and was considered a "puppet" of the BIA and the federal government. Backed up by the BIA police and the reservation police known as the "GOON squad" (GOON stood for "Guardians of the Oglala Nation"), he used violence and intimidation to carry out his unpopular rule. Many incidents of harassment and physical abuse of tribal members occurred. When Wilson and the FBI did not respond to efforts to resolve the murder of an Oglala named Raymond Yellow Thunder, Pine Ridge traditional elders appealed to AIM for help.

Violent incidents and unrest continued. In February 1973, 300 traditionals (Native Americans who wished to retain Indian tradition and identity) and AIM members, including Peltier, occupied the village of Wounded Knee, in southwestern South Dakota—where the U.S. Cavalry had slaughtered hundreds of Sioux in 1890—to protest the abuses of Wilson and the GOON squad. A 71-day siege by the FBI, U.S. marshals, and BIA police ended when U.S. government representatives agreed to investigate conditions on the Pine Ridge Reservation and Fort Laramie Treaty violations. The investigations never took place. An estimated 300 unexplained murders or "accidents" occurred during this period. At the request of Oglala Sioux chiefs who feared for their people in the lawlessness at Pine Ridge, Peltier and six other AIM members returned in March 1975 to establish a spiritual camp near Oglala to protect the people.

Convicted of deaths of FBI agents

In the late morning of June 26, 1975, FBI agents Ronald Williams and Jack Coler entered the Jumping Bull property near Oglala, supposedly to serve a warrant for robbery on a young Oglala named Jimmy Eagle. There were gunshots, and the two agents and a young Coeur d'Alene Indian, Joe (Killsright) Stuntz, were killed. FBI agents, BIA police, and other law enforcement agencies moved in, and the standoff continued for the rest of that day. While police searched for someone to charge with the murder of the FBI agents (no one has yet been charged with the death of Joe Stuntz), the U.S. Civil Rights Commission was called in to investigate the FBI's search tactics. The Justice Department never investigated the issue of FBI civil rights violations.

In November 1975, Peltier, Jimmy Eagle, Bob Robideau, and Darrelle Dean ("Dino") Butler were indicted for the deaths of agents Williams and Coler. Peltier had fled to Canada where he asked for asylum (protection from arrest), figuring he had little chance of a fair trial. In February 1976, he was arrested in Alberta, Canada, and extradition hearings soon began in Vancouver. A Lakota woman named Myrtle Poor Bear claimed she'd seen Peltier commit the murders. She later changed her story, saying that an FBI agent had said she might meet the same end as AIM member **Anna Mae Aquash** (see entry), who had been found shot in the head on the Pine Ridge Reservation right after Peltier's arrest. Aquash had earlier told the FBI she knew nothing about the murders of the agents and would not cooperate with them.

In the summer of 1976, Dino Butler and Bob Robideau were acquitted of the murders of the FBI agents on the grounds of self-defense, and in September charges were dropped against Jimmy Eagle for lack of evidence. That left Peltier, and on December

Leonard Peltier being deported from Canada to face murder charges, 1976. In 1994 the Justice Minister of Canada authorized a review of his extradition.

18, on the basis of Myrtle Poor Bear's story, he was extradited to the United States.

Peltier's murder trial began in Fargo, North Dakota, on March 4, 1977. The prosecution claimed that Peltier and others "ambushed" the FBI agents. The largely circumstantial evidence centered around a single shell casing from a .223 caliber AR-15 rifle that was linked to Peltier and a red and white van in which Peltier was allegedly seen entering and leaving the Jumping Bull property where the killings had taken place. The defense was not allowed to present the majority of its case.

No one testified in court to having seen Peltier commit the murders. Even the prosecution found "unbelievable" an FBI special agent's statement that he saw Peltier at the scene through his seven-power rifle telescope from a half mile away. Evidence of violence on the Pine Ridge Reservation, the persecution of AIM by the FBI, and FBI tampering was concealed from the jury. On April 18, 1977, the all-white jury convicted Peltier of both murders. On June 1, Judge Paul Benson sentenced him to two consecutive life terms. He was eventually sent to Marion Federal Penitentiary in Illinois.

Appeals for new trial denied

Peltier's lawyers appealed his conviction before the U.S. Court of Appeals for the Eighth Circuit in December 1977. The appeal was denied on the grounds of the evidence of the murder weapon. The lawyers also filed a petition with the U.S. Supreme Court, but in March 1979, the Court refused to review the case. In April 1979, Peltier was transferred to Lompoc Prison in California.

Upon learning of a plan to kill him, he and three other inmates escaped from Lompoc. Peltier was recaptured in late July 1979. He was tried, convicted, and given seven additional years in prison for the escape, but the conviction was reversed by the Ninth Circuit Court of Appeals.

A second appeal was filed a few years later. Thanks to the government's Freedom of Information Act, which gives citizens the right to government information about them, newly released FBI documents revealed that the critical shell casing could not be linked to the rifle allegedly used by Peltier. Even the prosecution testified that they did not know who did the killings. But again, in December 1982, Peltier was denied a new trial. In 1984 another hearing on ballistics (the study of the characteristics of firearms) evidence failed to overturn Peltier's conviction, and in October 1987, the U.S. Supreme Court again refused to hear his case.

The Eighth Circuit Court denied Peltier's third and final appeal on July 7, 1993. This time, the Court upheld his conviction on the "alternative theories" ruling, stating that he was guilty of committing the murders or of "aiding and abetting" them. In December 1993, the U.S. Parole Commission denied Peltier parole. He was told to reapply in 15 years.

Public support for Peltier grows

Over 20 million people worldwide have signed petitions and written letters of support for Peltier. There are some 150 support groups throughout the United States, and support organizations also exist in Canada, Europe, Australia, and Japan. After Peltier's final, unsuccessful appeal, his lead attorney, Ramsey Clark, submitted a formal application for executive clemency on November 22, 1993. Petitions for clemency with more than 500,000 signatures were submitted to President Bill Clinton in December 1993. Also, in the spring of 1994, the Justice Minister of Canada authorized a review of Peltier's extradition from Canada. The rock group Rage against the Machine also drew attention to Peltier's plight in their concerts and in a popular video.

In the epilogue of the 1991 edition of *In the Spirit of Crazy Horse,* the most well-known account of the events on the Pine Ridge Reservation, writer Peter Matthiessen described meeting an individual—"X"—who maintains that he actually shot the FBI agents. This person told Matthiessen that he wished others to know of Peltier's innocence but did not intend to reveal his own identity to authorities.

In 1986 Peltier received Spain's Human Rights Award for "defending the historical and cultural rights of his people against the genocide of his race." In 1993, he was nominated for the Nobel Peace Prize. From Leavenworth Prison, Peltier directs the efforts of the Leonard Peltier Defense Committee (LPDC), established in 1985 to lobby support for his release. He is involved in social and charitable causes and the Native American rights movement. He is also a painter.

Yet, as Peltier has written in the LPDC's newsletter, *Spirit of Crazy Horse,* "I have had to stare at photographs of my children to see them grow up. I have had to rely on restricted telephone calls to be linked to my mother and grandchildren. I miss having dinner with friends. I miss taking walks in the woods. I miss gardening. I miss babies. I miss my freedom." And of his ordeal in the summer of 1975, Leonard Peltier has said, "In honesty, I wish I hadn't been at that camp, but I do not regret that I was one of those who stood up and helped to protect my people."

Further Reading

Churchill, Ward, and Jim Vander Wall, *Agents of Repression: The FBI's Secret Wars against the Black Panther Party and the American Indian Movement,* Boston: South End Press, 1990.

Deloria, Vine, Jr., *Behind the Trail of Broken Treaties,* New York: Delacorte, 1974.

Matthiessen, Peter, *In the Spirit of Crazy Horse,* New York: Viking, 1991.

Messerschmidt, Jim, *The Trial of Leonard Peltier,* Boston: South End Press, 1983.

Outside, July 1995, pp. 44-55 and 120-126.

Stern, Kenneth S., *Loud Hawk: The United States Versus the American Indian Movement,* Norman: University of Oklahoma Press, 1994.

"War against the American Nation: Leonard Peltier," in *It Did Happen Here: Recollections of Political Repression in America,* compiled by Bud Schultz and Ruth Schultz, Berkeley: University of California Press, 1989, pp. 213-29.

Peter Pitseolak

Inuk photographer and writer
Born 1902
Died 1973

Peter Pitseolak left a personal account that captured in pictures and in words the final moments of Eskimo camp life and the mixed feelings that accompany a new era.

Peter Pitseolak was an Inuk photographer whose work shows the changes experienced by the Inuit (formerly called the Eskimo) from the late 1930s to the early 1970s. His legacy of over 2,000 photographs and negatives captured the last days of Eskimo camp life and the changes brought about by southern and European influences. Also an accomplished artist and a community leader, Pitseolak himself played a vital role in the history he caught with his camera. Without his efforts, many of the details of traditional Eskimo culture would have been lost. Equally important, however, is the personal narrative that he left along with his pictures, which gave historians a chance to see the changes in Eskimo life during the twentieth century from a Native's point of view.

Pitseolak wrote his autobiography, *People from Our Side,* in Inuit syllabics, a writing system that differs from an alphabet in that its characters represent syllables rather than letters. In this book he guessed that he was born in 1902, one year after the "first religious time," the period in which Christianity made its first inroads into Cape Dorset, Baffin Island. The son of Inukjuarjuk, a hunter, and his third wife, Kooyoo, Pitseolak claimed to remember being born. Recalling a dreamlike process of traveling through a narrow channel, like a "crevice in the ice," and then opening his eyes to find the "two little cliffs" of his mother's thighs, Pitseolak stated that he was born with a smile and did not cry, recollections that were supported by family members.

A precocious youngster, Pitseolak learned both the Eskimo and English alphabets before he was able to talk from the first Christian minister to go to the North, Okhamuk, who taught the Eskimos religion through song. As Pitseolak matured into adulthood, he was known for his intelligence and wisdom and was placed in positions of leadership with fur trading companies such as Hudson's Bay and the Baffin Trading Company.

A photographer by accident

While hunting one day in the 1930s, Pitseolak met a white man who was afraid of approaching a polar bear but wanted a picture of the creature. He asked Pitseolak to take the photograph, and Pitseolak—though a little nervous himself—agreed. This was his first picture and the beginning of a lifelong career. In the early 1940s, while working for Baffin, he obtained his first camera, a box-type model that was simple to use. A few years later, he received a more advanced model—a large 122 with focus settings—from a Catholic missionary. This allowed him to improve the quality of his pictures.

Pitseolak studied various film developing techniques as well. Having first learned the process by watching a white man, he soon grew dissatisfied with his efforts and began to try his own methods. By washing the film longer and at a lower water temperature for instance, Pitseolak was able to produce higher-quality pictures and was often asked for help by white men, including the Catholic missionary who gave him his camera.

Pitseolak's photographs capture numerous aspects of the Inuit life of his time and usually feature family members, such as his wife, Aggeok, their five children, and friends in everyday activities. Although the best of Pitseolak's pictures display his photographic abilities, his work is generally valued more for the perspective it provides on an Eskimo culture in transition. As Dorothy Harley Eber, who compiled and edited *People from Our Side,* concluded, "Peter Pitseolak photographed the people around him and their everyday life. In doing so he photographed an era—a period when people still got their food from the land, but when camp bosses sometimes put up small wooden houses in their camps, when planes made mercy flights, and when, eventually, a plastic igloo went up in Cape Dorset." Aware that he was documenting a vanishing culture, Pitseolak dedicated his work to his 35 grandchildren, setting up many of his pictures so that the camera might "show how for the future."

Writings told of an era's end

In addition to leaving behind a huge collection of photographs to various museums in Canada, Pitseolak used his writings to set down his own feelings about the changes he witnessed. Taking care to note both the

Peter Pitseolak, his wife, Aggeok, and their adopted son, Mark Tapungai, c. 1945

advantages and disadvantages of southern and European influences, Pitseolak commented on everything from the Christian religion to igloo construction.

Rather than simply mourning the loss of the old ways or completely embracing the ways of the *kadluka*—the Eskimo word for "white man"—Pitseolak stressed the importance of adapting to change while preserving one's heritage. For instance, he spoke of his acceptance of the "kadluka's" religion, but condemned the hypocrisy of the selfishness

Pitseolak's photograph of a summer camp outside Cape Dorset, c. 1946. Most of Pitseolak's photographs capture family and friends engaged in everyday activities.

and greed that often accompanied it. He found praise for the new methods of igloo construction while taking pride in the *tao-teeghroot,* a type of violin invented "way before the white men came," and therefore "true Eskimo."

When Pitseolak died in 1973, he left behind him not only thousands of photographs, but also his books *People from Our Side, Out of My Life,* and *Peter Pitseo-lak's Escape from Death.* These have given the reading public a personal account that captures in pictures and in words the final moments of Eskimo camp life and the mixed feelings that accompany a new era.

Further Reading

Pitseolak, Peter, *People from Our Side,* compiled and edited by Dorothy H. Eber, Bloomington: Indiana University Press, 1975.

Pitseolak, Peter, *Peter Pitseolak's Escape from Death,* 1977.

Pitseolak, Peter, *Pictures Out of My Life,* Seattle: University of Washington Press, 1972.

Pocahontas

Powhatan-Renapé diplomat
Born c. 1595, Virginia
Died 1617, Gravesend, England
Also known as Matoaka ("She Is Playful"),
    Rebecca Rolfe

Pocahontas "at the minute of my execution . . . hazarded the beating out of her own braines to save mine."—Captain John Smith

The story of the Powhatan-Renapé princess Pocahontas is one of the earliest and most deeply rooted legends of the American past. Most Americans learn as schoolchildren the fabulous tale of the Indian princess who rescues Captain John Smith, the Englishman she loves. And even if they hadn't learned it in school, the 1995 Disney film *Pocahontas* brought the legend to life for millions of children. If the story is true, Pocahontas may have had a strong impact on English settlement in the New World. Her relationship with Smith and the English settlers helped preserve the colonists through the long winters when they faced starvation.

Much of what we know about Pocahontas's early life comes from the writings of Captain John Smith. Smith was an adventurer with the Virginia Company, the corporation licensed by King James I to explore the coast of North America and harvest its resources. The company established the settlement of Jamestown, named after the English king, in May 1607, on the shores of the James River in Virginia, near Chesapeake Bay. The settlement was plagued in its early years by jealousy and disagreement among its leaders. Smith himself spent some time in prison for insubordination (not obeying the people in charge).

John Smith and the Powhatans

In December 1607, Smith was on an expedition up the Chickahominy River, in Virginia, exploring the region for new tribes to trade with, places to look for gold, and possible access to the Pacific Ocean. He apparently got too near a treasure house of the powerful local overking, **Powhatan** (see entry). Powhatan's agents caught Smith there and took him to the king.

What happened after that is confusing. Smith claimed that he wrote a letter to Queen Anne, wife of James I, in 1616, stating that Pocahontas "at the minute of my execution . . . hazarded the beating out of her own braines to save mine." Writing about himself in the third person, Smith provided a more detailed account in 1624 in his book *Generall Historie of Virginia*. He said that Powhatan fed him well, but then "two great stones were brought before Powhatan: then as many [of the Indians] as could layd hands on him, dragged him to them, and thereon laid his head, and being ready with their clubs, to beate out his braines, Pocahontas the Kings dearest daughter," unable to persuade the others with words, put her head over his and thus saved his life.

Some modern historians have questioned Smith's version of the events in Powhatan's camp. They believe that Smith, a self-promoter, created the story of Pocahontas to

Engraving of Pocahontas from John Smith's *The Generall Historie of Virginia,* 1624.

make himself more famous. In fact, in Smith's earliest version of his meeting with Powhatan, there is no mention of Pocahontas at all, and no threat of an execution. According to an account Smith wrote only a year after the incident, he was taken before Powhatan and questioned about the English presence in the area. After Smith answered Powhatan's questions, the king sent him back to Jamestown.

On the other hand, Smith's story of Pocahontas may have been based on fact. When young Indian men of certain tribes were initiated (accepted by means of a ritual) into full tribal membership, they often went through a ceremony that involved a mock,

or pretend, execution like the one Smith describes. At some point during the execution a sponsor had to speak up for the young man. If this was Smith's initiation ceremony, then Pocahontas served as Smith's sponsor in the tribe. This interpretation makes her behavior toward the English colonists more understandable.

The Willful One

Pocahontas seems to have deserved her name, which means something like "the willful one." Smith believed that her father spoiled her and could refuse her nothing. Yet if Pocahontas did regard the English colonists as her responsibility, then she took her duties toward them seriously. During the hungry early months of 1608, she supplied the colonists with food after their own supplies and homes burned.

Pocahontas also served as a go-between in negotiations between her father and the English settlers. In April 1608, one of Smith's fellow captains of the Virginia Company had made the mistake of exchanging English steel swords for turkeys. When Smith refused to barter more of his limited supply of weapons, the Powhatan began to ambush settlers for their swords, guns, axes, spades, and shovels. Smith responded by taking seven Native hostages, who confessed that they were acting under their king's orders. In mid-May, Powhatan sent Pocahontas to Smith as a negotiator, and it was to her that Smith released his captives.

Despite Pocahontas's efforts, relations between her father and the colonists worsened. The overking was alarmed by the arrival of more colonists and believed that the English intended to take his land. An attempted crowning of Powhatan according to English rituals (the plan of some Virginia Company officials in London) did nothing to ease his suspicions. In the autumn of 1608, Powhatan forbade all trade with the English. Faced with another hard winter on inadequate rations, Smith decided to confront Powhatan at his capitol, Werowocomoco, and force him to trade under threat of war.

In January 1609, Smith and Powhatan met on the banks of the Pamunkey River. According to Smith, who sought grain, Powhatan's major concern was to find out when the English would be leaving. He believed that the colonists desired Indian land, not trade. This was the major break between the English and the Powhatans. Recognizing that Smith did not intend to leave without the grain he wanted, Powhatan decided to remove himself and his family—including Pocahontas—to the town of Orapaks, about 50 miles from Jamestown.

Smith and his men were stranded at Werowocomoco because the barge on which they had meant to carry the grain had been grounded by low tide. They were forced to spend the night in the partly deserted town. Powhatan had planned to attack and destroy the English party, but Smith and his men were saved once again by the princess. According to Smith, she warned them of her father's plan, and they escaped.

Because of this action, some modern Native Americans consider Pocahontas a traitor to her people. She was at most 14 or 15 years old, yet according to Smith, she went alone, at night, in winter weather, in defiance of her father's wishes. Whether this was because of her feelings of responsibility toward the English she had sponsored or her

love of Smith, is not known. The English captain offered her gifts as a reward, but she refused them, explaining that if they were seen by others in the tribe she would be killed. It was the last Smith would see of her for about eight years.

Travels to England

For a time Pocahontas largely disappeared from the history of the Jamestown colony. There is some evidence suggesting that she helped hide occasional fugitives who fell into Powhatan's hands, sending them back to the settlement. Smith himself suffered a serious wound—gunpowder he had in a pouch at his side exploded, stripping the flesh off one leg—and he went back to England in early September 1609. He returned home under a cloud of suspicion because men he had removed from power in Jamestown had also returned, and they had pressed charges against Smith.

In about 1610 Pocahontas apparently married one of her father's supporters, a man named Kocoum. He may have been a member of another tribe, which would explain why by 1613 Pocahontas had left her father's territory and was living among the Patawamakes. There the English reentered her life again.

After Smith left Jamestown, a sea captain named Samuel Argall took his place in the colony. The colonists were still suffering from Powhatan's refusal to trade with them. In late December 1612, while looking for new trading partners, Argall met the chief of the Patawamakes, a man named Iapazaws. Through his relationship with this chief, Argall learned where Pocahontas was living. He realized that Powhatan, who had been waging a sort of guerrilla war against the English for years, might negotiate if he knew his daughter was in the hands of his enemies, the settlers. He coaxed Pocahontas on board his ship and sailed off with her to Jamestown.

Pocahontas's presence in their midst did not help the colonists' negotiations with the Powhatan tribes. Powhatan was willing to release some English hostages he had taken, but the guns, swords, and tools he had seized were another matter. He claimed that they had been stolen from him. Powhatan did most of his negotiations through his brother and successor Opechancanough, who distrusted the English and was eager to fight them. After one attack, Governor Dale of Jamestown and Captain Argall took Pocahontas to shore to negotiate for them, but she refused. According to a letter by Dale, she wouldn't talk to her tribe except to say that if her father loved her, he wouldn't care more about his weapons than he did about her, and that she would stay with the English, who loved her.

One Englishman certainly did love her. John Rolfe had gone to Jamestown to grow tobacco, the colony's first successful cash crop and the primary basis of the Virginia economy for about 300 years. Rolfe was a devout Christian, and he had courted the captive princess while she was in the care of Alexander Whitaker, the parson of the new community upriver from Jamestown called Henrico. Whitaker instructed Pocahontas in the Christian religion and presided when she accepted the faith and was baptized, taking the name Rebecca.

Rolfe carefully considered his position and wrote a long letter to Governor Dale, stating his desire to marry Pocahontas. Governor Dale approved, and so, when he was contacted, did Powhatan. The couple married at Jamestown in April 1614. Their marriage began the Peace of Pocahontas, a friendship between the English and Powhatan tribes that lasted for many years.

For three years, the couple prospered. In 1615, Pocahontas had a son, Thomas. The London owners of the Virginia Company recognized that the colony owed its existence to the princess and voted to award her an annual payment for the rest of her life. In addition, they decided to pay for her and her family to travel to England. There she would meet the king, be presented at court, and be a living advertisement for the company's success. In 1616 the Rolfes sailed for London, accompanied by the retired governor Dale and Powhatan's representative Uttamatamakin or Tomocomo. The Powhatan princess was soon the talk of the town. She was admitted into the queen's presence, and later was received by the king. Her husband didn't have the same opportunity, partly because James I was upset that Rolfe had married a foreign princess without his permission, and partly because he was offended by Rolfe's association with tobacco, a plant the king despised.

Pocahontas apparently enjoyed court life. However, in the late winter or early spring of 1616 and 1617, her health began to fail. Rolfe took her to the village of Brentford outside London. Smith visited her there and wrote that she spoke to him in a way that suggested she would not have married Rolfe if she'd known that Smith was still alive.

The Rolfes left for Virginia in mid-March 1617. By that time, however, Pocahontas was critically ill, probably with tuberculosis or pneumonia. She was able to continue only to Gravesend, toward the mouth of the Thames River. She died there and was buried on March 21, 1617. She was 22 years old. The site of her grave has since been lost.

John Rolfe died in 1622, shortly before Pocahontas's uncle Opechancanough launched a massacre of the English, killing about a quarter of the Jamestown colony's population. John Smith survived until 1631. He helped establish English colonies in what is now Massachusetts. Pocahontas's son Thomas survived his mother. When he was in his early twenties, he traveled to Virginia, where he took over the management of the Rolfe lands. He married, and his blood continues in the veins of the first families of Virginia, the Tidewater aristocracy who ruled the colony and much of the state until the time of the American Civil War in the 1860s.

Further Reading

Barbour, Philip L., *Pocahontas and Her World,* Boston: Houghton Mifflin, 1969.

Mossiker, Frances, *Pocahontas: The Life and the Legend,* New York: Knopf, 1976.

Native American Women, edited by Gretchen M. Bataille, New York: Garland Publishing, 1993.

Rountree, Helen C., *Pocahontas's People: The Powhatan Indians of Virginia through Four Centuries,* Norman: University of Oklahoma Press, 1991.

Smith, John, *Capt. John Smith ... Works, 1608–1631,* edited by Edward Arber, [Birmingham], 1884.

Young, Philip, "The Mother of Us All: Pocahontas Reconsidered," *Kenyon Review,* volume 24, 1962.

Pontiac

Ottawa-Chippewa tribal leader
Born c. 1720, Ohio
Died 1769
Also known as Obwandiyag

Pontiac was the force behind the strongest Indian resistance movement that the English-speaking settlers had yet encountered, or ever would encounter, on the North American continent.

Pontiac was the war chief of the Ottawa and the leader of the Pontiac Rebellion of 1763, one of the greatest Indian alliances in the history of America. A gifted leader and military tactician, he was the force behind the strongest Indian resistance movement that the English-speaking settlers had yet encountered, or ever would encounter, on the North American continent.

Although little is known about Pontiac's youth, it is believed that he was born around 1720 along the Maumee River in Ohio to an Ottawa father and a Chippewa mother. When Pontiac was born, the Ottawa nation was located at Michilimackinac, at Saginaw Bay, and at the Detroit River. As his influence and prosperity increased, he may have had more than one wife and several children. It is known that he had at least one wife, Kantuckeegan, and two sons, Otussa and Shegenaba.

An Ottawa childhood

Even though there are no records of his youth, it is assumed that Pontiac spent his

Pontiac

evidently demonstrated a particularly strong aptitude was the art of fighting and making war, from the initial stage of building enthusiasm for battle to the final stage of torturing prisoners. An Ottawa family was traditionally responsible for their child's education, and usually relied largely upon oral lessons and the example of others—both techniques emphasizing practical knowledge—rather than formal schooling.

The political organization of the Ottawa nation was simple and unstructured. Each village had several chiefs who served for an indefinite period of time. Heredity did not always play a part in who was selected chief; rather, a chief was chosen based on his capability and his ability to lead others, and he would retain his influence only as long as he was successful in battle. Pontiac's particular brand of authority was such that he was able to lead his own people effectively and he also gained the influence necessary to forge alliances with other tribes.

During Pontiac's early years, the Indians and the French enjoyed a mutually beneficial relationship. The Indians traded furs for French arms and other goods. Through these transactions, the Ottawa gradually replaced their bows and arrows with guns. Guns became the primary means of obtaining food and ensuring protection, and, as a result, the Ottawa increasingly relied on the goods of the French traders for survival. Their former way of life was lost.

Initially, Pontiac was inclined to be as cordial to the English settlers as he was to the French traders. However, this attitude changed when it became apparent that the English conduct toward Native peoples differed vastly from French interactions with

childhood and young adult years in a manner characteristic of the Ottawa. The first ceremony that would have concerned Pontiac was the naming ceremony. Ottawa babies were not named until they were a few months old. The exact meaning of the name Pontiac has never been determined, but nineteenth-century Ottawa tradition referred to him as Obwandiyag (pronounced Bwon-diac). The English spelled his name Pontiac, as this was probably the way it sounded to them.

As an Ottawa boy, Pontiac was taught skills that would enable him to hunt and to survive in the woods. In addition, he was probably encouraged to use the white men's weapons and tools, which were usually obtained from the French traders. Doubtless, Pontiac was also taught the customs and traditions of his tribe. One tradition at which he them. In particular, Pontiac took exception to several policies established by Lord Jeffrey Amherst, who was the British commander-in-chief in America. One particularly damaging order prohibited the British from trading gunpowder and ammunition to the Indians, who had become highly dependent on their weapons.

Further, the English displayed an increasingly aggressive attitude toward the Indians' land, indicating that they were interested in settling the entire country instead of just establishing military and trading posts. They also discontinued extending credit to the Indians. Credit was particularly important because the Indians often needed supplies to survive the winter. When spring arrived, they would repay the debt with furs. Another source of conflict was the attitude of the English toward them; they treated the Indians as though they were an expensive inconvenience. By 1763, the entire area seethed with hostilities.

Forges an alliance and launches attacks

Pontiac believed that if the tribes presented a united front and gained support from the French, the encroaching British could be forced from the Great Lakes region. His objective was to mount one enormous and simultaneous surprise attack on all of the British forts and settlements in the area. Part of Pontiac's plan may have been influenced by a religious leader known as the **Delaware Prophet** (also known as Neolin; see entry). The Delaware Prophet preached the rejection of the white man's lifestyle and spoke in favor of a return to traditional Indian customs. He depicted the

hazards of associating with white men by creating a series of deerskin paintings. The pictures showed the white men getting in the way of the Indians' happiness and prosperity; further, they illustrated the sins that the Indians had begun committing as a result of their interactions with Europeans (particularly the English) and their way of life.

While these images had a profound effect on the Great Lakes Indians, many disagreed with the Delaware Prophet about how to resolve the problem. In his teachings, the Delaware Prophet believed Indians should resist English influences by rejecting the use of their guns and overcoming dependence on trade with them. Many Great Lakes Indians—including Pontiac—viewed armed conflict as the only way to be free of the English settlers.

In an effort to achieve his goal of creating a united front of resistance to English troops and settlers, Pontiac sent red wampum belts to Indian tribes from Lake Ontario to the Mississippi River, calling them together in a conspiracy to attack all of the English-held posts in the region. Among the tribes who joined in Pontiac's efforts were the Seneca, Delaware, Shawnee, Miami, Ottawa, Ojibway, and Missisauga. Detroit, the most important fort of the Great Lakes region, was Pontiac's principal target.

In April 1763, Pontiac outlined his strategy in a speech to three Indian villages—Potawatomi, Ottawa, and Wyandot. He stressed the eviction of the British and a return to a traditional lifestyle. His speech served to provoke the warriors into action. On May 7, Pontiac approached Detroit under the guise of meeting for a council. Upon gaining access to the fort, he was to give the attack signal to his group of warriors whose weapons were hidden under blankets. However, reports of the imminent rebellion had reached Amherst, who sent reinforcements to Detroit. When it became apparent that the commander at Detroit had his men armed and prepared for the onslaught, Pontiac decided against giving the prearranged signal and retreated. Despite the presence of heavy reinforcements, Pontiac's warriors were restless for battle; to appease his followers, the chief returned to the fort two days later and launched an attack that proved to be unsuccessful.

Elsewhere in the Great Lakes region, other tribes participating in Pontiac's rebellion had greater success. Using various ploys, Indian warriors killed or captured all of the people at Fort Sandusky on May 16, at Fort St. Joseph on May 25, at Fort Miami on May 27, and at Fort Quiatenon on June 1. The Ojibway surprise attack at Michilimackinac on June 2 was probably the most notorious incident of Pontiac's war. During a game of lacrosse, the Indian players sent a ball over the stockade wall and then all went in to retrieve it. Once they gained access to the fort, the Ojibway began killing and taking prisoners.

In the middle of June, the Seneca joined in the rebellion. First they attacked Fort Venango, leaving no survivors; a couple of days later, they attacked Fort Le Boeuf, but the English were able to escape before the fort was destroyed. The Seneca then joined forces with the Ottawa, Ojibway, and Wyandot and carried out a successful siege leading to the surrender of Fort Presque Isle on June 20. In a little more than a month, nine British forts had been seized and one had been deserted. However, the Detroit post and Fort Pitt in Pennsylvania remained intact.

During the standoff at Detroit, the English troops successfully held off Pontiac's combined Indian force of about 900 warriors by receiving reinforcements via the water route from the Niagara. For his part, Pontiac also fortified his Indian force so that the siege gradually turned into a stalemate. In the meantime, at Amherst's suggestion, the English forces at Fort Pitt used a crude form of biological warfare to hold off the Indian siege there. Smallpox-infected blankets and handkerchiefs were discretely circulated among the warriors, resulting in an epidemic among the Indians in the Ohio towns of Delaware, Mingo, and Shawnee. The smallpox epidemic lasted until the following spring.

While Pontiac's War spanned a large region, the main concentration of fighting occurred in the Detroit area and along the English supply line stretching from Fort Niagara on Lake Ontario, along the Niagara River, and across Lake Erie to Detroit. Even though the losses were frequent along this supply route, some vessels did make their way through to provide necessary reinforcements to the beleaguered forts.

Periodically, the English attempted to mount offensives to break the stalemate in the Detroit area. One mission, which occurred in late July 1763, had particularly devastating results. Part of a British relief expedition making its way toward the fort at Detroit attempted a surprise night raid on Pontiac's camp located five miles to the north. The Indians were ready for them. They ambushed the soldiers as they crossed a bridge near a small stream. After 19 soldiers were killed and 42 were wounded, the English troops were forced to retreat.

The early weeks of Pontiac's War proved favorable to the Indian allies, but obstacles to future success were obvious from the onset. Many tribal leaders were critical of the acts of torture and cannibalism committed during drunken celebration parties at the Ottawa camp near Detroit. Kinochameg, son of the Ojibway leader Minevavana, traveled from northern Michigan to deliver a speech denouncing the abhorrent treatment of prisoners. In addition, representatives of the Delaware and Shawnee tribes spoke at a council meeting and informed everyone there that hostilities in the Great Lakes area were damaging the fur trading business with their French allies. The military confrontations often generated violence and brutality throughout the region that were not limited strictly to the battlefield. Isolated Indian raids on white settlements along the frontier from New York to Maryland provoked reprisals against Indians who were not even involved in Pontiac's War.

Throughout the war, Pontiac remained confident in his belief that the French would ultimately come to the Indians' aid. What the Indian chief did not know was that England and France had already signed a peace treaty in London the previous February. When Pontiac became aware of this fact he lost any real hope that the Indians would be able to win the war.

With winter approaching, his warriors were becoming increasingly restless about providing adequate food and shelter for the survival of their families. At this time, Pontiac received a letter dated October 20, 1763, from Major de Villiers, the commander of the French Fort de Chartres on the Mississippi River, advising him to end the war campaign. The next day, Pontiac declared an end to the siege of Detroit and retreated to the west, but he continued his opposition toward the English throughout the next year. However, with little leadership or direction, the Indian alliances gradually broke up and, apart from scattered Indian raids and attacks, armed hostilities began to cease between the tribes and the English.

Signs peace treaty

At a site along the Wabash River, Pontiac finally agreed to a preliminary peace pact with the British in 1765. He also assisted the English in peacefully subduing several remaining rebel Indians, earning their admiration and respect by his actions. However, he embittered many of his Indian followers for failing to win the war and more so for benignly cooperating with the enemy once peace was established. The next year, Pontiac signed a formal peace treaty at Oswego and was pardoned by the English for his involvement in the rebellion.

The vanquished chief remained the target of hostile Indians in the years that followed the conflict, and in April 1769, on a trip to a trading post at Cahokia, Illinois, Pontiac was stabbed to death by Black Dog, a Peoria (Illinois) Indian. It has been speculated that Black Dog was paid by the some uneasy English officers who continued to think of Pontiac as a threat to their well being. Other accounts indicate that Pontiac's assassination was discussed in an Indian council and Black Dog was chosen by the council to carry out the task. Pontiac's exact burial location has never been determined.

Pontiac has emerged as one of the most talented and determined Native American military tacticians who challenged and nearly halted the spread of white settlers into the American frontier. The failure of the Pontiac Rebellion of 1763 was not due so much to a breakdown in the tribal leader's military strategy or Indian support as to his inability to forge an effective alliance with the French against the English. Nevertheless, the war that Pontiac waged represents a significant milestone in European and Native American relations, for the Indians would never again have a serious opportunity to stem the tide of encroaching white settlers who took Natives' land and pushed them farther and farther west.

Further Reading

Dockstader, Frederick J., *Great North American Indians,* New York: Van Nostrand Reinhold Co., 1977, pp. 35, 217-219.

Peckham, Howard H., *Pontiac and the Indian Uprising,* New York: Russell & Russell, 1947.

Waldman, Carl, *Who Was Who in Native American History,* Facts on File, Maple-Vail Book Mfg. Group, 1990, pp. 279-280.

Powhatan

Powhatan-Renapé leader
Born c. 1548
Died 1618
Also known as Wahunsonacock ("He Makes an Offering by Crushing with a Falling Weight" or "He Knows How to Crush Them"), Ottaniack ("Possessor"), Mamanatowick ("He Who Exceeds" or "He Who Is Very Superior"), Priest, and "I Dream"

Powhatan proved to be a capable adversary of the English, ruining their schemes while gathering arms and intelligence for a war to expel the invaders.

Powhatan, or Wahunsonacock, as he was known before the English came into his region, was a major leader of the Renapé speaking people of what is now Virginia. He formed a confederacy of more than 30 tribes and was the main political force in the area at the time the English were trying to establish their first permanent settlements, most notably Jamestown. Although he was suspicious of English ways, Powhatan maintained generally peaceful relations with the English, using his diplomatic skills to avoid confrontation and to stay one step ahead of the colonists' efforts to take power and land from himself and his people. The peace he built lasted only a few years after his death, when his brother Opechancanough led the Powhatan in uprisings against English settlers.

Named for place and visions

Powhatan was born sometime between 1532 and 1548, in a village called Powhatan, which is today the site of Richmond, Virginia. By the late 1500s, he presided over the Powhatan Confederacy, an alliance of Indian tribes and villages stretching from the Potomac River to the Tidewater region of Virginia. Powhatan inherited from his father a confederacy of six tribes, but the ambitious leader quickly expanded his domain. Estimates of the size of the Powhatan Confederacy range from 128 to 200 villages consisting of eight to nine thousand inhabitants and encompassing up to 30 tribes. In 1612, Powhatan's family reportedly numbered 20 sons and 10 daughters (one of whom was **Pocahontas**) and he was said to have had 12 or more wives.

Communities under Powhatan's power received military protection and adhered to the confederacy's well-organized system of hunting and trading boundaries. In return, subjects paid a tax to Powhatan in the form of food, pelts, copper, and pearls. Europeans who visited Powhatan in the 1600s have described a large structure filled with "treasures," probably the chieftain's storehouse and revenue collection center.

Captain John Smith, the leader of the Jamestown colony, described Powhatan around 1608 as "a tall well-proportioned man ... his head somewhat gray.... His age is near 60; of a very able and hardy body to endure any labour." Others who knew the chieftain described him the same way. One colonist described him as regal and majestic: "No king, but a kingly figure."

Distrusted English

Powhatan and his society were greatly influenced by Spanish attempts to set up a mission in the area in 1570 and efforts by the English to colonize the Roanoke region in the 1580s. The Europeans introduced new diseases, including venereal disease, that greatly reduced the population of the region. In the early 1600s, English ship captains began to raid for slaves along the American coast. In 1605 or 1606 a ship raided the Powhatan and Rappahannock river areas, killing the chief of Toppahannock and carrying off others as slaves.

When the Jamestown expedition landed on the shores of Powhatan's domain in 1607, the English were unaware that they were trespassing on a land ruled by a shrewd and well-organized head of state. Powhatan, approximately 60 years old at the time, could easily have demolished the faltering community, but instead chose to tolerate the English for a time, probably out of a desire to develop trade with them. But despite his interest in gaining metal tools and weaponry, Powhatan was very suspicious of the English colonists. The independent Powhatan villages at the mouth of the bay shared his distrust of Europeans, and attacked the settlers when they came ashore.

In the early 1600s Powhatan usually resided at Werawocomoco ("Good House"), located on the north side of the lower Pamunkey (York) River. Reportedly, he had a large house in the territory of each of the "kingdoms" he had inherited. Powhatan also kept a treasure house on the upper Chickahominy called Orapacks. John Smith was made prisoner in late 1607 or early 1608 for

The English crown Powhatan

coming too close to this place, or perhaps for other actions. He was threatened with execution but, according to his own story and the many legends that have arisen, Smith was rescued by Powhatan's daughter Pocahontas, who later persuaded her father to send food to the starving colonists. By most accounts, the Jamestown settlers would have perished from starvation during their first winter had it not been for the help of the Powhatan.

Worthy adversary

English writers depicted Powhatan as a man of extreme power. They were impressed by the guards who surrounded him and his home. Certainly Powhatan received tribute from many republics but many others were only weakly attached to his confederacy. Several tribes on the north side of the Powhatan River had at least some degree of self-rule. Further north, Powhatan's power seems to have ended at the

Mattaponi River. The English may have wished to portray Powhatan's power as greater than it was, because they wanted to control the region. This would be easier to do if all the power belonged to one person. They hoped to make Powhatan a subject of the king of England, because that way everything he ruled would belong to England as well. The more territory and power Powhatan controlled, the more land and authority the English could grab if they could gain his loyalty. Thus, for reasons of diplomacy, the colonial leaders courted Powhatan. In 1609 he was offered a crown from the king of England and reluctantly agreed to have it placed ceremoniously on his head. In return Powhatan sent the king his old moccasins and a mantle.

Powhatan proved to be a capable adversary of the English, quietly undermining their schemes while gathering arms and intelligence to prepare his people for a war to expel the invaders. His strategy included sending several of his counselors to England, to discover the empire's strength and intentions. Uttamatamakin (Tomocomo), sent to England with Pocahontas in 1616, was one such observer. In the court of English king James I, Uttamatamakin became known as a vigorous defender of Renapé religion and values in arguments with the English.

Pocahontas was captured by the English and converted to Christianity. In 1614 she married John Rolfe, a Jamestown colonist who was later credited with founding Virginia's tobacco industry. Powhatan managed to maintain peace in his domain for several years after his daughter married Rolfe. In 1617 Pocahontas died suddenly as she was returning to Virginia, and in the following year her father died also. It was left to Powhatan's brother Opechancanough to wage the war of liberation that may have been Powhatan's plan all along.

Further Reading

Rountree, Helen C., *Pocahontas' People: The Powhatan Indians of Virginia through Four Centuries,* Norman: University of Oklahoma Press, 1990.

Rountree, Helen C., *The Powhatan Indians of Virginia: Their Traditional Culture,* Norman: University of Oklahoma Press, 1989.

Travels and Works of Captain John Smith, Volume 1, edited by Edward Arber, Edinburgh: Grant, 1910.

Red Cloud

Oglala Sioux tribal leader, warrior
Born September 20, 1822, Dakota Territory
Died December 10, 1909, Pine Ridge
         Reservation, South Dakota
Also known as Makhpiya-luta or Makhpia-sha

"Washington took our lands and promised to feed and support us. Now I, who used to control 5,000 warriors, must tell Washington when I am hungry. I must beg for that which I own."

A powerful leader of the Sioux Nation, Red Cloud was known for fighting against U.S. occupation of the Dakota Territory and later for trying to establish peaceful relations between his people and the U.S. government. Not much is known about his early life, and most of what historians have written about him focuses

Red Cloud

more on his military deeds and his statesmanship than his personal life. Best known for successful military tactics against U.S. troops, gold miners, and settlers that put fear in the hearts of travelers and temporarily gained the Sioux control over their lands, Red Cloud was also a gifted orator and diplomat, and a powerful leader who sought the welfare of his people.

There are many stories regarding Red Cloud's name. Some say it was derived from a meteor that streaked red across the sky on the night of his birth, September 20, 1822. (Dakota winter counts, the colorful calendars that Sioux painted on hides, confirm his birth in 1822.) Others have said the name Red Cloud was a family name in use long before his birth. Still others have related that the name came from the way the Sioux chief's red-blanketed warriors covered the hillsides like a red cloud. The place of his birth has also been questioned. Red Cloud himself often referred to his birth on the Platte River, but he may have said this to justify his claim to that territory.

Red Cloud was raised by an Oglala headman, Smoke, his mother's uncle. As a youth, Red Cloud quickly earned a reputation for bravery and cunning in raids against the Pawnee and Crow. He took his first scalp on an expedition against the Pawnee when he was 16 years old. He suffered for the rest of his life from a near-fatal wound he received when he led his first war party. At the age of 19, he shot his uncle's rival, Bull Bear, the most powerful Oglala chief. By the time he was 40, Red Cloud was a top warrior among the Bad Faces band of the Oglala group of the Teton Sioux, who had fought successfully against the Pawnee, the Crow, the Utes, and the Shoshonis.

Battles whites in Red Cloud's War

Until the spring of 1865, the Oglala kept the peace with white travelers through their lands. But the discovery of gold in Montana increased the traffic through their hunting grounds, particularly over the Bozeman Trail. Frontiersmen searching for gold followed this path from Wyoming to Montana, even though it cut across Oglala and Brulé Sioux land. The first Oglala attack on trespassers was at the Platte Bridge on July 25 and 26, 1865. Later, the Oglala confronted James A. Sawyer's surveying party near Pumpkin Buttes. Historians disagree about

Red Cloud's role in those two battles, but there is no doubt about his significance in Sioux attacks on gold miners from 1866 to 1868. The army set up a series of forts along the trail to protect the miners, but the Sioux kept up their attacks. The series of battles during that time became known as Red Cloud's War.

In the spring of 1866, government officials were optimistic about making peace with the Sioux and their allies the Northern Cheyenne. The final treaty was to be signed at Fort Laramie. The negotiations began June 3 and went smoothly until Colonel Carrington and his troops entered the scene. Red Cloud apparently took their arrival as a sign that the soldiers intended to take possession of the Bozeman Trail by force whether or not the Indians agreed to sign the treaty. He spoke angrily to the peace commissioners for pretending to negotiate for lands they had already taken and persuaded his warriors to leave the council and begin defending their homeland.

The government officials continued the meetings, getting the signatures of several other chiefs, including the Brulé Sioux leader Spotted Tail. The tribes who signed the treaty had little interest in the lands affected by the Bozeman Trail, which was mainly the hunting ground of Red Cloud's people. But without Red Cloud's signature on the treaty there could be no peace. Red Cloud initiated raids on American travelers and made blockades in the trail, sometimes cutting off all passage. The most famous skirmish occurred when the Sioux ambushed a small detachment of fort troops who were out on wood detail. Captain William J. Fetterman, trying to rescue the woodcutters, led a cavalry attack on the Sioux on December 21, 1866. Every one of his soldiers was killed. Although often named as the leader of the attack on Fetterman, Red Cloud may not even have participated in the battle. It was clear, however, that persuading him to agree to a treaty would not be easy. In the meantime, the Bozeman Trail was in effect closed because of the threat of Red Cloud's warriors.

Toward the end of the following summer, Sioux warriors again put pressure on Bozeman Trail forts. In the Hayfield Fight on August 1 and in the Wagon Box Fight the next day, the Sioux lost many warriors but successfully drove the hay-cutting and wood-cutting parties back to their forts. Encouraged by their success, the Sioux continued attacking isolated parties on the roads, making travel hazardous. The majority of their warfare was concentrated at Fort Fetterman on the Bozeman Trail and on the Union Pacific Railroad line in Nebraska.

On April 29, 1868, a council of government officials and Sioux leaders drew up the Treaty of Fort Laramie. This treaty reserved the western half of South Dakota plus a small section of North Dakota and officially named the entire Powder River area as "unceded Indian Territory." Red Cloud sent the message that he would not sign any treaty until Fort Phil Kearny and Fort C. F. Smith were removed. By the summer of 1868, Red Cloud's reputation among the settlers was so fearsome that it was clear to all that his signature would have to be on a treaty for it to be of any value. With the completion of the Union Pacific, a new road to Montana could be established west of Fort Laramie, making the Powder River road through the disputed lands unnecessary. By August 1868, the forts were abandoned and Red Cloud signed the treaty. With the Treaty of Fort Laramie, the Indians won a significant victory against the United States and dictated, to a large extent, the official terms of peace.

Disagreement over treaty

When Red Cloud finally signed the treaty, he made it clear that he did not agree with some of its terms. Many of the Sioux believed that because he did not sign the treaty until he described his objections, those points were addressed in the treaty agreement. One of the major areas of disagreement was the location of Red Cloud's agency. The government wanted to locate the distribution center for the Sioux at Fort Randall on the Missouri River, while Red Cloud intended to continue using Fort Laramie as a base. For the next two years, Red Cloud went to Fort Laramie for supplies.

In April 1870, Red Cloud announced that he wanted to visit the Great White Father—U.S. President Ulysses S. Grant—in Washington, D.C., to discuss the treaty and the reservation plans. This first trip to Washington and to New York City was a public relations success for Red Cloud. He won much non-Indian support with a speech he made at the Cooper Institute. The government compromised on the location of the agency, first locating it on the Platte River near the present Nebraska-Wyoming border.

Attempts to negotiate with government

After a second trip to Washington, and because of problems with local white set-

tlers, Red Cloud agreed to move the agency farther north in Nebraska to the White River, close to Spotted Tail's agency. But the spirit of compromise was not to last. In 1874, gold was found in the Black Hills and interested parties pressured the government to take this land out of Indian hands, even though the Fort Laramie treaty stated that it belonged to the Sioux. Hoping to buy the land from the tribe, the government again invited Red Cloud and others to Washington for negotiation. Red Cloud's main purpose for visiting Washington again was to protest the quality of goods distributed at the agency.

Negotiations for the Black Hills were doomed from the start, partly because of disagreement among the Sioux. Some, like Red Cloud and Spotted Tail, were willing to sell the land for the right price. Others, such as **Crazy Horse** and **Sitting Bull** (see entries), went to war to try to prevent loss of more land. Red Cloud spoke out for peace with the whites, but many of his young warriors joined the militants and fought at the Little Bighorn in 1876 (the battle also called Custer's Last Stand, in which several bands of Sioux battled Colonel George Armstrong Custer's forces and killed every one of his men). The government accused Red Cloud of secretly encouraging the warriors and appointed Spotted Tail chief of both agencies. More arguments over the location of the agencies followed, but a new compromise was reached by 1878, after Red Cloud refused to move his people to the Missouri River location chosen by the government. The Red Cloud agency was finally located in southwestern South Dakota and renamed the Pine Ridge Reservation.

Although Red Cloud lost the support of many of his own people by giving in to government demands, he continued to insist on better conditions. His speeches fill pages of government reports. He continually requested that the government meet the demands of treaties. In 1881 he requested the dismissal of agent McGillicuddy at Pine Ridge, setting off a contest for control of the agency that led to McGillicuddy's removal in 1886.

By the time of the Wounded Knee Massacre—in which the U.S. cavalry brutally slaughtered 300 Sioux men, women, and children in 1890—Red Cloud had lost the following of the militant warriors. He was even taken from Pine Ridge as a captive by his own people. During his later years, the once powerful warrior lost his sight. His son and daughter helped him return to Pine Ridge, where he was given a two-story frame house as a reward for his peaceful settlement on the reservation. He was baptized in the Catholic church.

Criticizes government

Toward the end of his life, Red Cloud continued to criticize the government for not fulfilling treaty promises and for giving his people the most worthless land to live on. As he told Warren K. Moorehead in an interview published in the *Transactions of the Kansas State Historical Society,* "Washington took our lands and promised to feed and support us. Now I, who used to control 5,000 warriors, must tell Washington when I am hungry. I must beg for that which I own." And in a July 4, 1903, speech—published in James R. Walker's book *Lakota Belief and Ritual*—Red Cloud proclaimed, "I was born a Lakota and I have lived a Lakota and I shall die a Lakota. Before the white man came to our country, the Lakotas were a free people.... The white men made the laws to suit themselves and they compel us to obey them."

Red Cloud suffered criticism from his community for agreeing too quickly to the white man's demands, and he was also criticized by the government for preventing his people from making progress. As a leader, he did the best he could to guide his followers through the loss of their traditional way of life, a course made more difficult by inconsistent government policy. He died December 10, 1909, on the Pine Ridge Reservation and was buried in the cemetery at Holy Rosary Mission with the full rites of the Catholic church. A simple monument marks his grave.

Further Reading

Fielder, Mildred, *Sioux Indian Leaders,* Superior, 1975.

Hyde, George E., *Red Cloud's Folk: A History of the Oglala Sioux Indians,* Norman: University of Oklahoma Press, 1937.

Moorehead, Warren K., "The Passing of Red Cloud," in *Transactions of the Kansas State Historical Society, 1907-1908,* Volume 10, Topeka, 1908, pp. 295-311.

Native North American Almanac, edited by Duane Champagne, Detroit: Gale, 1994.

Olson, James C., *Red Cloud and the Sioux Problem,* Lincoln: University of Nebraska Press, 1965.

Red Cloud, "I Was Born a Lakota," in *Lakota Belief and Ritual* by James R. Walker, Lincoln: University of Nebraska Press, 1980, pp. 137-140.

John Rollin Ridge

Cherokee poet, editor, journalist, and author
Born March 19, 1827, Cherokee Nation East
(near present-day Rome, Georgia)
Died October 5, 1867, Grass Valley, California
Also known as Chees-quat-a-law-ny
("Yellow Bird")

John Rollin Ridge had the heart and soul of a poet but was forever haunted by dreams of murderous revenge.

John Rollin Ridge's family history placed him right in the middle of a deadly struggle between different factions (groups in opposition) of the Cherokee people. After he witnessed the assassination of his father when he was 12, Ridge fled to Arkansas with his family, was educated in the East, and made his name in California as an author and editor. He never returned to the Cherokee Nation. Shortly before Ridge's death at age 39, his uncle, Stand Watie, sent him, as a representative of the Southern Cherokee, to treaty negotiations in Washington, D.C. He took part in the talks and then returned to California, where he died of "brain fever" in October 1867.

Depending on the source, Ridge was either three-eighths or one-half Cherokee. He was born in the Cherokee Nation East on March 19, 1827. This area, soon to be part of Georgia (near the city of Rome), was home to many of the Ridges and their relatives. His father, John Ridge, and grandfather, Major Ridge, were outstanding and prosperous Cherokee citizens and tribal leaders.

Ridge's mother was Sarah Bird Northrup of Connecticut. She had married John Ridge when he attended the Cornwall Indian School in Connecticut. His parents' marriage "was opposed by both families and so scandalized the Yankee 'do-gooders' that they soon closed their Indian school," Ridge wrote in an essay published in *A Trumpet of Our Own.*

Both Ridge's father and his grandfather were active in Cherokee politics and believed in assimilation, the blending of the tribe with white society. They were key members of the "Treaty party," a group of well-to-do slave-holders, merchants, and plantation owners who believed that the Cherokee land in Georgia should be sold to the U.S. government and that the Cherokees should move voluntarily and peacefully to new lands west of the Mississippi. They thought resistance to leaving Georgia would be a disaster for the Cherokee, both as individuals and as a nation.

The "Ross party," led by Cherokee principal chief John Ross, on the other hand, believed that negotiating with the federal government and using the U.S. court system would allow the Cherokee to stay in what was left of their ancestral lands. In accordance with this majority position, Major Ridge wrote a law that provided that any Cherokee who sold or bargained away tribal land would be judged guilty of a serious offense against the tribe. This offense would be punishable by death. In spite of this, Major Ridge and John Ridge, along with their relatives **Elias Boudinot** (see entry) and Stand Watie, signed the Treaty of New Echota in 1835, agreeing to move to Indian Territory (Oklahoma). The treaty led to the death of many Cherokees when they were relocated to Indian Territory (present-day Oklahoma) along the Trail of Tears—the forced march in 1838 to their new home—and most of its signers, including Major Ridge, were assassinated in the Cherokee Nation West on June 22, 1839. The murderers were widely believed to be followers of John Ross who were, ironically, upholding the law that Major Ridge himself had written.

Father's murder

Ridge witnessed his father's murder when he was 12. The scene and its story haunted him for the rest of his life and he told it whenever possible. His father was dragged from the house and stabbed to death by armed men. His mother took the children and fled to Fayetteville, Arkansas, only 50 miles away but outside of the Cherokee Nation. In 1841 Ridge was sent east to Great Barrington School in Massachusetts. He soon returned to Arkansas, however, where he worked with the missionary Cephas Washburn. Ridge excelled in school and particularly enjoyed studying the classics.

In 1847, before Ridge was 23, he married Elizabeth Wilson; they had one daughter, Alice Bird Ridge (Beatty). Ridge always had a quick temper and a strong desire for revenge against the Ross faction. He claimed to be actively involved in the guerrilla warfare (irregular fighting, using harassment and sabotage) between the Ross and the Ridge factions in the late 1840s. In May 1849, he shot and killed David Kell, a Ross follower and local judge. It was widely thought that the dead man had been assigned to kill Ridge and the intended victim had merely gotten the advantage over him. Even so, Ridge fled to Missouri (leaving his wife

John Rollin Ridge

and daughter in Arkansas) rather than risk a trial in the Ross-controlled Cherokee Nation. Ridge's thirst for revenge is revealed in letters such as the one to his uncle, Stand Watie, in which he says, "The feeling here is that of indignation against the Ross party. They would be glad to have every one of them massacred."

Sought his fortune in California

Ridge had seen the fortunes of his father and grandfather dry up, and he himself was never prosperous. He decided to go to California in an effort to seek his fortune. This move was probably supported (and maybe even paid for) by his mother and grandmother. They did not want him to return to the Cherokee Nation because he would face trial there for the Kell murder. Gold had been discovered in California, and Ridge knew he could earn a living with his pen or his hands, or both. He set out with his brother, Aeneas, and their black slave, Wacooli, on the "northern route" to California.

Their trip was full of hardships, but they arrived in California in August 1950. Ridge went to Yuba City, where he tried trapping, trading, and mining. Having little success in these fields, he became deputy clerk, auditor, and recorder for the county. He moved to Shasta City in late 1851, and his wife and daughter joined him in 1852, the year he wrote his famous poem "Mount Shasta." Critics in California considered it one of his best.

Ridge spent his time in California in various pursuits before he became editor and partial owner of a newspaper. During his residence in California he made his home at Marysville, Weaverville, Red Bluff, Sacramento, San Francisco, and Grass Valley. In 1854, he published his one book-length work, *The Life and Adventures of Joaquín Murieta.* This book about Joaquín Murieta, a legendary Spanish American "bandit" who raided American gold fields, remains popular to this day, although Ridge apparently earned no money from the book. He continued to write poetry and articles for whichever newspaper he worked for or owned at the time, leaving behind him a legacy of poems and fiction. He was also a prolific political essayist, writing often in defense of the political rights of the Cherokee, Creek, and Choctaw. Oddly, although California Indians were suffering greatly from political oppression and even system-

atic killings at the time Ridge lived there, he never wrote in defense of the California tribes.

He was the first editor of the *Sacramento Bee,* founded in February 1857 and still published in the 1990s. In 1857 Ridge edited the *California Express,* and in August 1858 he left that position for part ownership and editorship of the *Daily National Democrat.* In the period before the Civil War (1861-65), he spoke out strongly against secession, or the separation of the slaveholding Confederate states of the South from the rest of the United States. In 1861, Ridge became the political editor of the *San Francisco Herald,* where he supported Stephen Douglas against Abraham Lincoln in the presidential race. In 1863 he founded the *Trinity National* after moving to Weaverville in Trinity County. His last move was to Grass Valley, where in June 1864 he bought a quarter interest in the *Grass Valley National.*

Represented Cherokee interests in Washington, D.C.

After the American Civil War, representatives of the Five Civilized Tribes—as the Cherokee, Creek, Chickasaw, Choctaw, and Seminole were known—went to Washington, D.C., to negotiate new treaties. The Cherokee had split during the war; John Ross headed the group that supported the Union and Stand Watie headed those who supported the Confederacy. Watie had been, according to most accounts, the last Confederate general to surrender. The Confederate Cherokee were not optimistic about the coming negotiations, and sending two opposing delegations to Washington did not help. Ridge was asked by his uncle to be a part of the southern group. Their aim was to divide Cherokee country into two nations, so that Confederate sympathizers would have their own territory and government.

The delegation was composed of Ridge's cousin, Elias Cornelius Boudinot, Stand Watie and his son, Ridge, and several others. During the negotiations, Ridge argued bitterly with Boudinot, the Cherokees' former representative to the Confederate Congress at Richmond, Virginia, and this family feud was part of the reason their mission failed. The U.S. government recognized the northern delegation as the one to represent the Cherokee Nation, which remained undivided. This was the only Cherokee work Ridge ever undertook after leaving the nation as a young adult. He stated many times that he longed to return to his own people, even at the risk of facing trial on the earlier murder charge, but it was not to be.

Ridge returned to California and died within a year, on October 5, 1867. He is buried in California, next to his wife and daughter, in Green Wood Cemetery near Grass Valley. Ridge had the heart and soul of a poet but was forever haunted by dreams of murderous revenge. Although he stated several times that he wanted to use his pen on behalf of his people, his only real efforts in that direction were in 1862, when he produced a three-part series on the American Indian for the *Hesperian,* a southern California women's periodical.

Further Reading

Cherokee Cavaliers: Forty Years of Cherokee History as Told in the Correspondence of the Ridge-Watie-Boudinot Family, edited by Edward Everett Dale and Gaston Litton, Norman: University of Oklahoma Press, 1939.

Ellis, Clyde, "'Our Ill Fated Relative': John Rollin Ridge and the Cherokee People," *Chronicles of Oklahoma,* winter 1990-1991, pp. 376-395.

Native North American Almanac, edited by Duane Champagne, Detroit: Gale, 1994.

Parins, James, *John Rollin Ridge: His Life and Works,* Lincoln: University of Nebraska Press, 1991, pp. 3, 32, and 105.

A Trumpet of Our Own: Yellow Bird's Essays on the North American Indian, Selections from the Writings of the Noted Cherokee Author John Rollin Ridge, edited by David Farmer and Rennard Strickland, San Francisco: Book Club of California, 1981.

Wilkins, Thurmond, *Cherokee Tragedy: The Story of the Ridge Family and of the Decimation of a People,* New York: Macmillan, 1970.

Louis Riel

Métis tribal leader
Born 1844, Red River Colony (now Winnipeg, Manitoba, Canada)
Died November 16, 1885, Regina, Saskatchewan, Canada

Louis Riel hoped his trial would become such a public spectacle that it would embarrass the Canadian government and they would set him free. They didn't.

L ouis David Riel, Jr., was a leader of the Métis people who led the Northwest Rebellions of 1870 and 1885, battles of resistance against European settlers in Manitoba. After the First Riel Rebellion, he drafted the Métis List of Rights and acted as president of the newly created Métis nation

Louis Riel

called Assiniboia. When settlers and the Canadian government still refused to recognize Métis land rights, he led the unsuccessful Second Riel Rebellion. Executed for high treason in 1885, Riel is remembered as a great hero by many, and calls for his posthumous (after death) pardon have been raised.

Riel was born in the Red River colony, in what is today part of metropolitan Winnipeg, Manitoba, the eldest of 11 children. Baptized Louis Riel, he later added the middle name David. His father, Louis Riel, Sr., was a French-Ojibway gristmill (a building equipped with machinery for grinding grain) operator and a political leader in his own

right. His mother, born Julie Lagimodiere, was a deeply religious Frenchwoman who had grown up in the West. Her influence, and the Catholic education he began at the age of seven, formed the basis for Riel's deep religious convictions.

Abandoned priesthood and law for rebellion

With his Catholic background, Riel entered the seminary of the Gentlemen of St. Sulpice at Montréal College in Québec province at the age of 14 to study to become a priest. He excelled in English, French, Latin, Greek, and philosophy, as well as math and science. His father's death in 1864, however, caused Riel to become moody and withdrawn. He finally left the college in March 1865 without receiving a degree. Riel abandoned his dream of becoming a priest, became a clerk in a Montréal law firm, and worked there for a year, intending to pursue a career in law.

Riel wanted to marry a young Montréal woman with whom he had fallen in love, but her parents wouldn't give their permission, perhaps because of his Métis heritage or his poverty. In any event, he decided to abandon law and return to Red River, leaving Montréal in June 1866. For the next two years he worked at a variety of odd jobs in Chicago and St. Paul, Minnesota, and he finally went home to Red River in Manitoba in July 1868. Within a year he led the First Métis Rebellion, also called the Northwest Rebellion or the Red River Rebellion.

To understand the rebellion, it is important to know about the Métis. *Métis* is French for "mixed blood." When the term is capitalized, it refers to a particular group of people with a unique cultural identity. Their history dates back to the early seventeenth century, when French fur traders traveled to the Canadian wilderness. Through casual relations with—and often marriage to—Native American women, these traders developed good relations with the Native Americans and succeeded in the fur trade. The children of these unions were the Métis.

The majority of these early Métis were French-Cree, but some were Scots and Cree. Many were also French and Ojibway, like the Riels. Caught between two very different worlds, the Métis often formed their own communities. These communities, with roots in both the Native American and the French Catholic traditions, took on their own characteristics. By the nineteenth century the Métis of Manitoba had became a distinct social, cultural, and political group.

The first rebellion and exile

The most important reason for the first Northwest Rebellion was land rights. In 1867, the Canadian colonies united and formed the newly independent Dominion of Canada. Two years later the Hudson's Bay Company sold its land holdings—known as Rupert's Land—to the new government. Because the government feared the intrusion of an influx of veterans who had fought in the American Civil War, it encouraged quick settlement.

In response to available new land, people began streaming into the Red River area. The new settlers were Protestants and English. They differed in language, customs, and religion from the Métis, and the interests of the French, Catholics, and Indians, including Métis land rights, were of little

concern to them. John Alexander Macdonald, the first prime minister of the Dominion of Canada, sent in surveyors to divide the land into 800-acre-square townships. This pattern would destroy Métis property lines, which were customarily laid out in strips that extended from the river, through woods, and then to fields. In October 1869, Riel and 16 others chased off the surveyors.

Meanwhile, William McDougall was on his way to Red River to become the territorial governor. He had with him 300 rifles to form and arm a militia (part of the armed forces of a country called up only in an emergency). Louis Riel organized the Comité National des Métis (Métis National Committee), an independent Métis government, and sent men to set up barricades at the border. His army of 400 caught up with McDougall at Fort Garry near Winnipeg. After a bloodless takeover, Riel used the fort to establish his base. He then sent a List of Rights to the prime minister in Ottawa, Canada's capital. Métis demands included land rights, freedom of language and religion, representation in the Canadian government, and assurance that they would be consulted on any decisions that involved Red River country.

The central government started negotiations with the Métis. In the meantime, McDougall, acting on his own, recruited and armed a militia. Discovering this, Riel's men forced the militia to surrender. By December McDougall had returned to Ottawa. Riel declared the Comité a provisional (temporary and unofficial) government and named the Red River area *Assiniboia*.

Riel was elected president of Assiniboia, although he was only 25 years old. He declared a state of amnesty (pardoning of

Louis Riel and the Métis Provisional Government at Red River

criminals for past offenses) and released all prisoners. One of those released, Thomas Scott, a member of the Canada Firsters group that made up McDougall's militia, plotted an attack on Fort Garry. The Métis army captured him and took him back to Fort Garry. After a trial, a jury of seven Métis sentenced Scott to death for attempted murder. Scott's execution turned eastern public opinion, except in the province of Québec, against Riel.

By terms of the Manitoba Act of 1870, Assiniboia entered the Canadian confederacy (an association of separate states or nations) as part of Manitoba. The central government guaranteed most of the Métis List of Rights but did not offer amnesty for Scott's execu-tion or other actions that took place during the rebellion. Riel, however, continued to oppose the settlement. When troops were sent to control the situation, he fled. Riel went from one Métis settlement to another, in Canada and the United States, during this period. In that time, the Métis twice elected him as their representative to Parliament. However, he never took the office.

In 1875 the prime minister pardoned Riel for his part in the rebellion. However, the conditions of the pardon required him to stay in the United States for five more years. He returned to Canada from 1876 to 1878, living most of this time under a false name in two mental institutions in Québec after an apparent nervous breakdown. He was diagnosed as suffering from delusions of grandeur. He had become a religious zealot and believed he was a modern prophet. When he was released Riel returned to the United States and became a citizen. He eventually found his way to Montana, where he married a Métis woman, Marguerite Bellehumeur, and settled down to teach Native American children at a Jesuit mission.

The Second Rebellion, trial, and death

While Riel created a new life for himself in the United States, English Protestants continued to violate the Manitoba Act and settled on Métis lands. Having lost much of what they fought for, many Métis moved west to the Saskatchewan River. The railroad was not far behind. By the 1880s settlers were moving into the Saskatchewan River area and ignoring Métis rights. Once again the Métis sought Riel's help.

Famed horseman and hunter **Gabriel Dumont** (see entry) found Riel in Montana in June 1884 and asked him to return to renew the battle to defend the rights of the Métis. Riel agreed on the condition that the rebellion not be a violent one. On his return to Canada, Riel formed the Provisional Government of Saskatchewan, drafted a bill of rights, and organized the Métis into a cavalry force of 300. When the government ignored their appeals, Riel approved a campaign of sabotage: occupying government lands, cutting telegraph wires, and taking hostages. The Métis also demanded the surrender of Fort Carlton.

Against Riel's wishes, the situation grew more intense and became violent. On March 26, 1885, at Duck Lake, Dumont's men defeated a band of Royal Canadian Mounties. Sympathetic Crees, sensing a possible Métis success, joined in the fight. The Canadian government responded by sending 8,000 troops to the region. In May, after many battles, the Métis surrendered. Sixteen Métis were dead and 30 wounded.

Riel surrendered, knowing he would be prosecuted for treason and for Thomas Scott's execution 15 years before. He hoped his trial would become such a public spectacle that it would embarrass the Canadian government and they would set him free. They didn't. While his lawyers tried to plead insanity, even calling in doctors to testify to that effect, Riel refused to go along with them as a matter of pride. The six-man jury found him guilty of high treason and the judge sentenced him to death. He repeatedly appealed his sentence, but in vain. He was hanged on November 16, 1885, at Regina, Saskatchewan, the site of his trial. To this day, Riel remains a hero to the Métis; his fate still divides French-speaking and English-speaking Canada.

Further Reading

Davidson, William McCartney, *Louis Riel, 1844-1885: A Biography,* Calgary, Alberta: Albertan Publishing Company, 1955.

The Diaries of Louis Riel, edited by Thomas Flanagan, Edmonton, Alberta: Hurtig Publishers, 1976.

Flanagan, Thomas, *Louis "David" Riel: "Prophet of the New World,"* Toronto: University of Toronto Press, 1979.

Giraud, Marcel, *The Métis in the Canadian West,* translated by George Woodcock, Lincoln: University of Nebraska Press, 1986.

Native People, Native Lands: Canadian Indians, Inuit and Métis, edited by Bruce Alden Cox, Ottawa: Carleton University Press, 1987.

Robbie Robertson

Mohawk singer-songwriter, guitarist, film composer, producer, and actor
Born July 5, 1944, Toronto, Ontario, Canada
Also known as Jaime Robertson

"So many things on this record were, like 'God, I know I heard that when I was little.' I kept telling the musicians, 'I don't know where this comes from, but it goes like this.' These things they just hide in the darkness and then come out, like scent you remember from when you were a kid."

Robbie Robertson's work with the rock group the Band in the 1960s established him as one of the foremost songwriters in rock music history. But that group's works about the American experience dealt almost entirely with the lives of white people, so it came as a surprise to many fans to learn—years after the Band's peak—that Robertson was part Indian. Though he treated Native American issues from time to time in his solos, he did his first full-scale work involving his Mohawk heritage when he assembled the score to the acclaimed 1994 television miniseries *The Native Americans*. He described the project as powerful and rejuvenating to *New York Times* writer Tony Scherman. The creative process, he mused, resembled "being in the desert looking for drops of rain," until he began work on the score. "All of a sudden I could put my hands out and it was just pouring down. Everything became wonderfully fertile."

Robertson was born in 1944 in Toronto, Canada. His father was a Jewish man named Claygerman whom the musician remembers as being fond of gambling; he died when Robbie—whose given first name was Jaime—was still quite small. "My mother was a Mohawk and my introduction to music as a child was at the Six Nations Indian Reservation," he recollected to Kristine McKenna of *Musician* magazine. The boy spent his summers there even after his mother's marriage to a man named Robertson. He was introduced to the guitar by his cousin Herb at age ten. "He showed me how to play my first chord," he told *Rolling Stone's* Steve Hochman. "It turned my life around." By age 16 he had left school and played with such bands as Robbie & The Robots, Thumper & The Trombones, and Little Caesar & The Consuls.

Joined Hawks, played with Dylan

It was when Robertson signed on as bassist for the touring outfit Ronnie Hawkins & The Hawks, however, that his music career really began. The year was 1959; the band played blues and rock in bars all over Canada. When the guitarist, Fred Carter, Jr., left the band, Robertson moved over to guitar. After splitting up with the band's leader Hawkins, the remaining members played as Levon Helm & The Hawks, fronted by drummer-vocalist Helm. The group recorded a single and looked at an uphill climb to stardom, but fate stepped in in the form of the folk singer-gone-electric Bob Dylan. The acclaimed songwriter heard some tracks they'd recorded behind bluesman John Hammond, Jr., and in 1965 chose the Hawks as his backing group for a rock-style tour.

Working with Dylan in his big pink house in Woodstock, New York, the group recorded a powerful body of work that would be passed from fan to fan on bootlegged tapes for years before being released in 1975 as *The Basement Tapes*. Heavily influenced by Dylan, the Hawks became the Band and recorded their debut album *Music from Big Pink,* named after the songwriter's house, in 1968. Among many enduring songs on the album is the classic single "The Weight," which was a bigger hit for artists like the Temptations and the Supremes who recorded it than it was for the Band; the original version, however, has since become a "classic rock" radio staple.

Their second album, simply called *The Band,* also became an icon of late-1960s rock, thanks to such powerful Robertson compositions as "Up on Cripple Creek" and "The Night They Drove Old Dixie Down," an emotional tale of the South's defeat in the U.S. Civil War. In 1974 the Band backed up Dylan on his *Planet Waves* and on a concert tour that became the phenomenally successful live album *Before the Flood*.

Moves into film composing after Band disbands

After a less-than-spectacular third album and several years of struggle, the Band decided in 1976 to dissolve the group. Their farewell concert featured guest performances by some of the biggest names in pop music, including Neil Young, Eric Clapton, Dylan, Joni Mitchell, Ringo Starr, and Van Morrison. The final concert yielded a smash documentary film directed by Martin Scorsese and a hit three-record set. Robertson then worked as a producer of a variety of

Robbie Robertson

artists; including the pop singer-composer Neil Diamond. He went on to star in the film *Carny,* writing the score for the film. Other films for which he composed the score include Scorsese's *Raging Bull, King of Comedy,* and *The Color of Money*.

In 1987, Robertson released his first solo album, *Robbie Robertson*. It contains a song, "Broken Arrow," that addresses his Mohawk background. "When I was with the Band, I felt like I couldn't really impose my heritage in that situation," he told *Rolling Stone*.

Robertson continued producing, scoring, and contributing to works by other artists into the 1990s, as well as putting out another solo effort, *Storyville,* which had little commercial success. By the time the TV mini-series *The Native Americans* came along in 1994, he said, "I was just the right man for the job." He had not been avoiding his heritage, he insisted in a *New York Times* profile, "When the band lived in Woodstock, I had an enormous tepee in my backyard. I used to go there and sort out the confusion in my life." He also read Native American history. Even so, he admitted, the racism he'd seen as a youngster convinced him not to wear his ethnic identity on his sleeve.

In praise of "poets and spokesmen and warriors"

For *The Native Americans,* Robertson both produced other Indian artists—from the group Kashtin to the flautist (flute player) Douglas Spotted Eagle—and contributed his own material. "I wanted to make a record we could send out to the rest of the world saying, 'I know you have no idea what Native American music is, but here's a taste,'" he informed Scherman of the *New York Times*. He also pointed out in the *Rolling Stone* profile that he purposely avoided "sympathetic feel-sorry-for-me music—'You took my land, you mistreated me.' We all know that. But what is much more powerful is to praise these great poets and spokesmen and warriors."

Perhaps most importantly for Robertson—whose daughter, Delphine, and son, Sebastian, appear on the album—is that the project connected him with elements of his past he hadn't even remembered. "So many things on this record were, like 'God, I know I heard that when I was little,'" he recalled to Scherman. "I kept telling the musicians, 'I don't know where this comes from, but it goes like this.' These things they just hide in

the darkness and then come out, like scent you remember from when you were a kid."

For Robertson—who made his reputation detailing the European-American experience with the Band in the 1960s—working on Native American music meant going back to his childhood. In another sense, though, it was not such a departure from his other work. As he'd told *Rolling Stone* years earlier, moving from rock to movie scoring to acting was not such a stretch: "It's all storytelling." Now, at last, he was telling a little of the story of his mother's people.

Further Reading

Musician, November 1994, p. 7.
New York Times, October 9, 1994, pp. H32, H38.
Rolling Stone, October 6, 1994, p. 27.

Will Rogers

Cherokee entertainer and humorist
Born November 4, 1879, near Oolagah, Indian
      Territory (now Oklahoma)
Died August 15, 1935, near Point Barrow, Alaska

"My ancestors didn't come on the Mayflower, but they met the boat."

Will Rogers was America's best-known humorist during the first three decades of the twentieth century. He began his entertainment career as a Wild West show trick rider and roper but easily and successfully made the transition to the stage, film, and radio. His down-home style and wit appealed to audiences of all types. Ironically, this proud part-Cherokee became known as America's "Cowboy Philosopher."

Born on November 4, 1879, on the family ranch near Oolagah, in Indian Territory (now Oklahoma), Rogers was the last of eight children of Clement Vann Rogers, a former Confederate army officer, rancher, banker, and leader in Cherokee affairs, and his wife, Mary America Schrimsher. Rogers proudly proclaimed throughout his life that he was an Oklahoma cowboy and one-quarter Cherokee Indian. "My ancestors didn't come on the Mayflower but they met the boat," he quipped in *Will Rogers: His Life and Times*.

Rogers attended the local one-room Drumgoole School for a while, but he was such a restless student that his parents enrolled him in Harrell International Institute in Muskogee, Oklahoma, a girls' boarding school that his sister Mary attended. He then spent four years at Willie Halsell College, a private boarding academy in Vinita, Oklahoma. Next he attended Scarritt Collegiate Institute in Neasho, Missouri, but his passion for roping led to his expulsion. After a two-year stay at Kemper Military Academy in Booneville, Missouri, the 18-year-old Rogers quit school for good to travel and work. Though he never graduated, he had roughly the equivalent of a high school education.

Rogers always liked doing riding and roping tricks more than anything else. He went on his first roundup when he was just a toddler and learned to throw a rope from Uncle Dan Walker, a black cowboy, before he was five. Rogers won his first prize in a roping contest on July 4, 1899, in Claremore, Okla-

Will Rogers

homa, the place he always called home. He entered roping contests whenever he could, picking up tricks from his competitors. He continued to practice his repertoire of fantastic rope stunts throughout his life.

Launched career as actor and entertainer

After leaving school, Rogers worked on cattle drives and managed his father's ranch until he decided to make his way to Argentina in 1901. His world travels eventually landed him in South Africa, where he tended cattle for a couple of months before joining Texas Jack's Wild West Show in 1902. Rogers started as a trick rider in the

311

show, but soon his rope act earned him the billing "The Cherokee Kid—The Man Who Can Lasso the Tail Off a Blowfly." Texas Jack reportedly gave him some advice that he followed throughout his professional life: get off the stage before the audience has had enough.

In 1905 Rogers made his New York debut at Madison Square Garden. He broke into vaudeville the same year at Hammerstein's Roof Garden in New York City. His act consisted of riding his pony, Teddy (clad in felt-bottom boots buckled like galoshes), onto the stage and doing a variety of rope tricks to soft orchestra music.

During this early period of his career, Rogers married his longtime sweetheart, Betty Blake, and they had three of their four children. Rogers' career took off only after he started talking during his tricks, more because of his delivery and superb timing than any particular jokes. In general, he would concentrate on his lassoing, then make an impromptu remark half to himself.

Rogers was on the verge of being fired from a vaudeville show owned by famed impresario Florenz Ziegfeld, Jr., when he followed his wife's suggestion to use newspaper stories as a source of comedy. His constant reading gave him enough new material for three daily performances, which he prefaced with: "Well, all I know is what I read in the papers." He later used the same phrase in his newspaper column. Known as "the columnist of the theater," Rogers found over the years that the more serious the situation, the more the audiences laughed at his parody. In 1916 he joined Ziegfeld's tremendously popular Follies and appeared in several editions of the show until 1924.

Rogers' entertainment career extended beyond the vaudeville stage. He opened in his first Broadway musical, *The Wall Street Girl,* in 1912, and went on to perform in many stage successes in the United States and England. In 1918 Rogers appeared in his first motion picture, a silent film titled *Laughing Bill Hyde.* After signing a two-year contract with movie producer Samuel Goldwyn, he moved his family from New York to California.

By 1929 Rogers had made the transition to talkies, starting with *They Had to See Paris.* Talking pictures allowed him to showcase his onstage persona and play himself. In all, he appeared in 17 motion pictures. He was probably the highest-paid actor of his time and certainly one of the best loved. He first aired on radio in 1926. Beginning in 1930, he gave a series of popular weekly broadcasts.

Became a columnist and commentator

Rogers's various careers overlapped considerably. In 1920, then widely known as a theatrical performer and movie actor, he wrote a series of articles for the *Los Angeles Record* about the Republican and Democratic conventions. Although asked to run for legitimate public office, he never did. By 1928 he was a recognized commentator on political conventions.

In 1922, Rogers had started writing a humorous weekly newspaper column for the *New York Times.* The column later appeared in most American Sunday papers. Rogers is said to have been the most widely read—with an estimated 20 million readers—and frequently quoted newspaper columnist of his time. After two years, Rogers collected his favorite columns for a book, which, like some of his earlier film shorts, bore the title *The Illiterate Digest*. The well-received volume prompted reviewers to recognize him as "The Cowboy Philosopher," an "everyman" who skillfully voiced the feelings of the average American.

From the earliest days of his career, Rogers expressed concern for victims of misfortune, donating both his earnings and talents to charitable causes. He pledged ten percent of his 1918 salary to the American Red Cross and gave the organization $100 per week for the duration of World War I. As his popularity increased in the late 1920s, the press generously covered his continued humanitarian activities. He also was an advocate of relief for farmers and the unemployed.

Death of an aviation booster

Rogers visited every state of the Union and traveled around the world three times. An early booster of air travel and safety, he often flew around the country to his engagements. He flew with most of the outstanding aviators of the time and when unable to take a commercial flight, he would catch a ride on an airplane carrying the U.S. mail, weighing himself outfitted in flight gear and paying the equivalent sum as if he were a package. Rogers was in several plane crashes during his career. The third crash, which occurred in Chicago in 1929, left all of his ribs fractured.

In 1935 Rogers and his fellow Oklahoman aviator Wiley Post set off for what Rogers called "a vacation." It most likely would have been a flight to the former Soviet Union via Alaska if fate had not intervened. An aviation record holder, Post had donated his historic airplane to the Smithsonian Institution. For the Arctic trip, which Rogers was financing, Post piloted a craft assembled from parts to more than one model. Though certified as airworthy, the plane was hard to control in some situations.

On August 15, Post and Rogers stopped on Walakpa lagoon near Point Barrow, Alaska. Shortly after taking off for their next stop, the plane lost power and nosedived into the water, splitting apart and killing them both instantly. Reportedly, the last word Rogers typed on his typewriter was "death." Betty Rogers is said to have learned of her husband's death in Connecticut where their daughter, Mary, was starring in the play *Ceiling Zero,* about a young woman whose father dies in an airplane accident. Rogers died at the age of 55.

Final tribute

The *New York Times* dedicated four full pages to Rogers in the wake of his death, while general newspaper and radio coverage lasted for a week. In his memory, the nation's movie theaters were darkened; CBS and NBC television stations observed a half-hour of silence. A squadron of planes, each towing a long black streamer, flew over New York City in final tribute to this hero and friend of aviation.

Buried in California, Will Rogers's body was moved in 1944 to a gravesite beside that of his wife and their fourth child, Fred, who had died of diphtheria as an infant. The tomb sits in the garden of the Will Rogers Memorial at Claremore, Oklahoma. His chosen epitaph was one of his favorite sayings, "I never met a man I didn't like." In the 1990s Rogers's legend lives on in the Tony Award-winning musical *Will Rogers Follies,* among other tributes. He remains one of the most revered popular figures of the twentieth century.

Further Reading

Dockstader, Fredrick J., *Great North American Indians,* New York: Van Nostrand Reinhold Company, 1977.

Ketchum, Richard M., *Will Rogers: His Life and Times,* New York: American Heritage Publishing, 1973.

Rogers, Will, *The Autobiography of Will Rogers,* edited by Donald Day, Rogers Company, 1949.

Rogers, Will, *Ether and Me,* New York: Putnam, 1929.

Rogers, Will, *The Illiterate Digest,* A & C Boni, 1924.

Rogers, Will, *Letters of a Self-Made Diplomat to His President,* New York: A & C Boni, 1926.

Rogers, Will, *Rogers-isms: The Cowboy Philosopher on the Peace Conference,* New York: Harper, 1919.

Rogers, Will, *Rogers-isms: The Cowboy Philosopher on Prohibition,* New York: Harper, 1919.

Rogers, Will, *Sanity Is Where You Find It,* edited by Donald Day, Boston: Houghton Mifflin, 1955.

Rogers, Will, *There's Not a Bathing Suit in Russia,* New York: A & C Boni, 1927.

Rogers, Will, *Twelve Radio Talks Delivered by Will Rogers during the Spring of 1930,* New York: E. R. Squibb & Sons, 1930.

Sterling, Bryan B., and Frances N. Sterling, *Will Rogers' World: America's Foremost Political Humorist Comments on the Twenties and Thirties—and Eighties and Nineties,* New York: M. Evans, 1989.

The Will Rogers Scrapbook, edited by Bryan B. Sterling, New York: Grosset & Dunlap, 1976.

Yagoda, Ben, *Will Rogers: A Biography,* New York: Knopf, 1993.

Sacagawea

Lehmi-Shoshone interpreter and guide
Born c. 1784, in present-day Idaho
Died c. 1812
Also known as Boinaiv ("Grass Maiden"),
    Sacajawea "(Boat Launcher"), and
    Tsakakawia ("Bird Woman")

"The Indian woman, to whom I ascribe equal fortitude and resolution with any person on board at the time of the accident, caught and preserved most of the light articles which were washed overboard."
—Meriwether Lewis

S acagawea was an interpreter and guide for—and the only woman member of—one of the most famous expeditions in history. Most of what we know about her life comes from the journals of Meriwether Lewis and William Clark, a lawyer and a clerk for a fur trading company. These men led an 1803 expedition, authorized by President Thomas Jefferson, to explore the recently purchased Louisiana Territory (area that extended from the Mississippi River to the Rocky Mountains and from the Gulf of Mexico into the states of Montana, North Dakota, and Minnesota). The Shoshone Indians also have many stories in their oral tradition about Sacagawea, and many living Shoshone trace their ancestry to her. Nevertheless, there is much controversy surrounding her story.

Captured by Hidatsa war party

Sacagawea's Shoshone name was Boinaiv, which means "Grass Maiden." She was born somewhere between 1784 and 1788 into the Lehmi band of the Shoshone Indians, who lived in the eastern part of the Salmon River area of present-day central Idaho. Her father was chief of her village. In 1800, when Boinaiv was about 12 years old, her band was camped at the Three Forks of the Missouri River in Montana. There they encountered some Hidatsa warriors. The warriors killed four men, four women, and a number of boys. Several girls and boys, including Boinaiv, were captured and taken back to the Hidatsa village.

At the Hidatsa camp, Boinaiv was given the name *Sacagawea,* which means "Bird Woman," by her captors. Historians disagree about the derivation and spelling of her name. It is sometimes written as *Sacajawea,* a name meaning "Boat Launcher" in Shoshone. Sometime between 1800 and 1804, Sacagawea and another girl were sold to (or won in a gambling match by) a trader, Toussaint Charbonneau, a French Canadian who lived among the Hidatsa. He eventually married both.

Joins the "Corps of Discovery"

In 1803, Jefferson and the U.S. Congress authorized a "Voyage of Discovery" in which a group of men would explore the territory between the Mississippi and Columbia rivers and attempt to find a water route to the Pacific Ocean. Lewis, who was Jefferson's secretary and confidante, and his friend Clark were assigned to lead the explorers. The expedition of some 45 men left St. Louis, Missouri, on May 14, 1804. They arrived at the Mandan and Hidatsa villages near the mouth of the Knife River in North Dakota on October 26, 1804. There,

Sacagawea

they built cabins in a clearing below the villages and settled in for the winter.

Lewis and Clark realized that they would need someone to help communicate with and obtain supplies from the Shoshone when they passed through their territory. In November they met Charbonneau; both he and his wife, Sacagawea, were hired as interpreters of the Shoshone language. Sacagawea probably hoped that the expedition would allow her to reunite with her people. The process of interpretation turned out to be quite complicated, however. Sacagawea talked with her husband in the language of the Gros Ventre people. Charbonneau then passed on Sacagawea's words in French to a member of the party who spoke French and English; that person then relayed the information along to Lewis and Clark in English. Sacagawea also extensively used sign language, which many in the party could interpret.

By the time the party had arrived in the Mandan villages, Sacagawea was pregnant. In February 1805 she gave birth to a boy, named Jean Baptiste Charbonneau. Even with an infant, Sacagawea and her husband were hired as interpreters. On April 7, 1805, Sacagawea—carrying her infant in a cradleboard—accompanied the expedition out of the Mandan villages for the trek west.

During the expedition, Sacagawea revealed to Lewis and Clark important passageways through the wilderness. She also quickly demonstrated her knowledge of edible plants along the course. Lewis wrote on April 9 that when the expedition stopped for dinner Sacagawea "busied herself in search for the wild artichokes.... This operation she performed by penetrating the earth with a sharp stick about some collection of driftwood. Her labors soon proved successful and she procured a good quantity of these roots." At many other points in the trip, Sacagawea gathered, stored, and prepared wild edible plants for the party, especially a plentiful root called *Year-pah* by the Shoshones.

On May 14, the party encountered heavy winds near the Yellowstone River. Charbonneau was at the helm of the *pirogue,* or canoe, which held some supplies and valuables gathered during the expedition. The explorers were onshore at the time. They both knew Charbonneau wasn't very comfortable in the water, but they could only watch in horror as the boat overturned. But Sacagawea was ready and able to handle the

situation. Lewis wrote, "The Indian woman, to whom I ascribe equal fortitude and resolution with any person on board at the time of the accident, caught and preserved most of the light articles which were washed overboard." The articles included the expedition's records of the trip. About a week later, Lewis recorded that a recently discovered river had been named in Sacagawea's honor.

On June 10, Sacagawea became ill and remained so for the next several days. This event is discussed at length in the journals of both Lewis and Clark, who were extremely concerned for her welfare. Both took turns tending to her. Her condition worsened until Charbonneau convinced her to take medicine. The explorers noted privately that if she died, it would be his fault.

Lewis wrote that Sacagawea's illness "gave me some concern as well for the poor object herself, then with a young child in her arms, as from the consideration of her being our only dependence for a friendly negotiation with the Snake [Shoshone] Indians on whom we depend for horses to assist us in our portage from the Missouri to the Columbia River." Sacagawea recovered from this illness, but a few days later, on June 29, she, her infant son, Charbonneau, and the servant York nearly drowned in a flash flood. Fortunately, Clark hurried the group to safer ground and all survived.

Reunion with the Shoshones

On July 30, 1805, the party passed the spot on the Three Forks of the Missouri where Sacagawea had been taken from her people some five years before. A little over one week later, at Beaverhead Rock, Sacagawea recognized her homeland and told the expedition that the Shoshone had to be nearby. On August 13, Lewis took an advance party on ahead to find and meet the Shoshone; Clark remained behind with Sacagawea and the rest of the group. The next day, Clark saw Charbonneau hit his wife and spoke angrily to him about it.

On August 17, Clark, Sacagawea, and the rest of the party found Lewis, who had met the Lehmi-Shoshone chief Cameahwait. Clark described what happened: "I saw at a distance several Indians on horseback coming towards me. The interpreter and squaw, who were before me at some distance, danced for the joyful sight, and she made signs to me that they were her nation." They sent for Sacagawea to interpret between Lewis and Clark and Cameahwait: "She came into the tent, sat down, and was beginning to interpret, when in the person of Cameahwait she recognized her brother; she instantly jumped up and ran and embraced him, throwing over him her blanket and weeping profusely ... after some conversation between them she resumed her seat, and attempted to interpret for us, but her new situation seemed to overpower her, and she was frequently interrupted by tears."

Sacagawea learned that her only surviving family were two brothers and a son of her eldest sister, whom she immediately adopted. She also met the Shoshone man to whom she had been promised as a child; however, he was no longer interested in marrying her because she had borne a child with another man. While among her people, Sacagawea helped to obtain horses, supplies, and Shoshone guides to assist in the expedition's trip across the Rocky Mountains.

Sacagawea monument in City Park, Portland, Oregon

Leaving her adopted son in the care of her brother Cameahwait, Sacagawea and the rest of the party traveled on, eventually following the Snake River to its junction with the Columbia, and on toward the Pacific Ocean. On October 13, 1805, Clark again commented on Sacagawea's value to the expedition, saying she "reconciles all the Indians as to our friendly intentions—a woman with a party of men is a token of peace."

In November, a lead party from the expedition reached the ocean. Sacagawea, who had heard that this group had discovered a beached whale, insisted that Lewis and Clark take her there. Lewis wrote on January 6, 1805: "The Indian woman was very importunate to be permitted to go, and was therefore indulged; she observed that she had traveled a long way with us to see the great waters, and that now that monstrous fish was also to be seen, she thought it very bad she could not be permitted to see either."

When the party separated on the return trip in order to explore various routes, Sacagawea joined Clark, directing him through the territory of her people, pointing out edible berries and roots, and suggesting that he take the Bozeman Pass—a mountain pathway that runs between what are now the states of Colorado and Montana—to rejoin the other members at the junction of the Yellowstone and Missouri rivers.

Two days after the parties were rejoined, on August 14, 1806, the expedition arrived back at the Mandan villages. Here Charbonneau and Sacagawea decided to stay. Clark offered to adopt their infant son Jean Baptiste, whom he had affectionately called "Pomp" on the trip. They accepted Clark's offer for a later time after the infant was weaned. On the return trip to St. Louis, Clark wrote a letter to Charbonneau, inviting him to live and work in St. Louis and telling him that Sacagawea deserved a "great reward" for her help on the journey. Charbonneau was paid for his services; Sacagawea, as his wife, received no money apart from his.

Controversy remains over Sacagawea's later years

There is reason to believe that Sacagawea lived for only a few short years after parting ways with the Lewis and Clark expedition. It may be that Charbonneau accepted Clark's invitation to go to Missouri and farm. On April 2, 1811, a lawyer and traveler named Henry Brackenridge was on a boat from St. Louis to the Mandan, Arikara, and Hidatsa villages of North and South Dakota. In his journal he mentioned meeting the Frenchman and his Snake Indian wife. Brackenridge admired Sacagawea's gentle personality and added that she tried to imitate European styles of clothing and manners. He also expressed regret that she looked ill and that she wanted to visit her people again but her husband wanted to live in a city.

Many historians believe that Charbonneau and Sacagawea, after leaving their son, Jean Baptiste, with Clark to raise in St. Louis (the boy grew up to become a respected interpreter and mountain man), took their infant daughter, Lizette, and traveled to the Missouri Fur Company of Manuel Lisa in South Dakota. An employee of the fur company, John C. Luttig, recorded in his journal on December 20, 1812: "This Evening the Wife of Charbonneau, a Snake Squaw died of a putrid fever she was a good and the best Woman in the fort aged abt 25 years she left a fine infant girl." Sacagawea was buried in the grounds of the fort. In addition, William Clark published an account book for the period 1825 to 1828, in which he listed the members of the expedition and whether they were then either living or dead. He recorded that Sacagawea was deceased.

Another theory of Sacagawea's life relates that Sacagawea left her husband, took her son, Jean Baptiste, and adopted son, Bazil; and went to live with the Comanches. There she married a man named Jerk Meat and bore five more children. Later, Sacagawea returned to her homeland to live with her Shoshone people at what was now the Wind River Reservation, Fort Washakie, Wyoming. She was called *Porivo* ("Chief") at Wind River and became an active tribal leader. She was reported by some Shoshones, Indian agents, and missionaries to have died at the age of about 100 in 1884 and to have been buried at Fort Washakie. Opponents of this theory argue that the woman who called herself Sacagawea was actually another Shoshone.

The Shoshones of Fort Washakie have started a project to document the descendants of Sacagawea. As of mid-1993, more than 400 Shoshones who can trace their ancestry to Sacagawea had been counted. Many among them believe that she indeed lived a long and full life.

From the time of her marriage, Sacagawea's life was bound to a group of explorers who wanted to help America gain western territory. In spite of separation from her people, illness, physical abuse from her spouse, and an infant to care for, Sacagawea made key contributions to the success of the Lewis and Clark expedition. Her skills as an interpreter and as liaison (go-between) between the Shoshone and the expedition, her knowledge of the plants and wildlife along much of the route, and her common sense and good humor contributed to the journey's success.

Sacagawea has become one of the most memorialized women in American history. A bronze statue of her was exhibited during the centennial (hundred-year) observance of the Lewis and Clark expedition in St. Louis in 1904. Another statue was commissioned by a women's suffrage group in Oregon, with the unveiling set to coincide with the Lewis and Clark Centennial Exposition in Portland, Oregon, in 1905. Statues were also built in Idaho, Montana, North Dakota, Oklahoma, and Virginia. In addition to the river in Montana named for Sacagawea by Lewis and Clark, other memorials include three mountains, two lakes, and numerous markers, paintings, musical compositions, schools, and a museum.

Further Reading

Clark, Ella E., and Margot Edmonds, *Sacagawea of the Lewis and Clark Expedition,* Berkeley: University of California Press, 1979.

Dawson, Jan C., "Sacagawea: Pilot or Pioneer Mother?" *Pacific Northwest Quarterly,* 83, January 1992, pp. 22–28.

Hebard, Grace Raymond, *Sacajawea: A Guide and Interpreter of the Lewis and Clark Expedition, with an Account of the Travels of Toussaint Charbonneau, and of Jean Baptiste, the Expedition Papoose,* Glendale, CA: Arthur H. Clark Company, 1933.

Howard, Harold P., *Sacajawea,* Norman: University of Oklahoma Press, 1971.

Reid, Russell, *Sakakawea: The Bird Woman,* Bismarck: State Historical Society of North Dakota, 1986.

Remley, David, "Sacajawea of Myth and History," in *Women and Western American Literature,* edited by Helen Winter Stauffer and Susan J. Rosowski, Troy, NY: 1982, pp. 70–89.

Buffy Sainte-Marie

Cree singer, composer, actress, and activist
Born February 20, c. 1942

Buffy Sainte-Marie's song "Now That the Buffalo's Gone" is thought by some to be the first Indian protest song.

It is likely that the first awareness many contemporary non-Indian Americans had of Indian rights came to them through the lyrics of a Buffy Sainte-Marie song. A unique and versatile performer who informs her audiences about the wrongs done to Native Americans, she is a highly respected spokesperson for indigenous people.

Early life

Beverly Sainte-Marie, a full-blooded Cree, was born in either 1941 or 1942 on the Piapot Reserve in Craven, Saskatchewan, Canada. She was orphaned in the first months of her life and adopted by Albert C. Sainte-Marie and Winifred Kendrick Sainte-Marie, a part-Micmac couple in Massachusetts who had lost an infant daughter about her age. Nicknamed Buffy as a child, she learned Micmac stories from her mother and taught herself to play an old piano at the age of four.

Later, Sainte-Marie composed poems and set them to her own tunes. She received her own guitar as a gift when she was a teenager and considers this as a major turning point in her life. She quickly mastered the instrument and could play in more than 30 tunings, developing a distinctive style for her haunting songs about Native history and modern issues. While she was a student at the University of Massachusetts, she played at local coffeehouses and clubs and drew large audiences, combining original compositions with folk and jazz favorites. She earned a bachelor's degree in philosophy (with many courses on Asian traditions) in 1963 and was named one of the top ten graduating seniors at the university that year.

A folk artist and activist

Soon after graduation, Sainte-Marie moved to New York City's Greenwich Village. This neighborhood was the center of the rapidly growing folk culture in the 1960s and supported a creative explosion of music and poetry. Enthusiastically embraced by the movement, Sainte-Marie regularly appeared at such clubs as the Gaslight Cafe, the Bitter End, and Gerde's Folk City. She signed a contract with Vanguard Records, which released her first long-playing album, *It's My Way,* in 1964. The following year, she played New York's famous Carnegie Hall, one of the most prestigious venues (places where performances are presented) in the nation.

Sainte-Marie possesses a unique singing style that includes traditional Native "vocables" (characteristic syllables without meaning that are repeated again and again) and the use of the Creek mouthbow. With her riveting songs about Indian oppression, Sainte-Marie soon became a political activist, using her music to relate the tragedies and triumphs of aboriginal (native)

North Americans. Her song "Now That the Buffalo's Gone" is thought by some to be the first Indian protest song. Other well-known Sainte-Marie songs are "Until It's Time for You to Go" and "Up Where We Belong," the Oscar-winning theme song of the film *An Officer and a Gentleman,* which she cowrote with Jack Nitzche. In the early 1970s, she wrote "Starwalker," which is sometimes called the theme song of the activist organization known as the American Indian Movement (AIM).

Although Sainte-Marie's early career focused on music, she was soon offered acting roles. She appeared on several television programs in the 1960s, including an important episode of *The Virginian* in which she insisted that all Indian roles be played by Indians. This episode, which also benefited from Sainte-Marie's assistance with the script, was praised as being true to life.

The singer-actress narrated part of the Oscar-award-winning documentary film *Broken Rainbow,* which told the story of a land dispute between the Hopi and Navajo people, and appeared as the Iroquois Clan mother/matriarch in Turner Entertainment's made-for-television movie *The Broken Chain.* A frequent guest on the children's television series *Sesame Street,* she has written for children (including the 1986 book, *Nokosis and the Magic Hat*) and for periodicals such as *Akwesasne Notes.* Never one to take herself too seriously, she has also done commercials for Ben and Jerry's ice cream.

Although performers are public people, some are able to maintain their privacy, and Sainte-Marie has succeeded in keeping her offstage life to herself. It is known that in 1967 she married Dewain Kamaikalani Bug-

Buffy Sainte-Marie

bee, a man of Hawaiian, American Indian, and European ancestry. It is believed that she has an adult son, Cody Starblanket. She has also been linked with the composer-musician Jack Nitzche and the actor Sheldon Peters Wolfchild.

Buffy Sainte-Marie continues to be an active voice in Indian affairs. She has played at concerts in support of **Leonard Peltier** (see entry), the AIM activist and political prisoner who is currently serving two life sentences at Leavenworth Prison, in Kansas. She founded the Native North American Women's Association, which sponsors art and education projects, and instituted a scholarship fund, Nihewan Foundation, for Native Americans who wish to attend law school. Although her recording schedule has slowed, she remains a unique singer-songwriter with an international following.

Further Reading

Contemporary American Indian Leaders, edited by Marion Gridley, New York: Dodd, Mead, 1972.

Native American Women, edited by Gretchen M. Bataille, New York: Garland Publishing, 1993.

Native North American Almanac, edited by Duane Champagne, Detroit: Gale, 1994.

Vogel, Virgil, *This Country Was Ours,* New York: Harper and Row, 1972.

Ramona Sakiestewa

Hopi weaver
Born 1949, Albuquerque, New Mexico

"My weaving comes out of Pueblo weaving. Unlike Renaissance and modern tapestries, mine are completely finished on both sides."

Ramona Sakiestewa is a contemporary fiber artist of the Southwest who dreams in color and pattern. Those dreams, translated into blankets, rugs, and tapestries, have brought her awards, important commissions, and a business of her own. Combining elements of ancient design and process with modern weaving method and technique, she is creating new directions and new traditions in Native American arts.

Born in Albuquerque, New Mexico, and raised there by her German-Irish mother, Sakiestewa still felt a closeness to the heritage of her Hopi father. She always loved fabric and even sewed doll clothes at the age of four. Her mother and stepfather were enthusiastic collectors of Native American art, and she worked with Indian art at an Albuquerque trading post. Especially interested in weaving, she studied books by two anthropologists (scholars who study human customs and beliefs), Ruth Underhill's *Pueblo Craft* and Kate Peck Kent's *Weaving of Cotton in the Prehistoric Southwestern United States.* Later in her life, she was able to work directly with Kent, and they became close friends.

While still in high school, Sakiestewa taught herself to weave on the vertical loom. Weaving—the interlacing of vertical threads with horizontal threads, or the "warp" with the "woof,"—is done on one of the many varieties of looms. The warp threads are pulled up on a frame and run through small holes called eyelets on vertical wires, or heddles. By raising and lowering the heddles, the weaver creates a space called the shed; the woof threads are moved through this space. Once a new line of interlaced threads is woven, a piece called the comb pushes it home.

In the late 1960s, Sakiestewa spent time in New York studying color and design at the School of Visual Arts. She became skilled at using the treadle loom—which has a foot-operated lever—and later took several short-term classes in Santa Fe, New Mexico. At first, weaving was just a hobby; she worked in arts administration and planned training programs for the Museum of New Mexico. She also helped establish ATLATL, a national Native American arts and cultural service organization. She married Arthur Sze, a poet, and had a son, Micah.

Combines the contemporary with the traditional

In 1975, Sakiestewa received her first commission from the Park Service at Bandelier National Monument near Los Alamos, New Mexico, to copy an Anasazi turkey feather blanket like those found at archaeological sites (places where scientists have dug up fossils, relics, artifacts, or other monuments of past human life) there. Through study and research, she learned the process of making yarn from plant fibers. She made one-of-a-kind rugs, using wool in its natural colors or hand-dyed with natural vegetable dyes. Becoming expert on the horizontal loom greatly increased her production, but her techniques remained linked to tradition. Sakiestewa told Betty Freudenheim in *American Craft,* "My weaving comes out of Pueblo weaving. Unlike Renaissance and modern tapestries, mine are completely finished on both sides."

Patricia Harris lists the sources of Sakiestewa's designs in *Fiberarts* magazine as "architecture, natural landscape formations, the colors of the land and vegetation ... traditional Navajo and Pueblo tribal designs, patterns from tapestry, pottery and basketry, ceremonial dance movements." Often, the patterns and designs appear to Sakiestewa in dreams. She told Freudenheim that she has extraordinary and intense dreams, in "full color, like a Cecil B. DeMille movie." She

has begun using fine wool yarn in 260 colors, imported from Sweden, and likes to see colors from different cultures and eras. Inevitably, she weaves in vivid hues and tries to get to the essence of particular color combinations.

The artist founded Sakiestewa Ltd., her own company, in 1982, a year after she began weaving full time. At first her products were strictly functional: floor rugs, upholstery fabrics, and pillows. Then she began producing one-of-a-kind rugs, with designs from historic textiles. By 1992 she had four looms, and with two part-time assistants working in a studio cottage next to her home, she was producing up to 30 tapestries a year. She sold her work at the annual Santa Fe Indian Market, at the Native American Arts show at the Heard Museum in Phoenix, Arizona, and through Indian-oriented art galleries.

Receives Wright commission

In 1989 Sakiestewa received a commission from the Taliesen Foundation for a series of 13 tapestries to be based on the drawings of Frank Lloyd Wright. Their purpose was to support the Taliesen West traveling museum project. Many of her works are done in series; she often works on several series simultaneously. Each series develops from her experience, her observations, her heritage, or her multicultural studies. For example, the "Basket Dance" series derives from early Southwestern basketry and textiles; the "Eastern Horizon" series uses astronomical configurations from Anasazi ruins; and the "Katsina" series is drawn from the many figures in the Hopi ceremonial calendar. From her experience in

South America, she derived the "Kutij" series; her trip to Japan led to the "Tenryuji" series. Working with Pendleton Woolen Mills of Oregon, she undertook the "Southwest Trails" blanket series.

An exhibit titled "Ramona Sakiestewa: Patterned Dreams" was held at the Wheelwright Museum of the American Indian in Santa Fe, New Mexico, in 1989. Her tapestry was also included in a touring show, "Women of Sweetgrass, Cedar, and Sage," an exhibition of contemporary Native American women artists, sponsored by ATLATL. In 1991, 12 of her Wright tapestries were collected in an exhibit in New Jersey. The thirteenth was touring with the "Wright Automatic House" traveling museum. Her tapestries, rooted in her culture, filled with history, yet boldly contemporary, chart new directions in Native American art.

Further Reading

Baizerman, Suzanne, *Ramona Sakiestewa: Patterned Dreams: Textiles of the Southwest,* Wheelwright Museum of Indian Art, 1989.

Freudenheim, Betty, "Crafts: 'Ancient Ones' Inspire Hopis," *New York Times,* April 21, 1991, p. 11.

Miller, Bobbi, "Ramona Sakiestewa," *Shuttle, Spindle and Dyepot,* spring 1992, pp. 34-37.

Will Sampson, Jr.

Creek actor and artist
Born 1934, Creek Nation Reservation,
    Okmulgee, Oklahoma
Died June 2, 1987, Houston, Texas

Will Sampson, Jr., once said that he prepared for his paintings of cowboys, Indians, and western landscapes in the same manner he studied for his acting roles: "I research thoroughly."

Through his acting debut as Chief Bromden in the hit 1975 movie *One Flew over the Cuckoo's Nest,* Will Sampson, Jr., became one of the most widely recognized Native American actors of his time. Sampson, who was born and raised on the Creek Nation Reservation in Okmulgee, Oklahoma, entered acting late in life, and it was only one of his professional interests. After a brief period in the U.S. Navy, he held a variety of jobs: construction worker, oil field worker, forest ranger, lumberjack, rodeo cowboy. He was also a professional and highly regarded artist, whose paintings have been exhibited in many shows, exhibitions, and galleries.

Begins acting career

Sampson was 40 years old when he began his acting career in 1974. While he was directing an art exhibition in Yakima, Washington, an old rodeo friend told him that the producer Michael Douglas was looking for a "big Indian" to play in his latest movie. An imposing six feet, seven inches tall, Sampson was easily "discovered." Sampson met with Douglas and starring actor Jack Nicholson. Before he would sign on for the part in *One Flew over the Cuckoo's Nest* he also read the Ken Kesey novel on which the film was based.

Sampson played Chief Bromden, a mysterious, alienated Indian living in a harshly dehumanizing mental hospital, who, by faking muteness, avoids any kind of engagement with the disturbingly ugly world. But then the rebellious, wise-cracking Randle Patrick McMurphy (played by Nicholson) enters the ward, pretending to be crazy in order to escape work detail while doing time on a prison farm. The other mental hospital patients, including Bromden, find strength and sanity in McMurphy's refusal to let his free spirit be broken. As it becomes clear that McMurphy will willingly die before he will lose his self-determination, it becomes equally clear that power is on the side of the mental hospital's head nurse, who will use any means available to "reform" McMurphy into submission. Watching McMurphy's doomed battle against the system propels Chief Bromden to use his own massive strength to quite literally break down the walls of repression and find freedom.

One Flew Over the Cuckoo's Nest won the top 1975 Academy Awards and is already considered a classic. Along with its well-known star, the film successfully used many nonprofessionals, including Sampson, in its cast. Sampson's portrayal of the mutely powerful Bromden received rave reviews.

Sampson took advantage of a variety of opportunities in the entertainment industry after his successful debut in film. His later movies included *Buffalo Bill and the Indi-*

Will Sampson, Jr., in *One Flew over the Cuckoo's Nest*

ans, *The Outlaw Josie Wales, The White Buffalo, Orca, Fighting Back, Alcatraz: The Whole Shocking Story, Poltergeist II: The Other Side,* and the title role in *Old Fish Hawk.* In 1982, Sampson won an award for best narration by the Alberta Film Commission for his work on *Spirit of the Hunt,* a major Canadian film.

He also worked in television and on stage. Television work included regular appearances in the series *Vegas, Born to the Wind,* and *The Yellow Rose.* He narrated the PBS documentary *Images of Indians,* which describes how Europeans and Americans have seen Indians through history. On the stage he played **Red Cloud** (see entry) in an American Indian Theater Company of Oklahoma production of *Black Elk Speaks.*

Continues work as artist

While his acting career grew, painting remained Sampson's greatest passion. His work was exhibited in the Smithsonian Institution and the Library of Congress, as well as in galleries. Sampson once said that he prepared for his paintings of cowboys, Indians, and western landscapes in the same manner he studied for his acting roles: "I research thoroughly. I've done paintings of all the great Indian chiefs and I studied everything about them." He contributed his influence, knowledge, and money to Native American causes, frequently educated students on the topics of Western art and Indian traditions, and participated in the fight against alcoholism.

Sampson had suffered from scleroderma, a chronic degenerative disease, for years. After complications associated with heart-lung transplantation, Sampson died of kidney failure in Houston, Texas, on June 2, 1987. He was 53 years old and married to his fourth wife.

Further Reading

Biographical Dictionary of Indians of the Americas, Volume 2, Newport Beach, CA: American Indian Publishers, 1991.

Native North American Almanac, edited by Duane Champagne, Detroit: Gale, 1994.

New York Times, June 4, 1987, p. D26.

Sanapia

Comanche medicine woman
Born 1895, Fort Sill, Oklahoma
Died 1984, Oklahoma
Also known as Mary Poafpybitty, Memory
      Woman, and Sticky Mother

Sanapia understood well the taboos, obligations, and responsibilities associated with being an eagle doctor and was not sure she wanted that kind of life.

Sanapia, the last known Comanche eagle doctor, was one of the most powerful Native American women on the Great Plains in the first half of the twentieth century. Raised in conflicting cultural and religious traditions, Sanapia was not sure she wanted to take on the highly traditional—and prestigious—role of an eagle doctor. In her later years she became concerned that there was no one to whom she could pass on her skills. Sanapia is best known to American society because she cowrote a book about her experiences as an eagle doctor, including the training in healing and the supernatural she received as a young woman. Through her autobiography, the traditional role of eagle doctor will certainly be remembered in generations to come.

Sanapia was a member of one of the northern bands of the Comanche community, the Yapai ("Root Eaters"), also known as Yamparika ("Yap Eaters"). In the spring of 1895, a group of Yapai Comanches traveled from Medicine Park, Oklahoma, to Fort Sill to obtain government rations (food and supplies). There, Sanapia was born—the sixth of 11 children—to a Comanche father who had converted to the Christian religion and a traditional (believer in the established religion and customs) Comanche and Arapaho mother.

Sanapia's ties to her tribe were strong: her paternal grandfather was an honored Yapai leader, and one of her mother's brothers was an Arapaho chief. According to custom, she was raised mainly by her maternal grandmother, who taught her about Comanche life and oral tradition (stories that are passed generation to generation by the spoken word). The elder woman directed young Sanapia to follow in the footsteps of her mother and another maternal uncle, both of whom were eagle doctors.

Sanapia's Comanche ancestors shared cultural and historical roots with the Shoshone people of the region, speaking the same language. Both groups had begun to move southward some time in the 1700s. Sanapia's people, the Yapai, were members of the northernmost of the Comanche bands and were probably the last to split from the Shoshone. They were also the most traditional and conservative (resistant to change). The Yapai Comanche today live south of the Washita River near Anadarko, Oklahoma, north of Fort Sill.

After they acquired horses from the Spanish in the late 1600s, Comanches became skilled at hunting buffalo. Theirs was a male-dominated society; women normally had low status. Shamans (priests who attempt to cure sickness and control events by magic) and medicine men had the most influence. The tribe's religion considered the Great Spirit as the source of all power. Humans could gain access to this power through dreams of spirits and other beings,

or one person could pass it to another through rituals. Because it was believed that Sanapia's guardian spirit and source of supernatural power was the eagle, she was called an eagle doctor.

As the buffalo population decreased in the nineteenth century, the Comanche people began raiding their neighbors as well as trading with them. Before the reservation years beginning in 1870, their trading was an important part of the economy in Texas, Old Mexico, and New Mexico. But contact with Europeans moving westward eventually put an end to the Comanche's nomadic (traveling to hunt or find food, rather than living in permanent settlements) life. First they were confined to reservations, then to allotments— small plots carved out of tribal lands—on which they were expected to survive as farmers. Their assimilation, or blending into mainstream society, wore away their traditional culture. Problems coping with this process were said to cause "ghost-sickness" among many Comanches, and the eagle doctor treated this sickness with spiritual, herbal, and psychological remedies.

Becomes an eagle doctor

When she was seven, Sanapia started her formal education at Cache Creek Mission School, where she studied for seven years. At the age of 13, she reluctantly agreed to allow her mother to begin training her in the ways of the eagle doctor. Sanapia understood well the taboos (forbidden things), obligations, and responsibilities associated with being an eagle doctor and was not sure she wanted that kind of life. But she had little choice. Earlier, her uncle had given her his blessing while treating her in childhood for influenza—in such a way that she could only recover if she agreed to devote her life to healing. He named her "Memory Woman," so that she might never forget her promise.

Following a set ritual, Sanapia first learned to identify, gather, and process Native plants used in medicines. She spent the next four years practicing healing skills and acquiring the eagle power, as taught by her mother, grandmother, grandfather, and uncle. They ensured that she developed the proper attitude toward her profession, as well as the needed skills and knowledge. In early-twentieth-century Comanche society, such training raised her status to a position equal to a man.

The supernatural power that Sanapia received in the last stage of her training was considered potentially dangerous. There was always a chance that new doctors could use their power for evil, so family approval was required before Sanapia's mother could pass the eagle power on to her. The final days of training—when this transfer of power occurred—were a period of solitude, meditation, and fasting for Sanapia so that her worthiness and courage could be tested by supernatural beings. Once she completed her training, Sanapia could not begin to practice as an eagle doctor for many years. Strict taboos prevented women who had not yet reached menopause (who had not stopped having their monthly periods), from exercising the powers of a medicine woman.

Guided toward healing through personal tragedy

Three important religious frameworks influenced Sanapia's life. Her mother represented the traditional Plains Indian spiritualism (religious ideas), which conflicted in many ways with her father's Christianity. Her uncle and paternal grandfather were Peyotists, members of a religion mixing aspects of Christianity with Native American beliefs and relying on rituals involving the hallucinogenic plant known as peyote. Never very involved in formal religion—and true to the individualistic Comanche nature—Sanapia combined elements of all three concepts in a set of beliefs that she thought appropriate for the role of medicine woman.

All of the varying influences on her beliefs came together in her adult life. Sanapia married three times. Her first marriage, at the age of 17, produced a son. She left her husband shortly thereafter and remarried within a year. She had two more children, a son and a daughter, in this second marriage. Sanapia was devastated by the death of her second husband in the 1930s, and she dealt with her grief by engaging in excessive drinking, gambling, and reckless sexual behavior. During this time of instability, her sister asked Sanapia to cure a sick child. Sanapia's cure was successful, and this led her to follow the path for which her mother had trained her many years earlier. She married her third husband some years later and at that time committed herself to the role of medicine woman.

An uncertain future

Tradition demands that one's medicine power should be transferred to a younger person who is worthy and willing to accept the position's responsibilities. Sanapia was concerned that she would not live long enough to pass on her power to another generation, so she allowed an anthropologist (a scholar who studies people's beliefs and customs), David E. Jones, to write a detailed account of her life and medicine ways, hoping the book would serve as a training manual. She predicted, however, that changing times would eventually bring about the end of the medicine way in the Comanche community. Sanapia died in Oklahoma in 1984. It remains unclear whether she passed her power on to another healer.

Further Reading

Foster, Morris W., *Being Comanche,* Tucson: University of Arizona Press, 1991.

Hagan, William T., *United States-Comanche Relations: The Reservation Years,* New Haven, CT: Yale University Press, 1976.

Jones, David E., *Sanapia: Comanche Medicine Woman,* New York: Holt, Rinehart and Winston, 1972.

Native American Women, edited by Gretchen M. Bataille, New York: Garland Publishing, 1993.

Seattle

Suquamish-Duwamish tribal chief
Born c. 1788, central Puget Sound, Oregon
Region (now Washington State)
Died June 7, 1866, Washington State
Also known as Seathl (Seatlh, Sealth),
See-yat, "Noah"

"My words are like the stars that never set. Whatever Seattle says, the great chief at Washington can rely upon with as much certainty as he can upon the return of the sun or the seasons."

As principal chief of the Duwamish people, Seattle was responsible for continued good relations between his people and the new white settlers in the Pacific Northwest. By consistently choosing not to fight the encroaching settlers, his people knew peace throughout the turbulent nineteenth century.

Seattle was born in about 1788 to Schweabe, his Suquamish father, and Scholitza, his Duwamish mother, in the central Puget Sound area of the Oregon Region (now Washington State). As a member of a patrilineal society—that is, one in which power was handed down from father to son—Seattle learned and spoke Schweabe's Suquamish dialect.

When Seattle was four years old, European settlers arrived in the Puget Sound area. By the 1830s, when he was in his midforties, Seattle had been converted to the Catholic religion by French missionaries and was baptized as *Noah.* With his new faith, he started morning and evening church services among Native Americans that continued even after his death.

The city

The California gold rush of 1849 filled the Pacific Northwest with settlers seeking the natural wealth of the area. Seattle was then principal chief of the united Suquamish and Duwamish nations. He spoke out for friendship, open trade, and the accommodation of whites.

Out of respect for their friend and ally, the whites at Puget Sound took Seattle's name for their own settlement in 1852. His people, however, believed that frequently mentioning a dead person would disturb that person's eternal rest. In order to use his name for their city, white settlers agreed to pay the chief in advance for the trouble that his spirit

Seattle

would have when his name was mentioned. Seattle received money from a small tax imposed on the settlers.

The land

As settlers continued to pour into the area, the U.S. government pressed the issue of purchasing land from the Indians. In December 1854, Seattle met with Washington territorial governor Isaac Stevens to discuss the sale of Native lands in exchange for smaller reservations and government money. His speech at this meeting was translated into English and written out by Henry A. Smith, a poet. Seattle agreed to help the whites and the U.S. government by moving the Puget Sound bands to a reservation.

In 1855, at the age of 67, Seattle became the first signer of the Port Elliott Treaty between the Puget Sound Indians and the United States. But soon after the treaty was made, the terms were broken by whites. This led to a series of Native American uprisings from 1855 to 1858, including the Yakima War from 1855 to 1856 in an area east of the Cascade Mountains, and the unsuccessful 1856 attack on Seattle's village by Nisqually warriors from west of the Cascade Mountains.

In accordance with the treaty, Seattle and his people moved to the Port Madison reservation, located west-northwest across Puget Sound from the current city of Seattle, on the east shore of Bainbridge Island. There he lived in the Old Man House, a large community building.

The speech

Seattle's 1854 address to the Washington territorial governor about the status of his people and their future was said to be very well expressed and moving. Unfortunately, at least four versions of the speech have been printed, and no one knows for sure which is the most accurate. Seattle spoke in either Suquamish or Duwamish, which was then translated immediately into Chinook, and then into English for the U.S. government representatives. The only surviving transcript came from the notes in English that were supposedly taken by Henry Smith as Seattle spoke.

On October 29, 1887, the *Seattle Sunday Star* published what Dr. Smith claimed was the basic substance of Chief Seattle's words, although it "contained none of the grace and elegance of the original." The text begins:

"Yonder sky that has wept tears of compassion upon my people for centuries untold, and which to us appears changeless and eternal, may change. Today it is fair. Tomorrow it may be overcast with clouds. My words are like the stars that never set. Whatever Seattle says, the great chief at Washington can rely upon with as much certainty as he can upon the return of the sun or the seasons." At the same time, Seattle showed in the speech that he understood that the United States might take his people's land if they didn't agree to sell it. He added that Indians found the idea of buying and selling parts of the earth very strange.

Two years later, in 1889, Washington became a state. A year after that, the city of Seattle put up a statue honoring its namesake, chief of the Suquamish and Duwamish peoples. Both of these Native American tribal bands are now extinct, but Seattle's speech has continued to fascinate scholars throughout the twentieth century. In the 1960s the poet William Arrowsmith put the speech into modern-day English.

Seattle was married twice and had six children, four of whom died in childhood. He passed away on June 7, 1866, at the age of 78, on a Washington reservation. His famous speech—even though historians disagree about different versions of it—remains an important document for understanding relations between Indians and whites.

Further Reading

Buerge, David, "Seattle's King Arthur: How Chief Seattle Continues to Inspire His Many Admirers to Put Words in His Mouth," *Seattle Weekly,* July 17, 1991.

Statue of Chief Seattle, Washington

Kaiser, Rudolf, "Chief Seattle's Speech(es): American Origins and European Reception," in *Recovering the Word: Essays on Native American Literature,* Berkeley: University of California Press, 1987.

Native North American Almanac, edited by Duane Champagne, Detroit: Gale, 1994.

Watt, Roberta Frye, *Four Wagons West,* Portland, OR: Binsford & Mort, 1934.

Sequoyah

Cherokee linguist
Born c. 1770, Taskigi, near present-day Vonore,
    Tennessee
Died 1843, Tamaulipas, Mexico
Also known as Sequoya (Sikwaji, Sikwayi),
    Sogwali (Sogwili), George Guess
    (George Gist, George Guest)

*Sequoyah was the unschooled genius
who single-handedly invented a written
language for the Cherokees. Up until
then, it was believed, no North American
Indian tribe had an alphabet. The fact that
a single uneducated person made one in
a relatively short time is amazing, a first
in world history.*

For years, American schoolchildren have known Sequoyah from his famous nineteenth-century portrait in the Library of Congress. Head wrapped in a traditional turban, smoking a long pipe, Sequoyah points to a tablet of 86 strange letters. The painting captures both Sequoyah's main accomplishment and the public's heroic image of him. He was the unschooled genius who single-handedly invented a written language for the Cherokees. Up until then, it was believed, no North American Indian tribe had an alphabet. The fact that a single uneducated person made one in a relatively short time is amazing, a first in world history. This has made some people question the story of Sequoyah. Others are happy to celebrate the legend of Sequoyah, whose life and genius were dedicated to his people's welfare.

Outline of Sequoyah's life

Sequoyah was born in Taskigi, an Indian village in Tennessee, the son of Nathaniel Gist, a white trader, and a part-Cherokee mother. Gist abandoned Sequoyah's mother while she was pregnant with him, and the boy grew up without formal education and speaking no English.

As a young man Sequoyah was a skilled hunter, trader, farmer, and silversmith (a person who makes objects of silver). He served in the U.S. Army under General Andrew Jackson in the war against the Creek Indians of 1813 to 1814. Around this time he took the English name George Guess, misspelling his father's last name. Disabled—by a war wound or a hunting accident—Sequoyah was forced into a less active life.

A linguist emerges

In 1809, while living in present-day Arkansas, he became fascinated by the "talking leaves" of nearby white settlers: the books and letters that allowed them to communicate over long distances. Sequoyah then began working on a written version of the Cherokee language. He recognized the importance of a written constitution and official records, and this was originally his main purpose in developing a written Cherokee language. At first he developed a pictographic (using pictures to represent concepts and meanings) version of the Cherokee language, but soon abandoned this approach in favor of a syllabary, which used eighty-six characters representing different syllable sounds. It took Sequoyah 12 years to finish the project.

At first, the Cherokee were suspicious of the syllabary, thinking Sequoyah was prac-

Sequoyah

ticing witchcraft. In 1821, however, boldly appearing before the Cherokee council, he explained the invention of his writing and demonstrated its practical values to the tribe. The system was easy to learn, and the Cherokee rapidly took to it. Sequoyah began traveling to teach the system to his people, and within a few years thousands of Cherokees could read and write.

Christian missionaries, inspired by a translation of the Bible into Cherokee, helped obtain a printing press with a Cherokee syllabary font. Soon, books and newspapers began tumbling from the Indians' own presses. In 1828 the *Cherokee Phoenix,* the first Cherokee newspaper, was published in both English and Cherokee. Also in 1828 the Cherokee constitution was ratified and written down. Sequoyah was invited to Washington, D.C., and his achievement was celebrated. The Cherokee people quickly adopted the technological (characterized by use of tools and machines instead of hand labor) advantages of the European-based civilization.

A Cherokee statesman

Sequoyah continued to play an active role in politics and linguistics. After the "Trail of Tears"—the devastating forced migration of the Cherokee and other southern tribes to Indian Territory (now Oklahoma) in 1838—Sequoyah helped his people once again. For several years after the relocation, two major factions arose among the Cherokee in Indian Territory. The later Cherokee arrivals to the new lands, who had come with the Trail of Tears or after, and the earlier migrants, called "Old Settlers," who had more or less voluntarily relocated at the urging of the government before the march, could not agree on a shared government for their new territory. As president of the Western Cherokee, Sequoyah sponsored the Cherokee Act of Union in July 1839, which helped provide a basis for a united government.

In 1842, Sequoyah set off on a long search to make contact with a Cherokee band rumored to have migrated to Mexico during the American Revolution in the late 1700s. He hoped to locate them by cross-referencing languages. In this last effort he failed; he died in the Mexican state of Tamaulipas. Among the many honors accorded to Sequoyah, later generations named a giant redwood tree and a national park in California after him.

Further Reading

Bird, Traveller, *Tell Them They Lie: The Sequoyah Myth,* Los Angeles: Westernlore Publishers, 1971.

Foreman, Grant, *Sequoyah,* Norman: University of Oklahoma Press, 1938.

Foster, George E., *Se-Quo-Yah: The American Cadmus and Modern Moses,* Philadelphia, PA: Office of the Indian Rights Association, 1885.

Kilpatrick, Jack Frederick, *Sequoyah of Earth and Intellect,* Austin, TX: Encino Press, 1965.

Woodward, Grace Steele, *The Cherokees,* Norman: University of Oklahoma Press, 1963.

Leslie Marmon Silko

Laguna Pueblo novelist and poet
Born March 5, 1948, Albuquerque, New Mexico

"I suppose at the core of my writing is the attempt to identify what it is to be a half-breed or mixed blooded person; what it is to grow up neither white nor fully traditional Indian."

L eslie Marmon Silko is best known for her 1977 novel *Ceremony,* in which she took the stories she had learned as a child and retold them in a modern setting. More than in anything else, Silko believes in the power of stories. She uses the novel form to create a powerful and moving experience for her readers, following in the Native American tradition of storytelling as healing, unifying, and promoting survival.

Silko was born in Albuquerque in 1948 and raised in Old Laguna on the Pueblo Reservation in New Mexico. Her father, Lee Marmon, and her mother, a Native American of mixed Plains ancestry born in Montana, created a home that reflected Silko's background of European American, Laguna, and Mexican lineage. Her father involved her and her two younger sisters in the same activities that boys would have pursued. He took them hunting, and Silko owned a horse by the time she was eight. Later, she helped round up and drive the family's cattle.

Silko's paternal grandmother, Lillie Marmon (born Francesca Stagner), was a Model A car mechanic. An influential role model for Silko, she used her skills to fix the machines in her son's coin-operated laundry even when she was elderly. Lillie had been educated at Carlisle Indian School and Dickinson College in Carlisle before her marriage to Hank Marmon. Her mother, Helen, was from an old Spanish family in the area, and Silko's Mexican ancestry can be traced to them. Hank (Henry) Marmon, Silko's grandfather, had attended Sherman Institute, an Indian School, in Riverside, California. He wanted to be an automobile designer, but such jobs were closed to Indians at the time. He returned home to clerk in a store but was interested in automobiles all his life.

Female-centered culture

The culture in which Silko grew up was female-centered. The Lagunas are matrilineal—power is handed down from mother to daughter—and women own the houses and

Leslie Marmon Silko

fields. The gods are female; the most important of them is Thought Woman, sometimes called Spider Woman. Because of the importance of the female in Laguna culture and Silko's strong female and male role models, it is not surprising that she incorporates male and female characters into her novel with equal ease and feels that she grew up without restrictions.

Because her mother was away at work, Silko was raised primarily by her great-grandmother, Marie Anaya Marmon, who was a full-blood from Paguate village, north of Old Laguna. Marie—or "A'mooh," as she was called—had attended the Indian School at Carlisle, Pennsylvania, and had married Robert G. Marmon and became a devout Presbyterian. Silko also saw much of her grandmother Lillie and her great-aunt Susie, wife of Walter K. Marmon, Hank's brother.

Lillie, Susie, and her great-grandmother told Silko the old stories.

In an interview with Kim Barnes, Silko discussed the way men and women are portrayed in her work. Explaining why her male characters are often weaker and more complicated than her women, she said, "I grew up with women who were really strong, women with a great deal of power ... within the family.... If someone was going to thwart you or frighten you, it would tend to be a woman; you see it coming from your mother, or sent by your mother." The women are the authority figures, and "your dad is the one who's the soft touch, and it's the mother's brother who reprimands you."

The Marmons, the European American men who figure so prominently in Silko's background, had gone to New Mexico after the U.S. Civil War with other men, including John Gunn (great-grandfather of Native American writer **Paula Gunn Allen**). They married Laguna women and stayed in the area. Silko grew up in the Marmon home in which her father was born, which was located outside the village.

Education and storytelling

Silko attended a Catholic school in Albuquerque, which seemed a little foreign to her, though she was secure enough not to feel that she herself was strange. She attended the University of New Mexico at Albuquerque; she married and then bore her first son, Robert, in 1966, when she was just 18 and a first-semester sophomore. In 1969 she graduated from the University of New Mexico with highest honors (summa cum laude) in English and high honors (magna cum laude) in her general course work.

She attended law school at the University of New Mexico in a program intended to produce Native American lawyers. In 1971, however, she received her first National Endowment for the Arts (NEA) discovery grant for short fiction. This discovery grant was awarded for her story "The Man to Send Rain Clouds," about an incident she read about in the paper. In 1967, she had written the story for a creative writing assignment and discovered that writing came easily to her. The story was published in the *New Mexico Quarterly* and was the beginning of her writing career.

Silko believes that storytelling is a birthright (a natural right) of the Lagunas. Children hear stories from the time they are very small, and storytelling is a way of life. She feels fortunate to have such a culture and believes that her skill is not just an accident. As a child, she loved to read stories from different places, and in high school she was interested in American authors such as William Faulkner, John Steinbeck, Flannery O'Connor, and Edgar Allan Poe.

Silko is never sure where her stories come from. Sometimes they come from her imagination, she feels, while others she must have heard and then forgotten. A case in point is "Tony's Story," which appeared in the 1974 collection *The Man to Send the Rainclouds: Contemporary Stories by American Indians* and was written while she was in college. It tells of the killing of a state policeman from the point of view of a Native American man who committed the murder because he thought the policeman was a witch. Silko thought she had invented this but later learned that what she thought she had imagined was fact. Her only conclusion was that she must have heard about the case as a small child and forgotten it.

Writing career accelerates

The early 1970s were very busy for Silko both in her personal life and in her writing career. In 1972, she gave birth to her second son, Cazimir. In 1973, she was awarded an NEA writers fellowship and a *Chicago Review* poetry prize, and her poetry chapbook (or small book of poems) *Laguna Woman* was published.

Silko often re-creates old Laguna stories in her poetry, sometimes giving them a modern twist. In the foreword to *Laguna Woman,* she says: "I suppose at the core of my writing is the attempt to identify what it is to be a half-breed or mixed blooded person; what it is to grow up neither white nor fully traditional Indian."

She taught for two years at Navajo Community College at Tsaile, Arizona, and learned about Navajo witchcraft beliefs, which appear in some of her works. She then moved with her husband, John Silko, to Ketchikan, Alaska, where he took a position as the supervising attorney for Alaska Legal Services. During the next two years, while Silko was writing her novel *Ceremony,* she was having severe migraine headaches and was constantly ill. Her sickness was like that of her main character, Tayo, a mixed-breed Laguna man back from World War II, and she said in an interview with Dexter Fisher that "as Tayo got better, I felt better." Silko named the novel *Ceremony* because "writing the novel was a ceremony for me to stay sane."

Ceremony was a hit with critics, the first Native American novel to be so widely noticed since N. Scott Momaday's *House Made of Dawn* in 1968. Like Momaday's novel, *Ceremony* explores the lives of World War II Native American veterans. But unlike the earlier novel, *Ceremony* focuses on the survival of the Pueblo people. Silko weaves the old stories into the text, alongside the modern story of her war veterans, working toward a magnificent healing story inspired by and dedicated to Thought Woman.

Personal difficulties

Silko returned to New Mexico and taught at the University of New Mexico, finding it increasingly difficult to teach and find time to write. She then moved to Tucson and taught at the University of Arizona. She had met the poet James Wright at a writer's conference in 1975, and after the publication of *Ceremony,* he wrote to tell her how much he liked the novel; they continued to write to each other until his death of cancer in 1980. In her letters of 1978—which were collected by Wright's wife, Anne, and published in 1986 as *The Delicacy and Strength of Lace*—Silko talks about her difficulties, which included a second divorce, a child custody battle, and financial troubles. Wright's supportive letters were important to her.

In the spring semester of 1979, Silko was on leave from the University of Arizona, Tucson; she taught writing at the University of Washington in Seattle and took time out to attend a three-week workshop at Vassar College, in Poughkeepsie, New York. The campus newspaper made much of her absence from the University of Washington, even though the English department had approved it, and Silko was upset. Money and time were pressing problems.

Situation improves

Upon returning to Arizona, Silko continued to teach and worked on four videotapes dedicated to Laguna stories and funded by the National Endowment for the Humanities (NEH). Her situation began to improve; in 1980 Silko won a Pushcart IV prize. She had also written a short story, "Storyteller," while she was in Alaska. This became the title story for her collection of photographs, short stories, and poetry entitled *Storyteller* and published in 1981. Most of her previously published short stories and poetry appear in this volume.

Also in 1981, Silko won the prestigious John and Catherine MacArthur Prize fellowship for work in fiction, poetry, and film. The award was $159,000, tax-free, over five years. She used this money to free herself from her teaching responsibilities so that she could work full-time filmmaking and writing. The book of letters between her and James Wright won the *Boston Globe*'s nonfiction prize. In 1988, Silko won the New Mexico Endowment for the Humanities "Living Cultural Treasure" award. In 1989, she was given the University of New Mexico's Distinguished Alumnus award. In 1991 she was awarded the Lilla Wallace–*Reader's Digest* Fund Writers award. Also that year Silko's 763-page *Almanac of the Dead,* her most controversial work to date, was published.

Silko sees *Almanac* as a sort of trial by novel. Her father, as tribal treasurer, used stories to testify for the Laguna land boundaries, and Silko collects stories in the form of a novel to show 500 years of European abuse and oppression of Native Americans and the land. She also tries to predict a part of the future. A huge tale of drug dealers, military tyrants, self-serving land developers, and corrupt Native Americans, *Almanac* is a graphic and disturbing novel. In an appearance at Ohio University's Spring Literary Festival in Athens, Ohio, in 1992, when questioned about the depressing nature of the novel, Silko said that maybe it wasn't supposed to be read. Nevertheless, Silko's complex and passionate work is a testimony to her belief in the power of words to preserve and support a culture.

Further Reading

Barnes, Kim, "A Leslie Marmon Silko Interview," *Journal of Ethnic Studies,* 13:4, winter 1986, pp. 83–105.

Evers, Lawrence, and Dennis Carr, "A Conversation with Leslie Silko," *Sun Tracks,* 3, fall 1976, pp. 28–33.

Ruoff, A. LaVonne, *Literatures of the American Indian,* New York: Chelsea House, 1991.

Seyersted, Per, *Leslie Marmon Silko,* Boise, ID: Boise State University Western Writers Series, Number 45, 1980.

Silko, Leslie Marmon, *Almanac of the Dead,* New York: Simon & Schuster, 1991.

Silko, Leslie Marmon, *Ceremony,* New York: Viking Press, 1977.

Silko, Leslie Marmon, *Laguna Woman: Poems,* Greenfield Center, NY: Greenfield Press, 1974.

Silko, Leslie Marmon, *Storyteller,* New York: Seaver Books, 1981.

Silko, Leslie Marmon (with James Wright), *The Delicacy and Strength of Lace: Letters between Leslie Marmon Silko and James Wright,* edited by Anne Wright, Saint Paul, MN: Greywolf Press, 1986.

Jay Silverheels

Mohawk actor
Born c. 1918, Six Nations Indian Reservation,
     Ontario, Canada
Died 1980

*"Children had better examples
in those days."*

A popular Native American actor, Jay Silverheels is perhaps best remembered as Tonto, the loyal Indian sidekick to television's *Lone Ranger* on the western series that ran from 1949 to 1957. He also performed in a number of films throughout the 1950s, 1960s, and 1970s. The first American Indian to be given a star on Hollywood's Walk of Fame, he has been credited with contributing to the development of positive images of Native Americans in both television and film.

Silverheels, a full-blooded Mohawk, was born Harold J. Smith on Six Nations Indian Reservation in Ontario, Canada. The Mohawks are a powerful tribe of the Iroquois Confederacy (an alliance of the Mohawk, Seneca, Oneida, Cayuga, and Onondaga formed in about 1570) who still occupy a large reservation in New York State and Ontario. The son of Captain A. G. E. Smith, a decorated Canadian soldier of World War I, Silverheels was a strong athlete. He won early fame in Canada as a champion lacrosse player. He was also skilled in hockey, football, and track, and won several awards in boxing and wrestling.

Launched acting career

Silverheels first traveled to the United States in 1938 while playing on Canada's national lacrosse team. Shortly afterward, he met the actor Joe E. Brown, who launched his acting career. For nine years Silverheels had only minor roles in western films, in which Native Americans were generally portrayed as villains. He had his first important role in 1947 when he played an Aztec warrior in *The Captain from Castile.* Despite being cast opposite the then famous actor Tyrone Power, Silverheels performed exceptionally well in several scenes, drawing the attention of numerous directors and producers.

In 1949 Silverheels was cast as Tonto in *The Lone Ranger* television series, an offshoot of the popular radio program created by Fran Striker in 1933. The role of Tonto was originally played on the screen by the veteran actor Chief Thunder Cloud, a Cherokee. Silverheels made the role fit his own style and became extremely popular in the process. As Tonto, Silverheels—along with Clayton Moore as the masked ranger—fought for law and order in the old American West. It was an unusual example of teamwork between an Indian and a white man in a western drama, as Tonto and "Kemosabe," as he called the ranger, often rescued each other from harm. Overall, Silverheels appeared in 221 television installments of *The Lone Ranger* before the series was cancelled in 1957. Reruns of the program were shown through 1961; afterward, it was widely syndicated (sold directly to local television stations).

Prospered in film

Silverheels's performance as Tonto, as well as his notable appearance in *The Cap-*

Jay Silverheels

tain from Castile, greatly contributed to his later success in film. A tall and handsome man, Silverheels was well liked by American audiences. He was therefore most often cast as a "good Indian," providing for a sharp contrast to the evil roles usually given to Native Americans in early American film. As a result, Silverheels has been credited, in part, with changing public opinion about American Indians through film.

While Silverheels appeared in many western pictures, a few performances were particularly important to his career. Among these was his 1950 portrayal of the Apache chief **Geronimo** (see entry) in *Broken Arrow,* which is often deemed the first film to depict American Indians in a sympathetic light. In 1964 Silverheels starred in *Indian Paint,* a

film about an Indian boy and his love for his horse, and in 1973 he costarred in *Santee,* the story of the relationship between a bounty hunter (person who hunts for fugitives to obtain a reward) and the son of a man he killed.

Silverheels also costarred in three Lone Ranger films during this period: *Lone Ranger* (1956), *Lone Ranger and the Lost City of Gold* (1958), and *Justice of the West* (1961). Throughout his career, Silverheels chose nonviolent projects in which American Indians and white people were able to coexist peacefully. Also characteristic of his work is an emphasis on the triumph of good over evil. According to Silverheels, "children had better examples in those days."

Contributions to the Native American community

In the 1960s, Silverheels founded and directed the Indian Actors Workshop in Hollywood. Through this workshop, he helped further the acting careers of several Native Americans at a time when roles for them were very limited. Silverheels was also active in numerous public service projects focusing on drug and alcohol abuse and the elderly. On July 21, 1979, he became the first American Indian actor to have a star placed in Hollywood's Walk of Fame along Hollywood Boulevard.

On March 5, 1980, Silverheels died of complications of pneumonia at the Motion Picture and Television Country House in Woodland Hills, California. At the time of his death, he was survived by his wife, Mary, and four children, Marilyn, Pamela, Karen, and Jay Anthony. Since then, a sports recreation center has been built in his honor on his home reservation in Ontario.

Further Reading

Corneau, Ernest N., *The Hall of Fame of Western Film Stars,* North Quincy, MA: Christopher Publishing House, 1969.

Indians of Today, fourth edition, edited by Marion Gridley, ICFP, 1971.

Native North American Almanac, edited by Duane Champagne, Detroit: Gale, 1994, pp. 770, 1160.

Time, March 17, 1980, p. 65.

Sitting Bull

Hunkpapa Sioux tribal leader and warrior
Born c. 1831, South Dakota
Died 1890
Also known as Tatanka Iyotake,
      Jumping Badger, "Slow"

To convince his warriors to quit the battle once it became obvious they had lost, Sitting Bull sat down in the midst of the fight to smoke.

Sitting Bull is certainly one of the best-known Indians in American history. Respected as a great warrior, chief, and holy man in the Sioux Nation, he held a unique post as the primary chief of several Sioux bands. Although he had a number of other talents, it is for his bravery and tenacity in defending his people against the white man's occupation of their land, destruction of their way of life, and desecration of their sacred places in the Black Hills of South Dakota that he is best remembered. Among his most famous achievements was his leadership at the Battle of the Little Bighorn, where Indian troops defeated U.S. General George Custer. He also gained public renown for his appearances in Buffalo Bill Cody's Wild West Show and for his lifelong refusal to obey treaties and compromises that hurt his people.

Made his name as warrior

Historians seem to agree that Sitting Bull was born near the Grand River during the Winter-when-Yellow-Eyes-Played-in-the-Snow, which was probably 1831. Until he first distinguished himself as a warrior at the age of 14, his name was Jumping Badger, but he was nicknamed "Slow." After "Slow" displayed courage in battle with the Crows, his father gave him the name of Sitting Bull and took for himself the name Jumping Bull.

By 1856, Sitting Bull was one of the two honored sash wearers of the Hunkpapa's Strong Heart warrior society. After receiving a bullet wound in the foot, which left him with a permanent limp, he was named leader of the Strong Hearts, and he was a cofounder of the elite Midnight Strong Hearts. As a leader, he successfully fulfilled his role as tribal hunter and kept the tribal hunting grounds cleared of competition from other tribes. He also left a legacy of songs, many composed for special spiritual occasions and others with more secular, or non-religious, content. He left behind him a wealth of pictographic images—stories told with pictures—detailing his exploits.

Sitting Bull's first wife died in childbirth in 1853, and his four-year old son died in 1857. That same year he adopted his sister's four-year old son, One Bull. In a raid on the Assiniboin that year, Sitting Bull adopted a young captive as his brother. This eventually

Sitting Bull

participated with several other bands of Sioux in fighting the troops. An 1864 defeat divided the Sioux leaders, however. Some were ready to surrender after seeing the firepower of the white army; others, like Sitting Bull, became more aggressive. The first official mention of Sitting Bull in U.S. documents was in a report on a raid that took place the following year.

Fights against Indian relocation to reservations

While Oglala leader **Red Cloud**'s (see entry) warriors fought against development of the Bozeman Trail—a path of forts that white miners seeking gold followed from Wyoming to Montana—Sitting Bull mounted a campaign against the forts on the Upper Missouri River. In 1867 he was made chief of several Sioux bands, with the Oglala **Crazy Horse** (see entry) as second in command. This was an unusual political organization for the Lakota, but indicates the respect and trust that many of the Sioux had for Sitting Bull as a leader.

As part of the government's peace policy, the Jesuit missionary Father Pierre-Jean De Smet met with Sitting Bull. He hoped to persuade him to give up the fight against the government's plan to settle the Sioux on reservation lands. Sitting Bull summarized his terms for peace: he did not propose to sell any part of his country; the whites must quit cutting timber along the Missouri River; and the forts of the white solders must be abandoned. His refusal to sign the 1868 Treaty led the government to get two other Hunkpapas to sign it and claim that these signatures represented the entire band. But they in no way represented the feelings of

led to a temporary truce between the Hunkpapa and Assiniboin. One Bull and his brother White Bull later in life provided firsthand information about Sitting Bull for researchers.

In 1862, the eastern Sioux in Minnesota rebelled against white settlement on their native lands. Several of the Dakota Sioux fled west and found refuge with the western Sioux, and white troops followed them. For the next few years, Sitting Bull's Hunkpapas

Sitting Bull, who was adamantly opposed to white settlement. For this reason, the government's accusations later on that Sitting Bull did not live up to the treaty held no meaning for him.

Sometime between 1867 and 1870, Sitting Bull adopted a rescued mail carrier. This man, Frank Grouard, provided him with information and advice about dealing with the white world. Sitting Bull's last attack was the war expedition against Fort Buford in 1870. The following year, again willing to negotiate for peace, Sitting Bull settled near Fort Peck. The difficult winter of 1872 caused a number of Sioux to go into the Milk River Agency for rations and clothing. By waiting out the Sioux, the government was able to divide them further. Even so, they failed to sway most bands permanently into the reservation system.

Throughout these years, Sitting Bull's bands also maintained their traditional warfare with the Crows and the Flatheads. Internal tribal society continued to change. Sitting Bull became a powerful leader in a newly formed secret society called the Silent Eaters. In 1875 or 1876, he also formed a visible group called the White Horse Riders, a kind of *akicita,* or police guard. In 1872, Sitting Bull acquired two new wives, replacing two earlier wives, one whom he had thrown out and the other who had died. These two new wives, daughters of Gray Eagle, stayed with him until his death.

On August 14, 1872, Sitting Bull led warriors out to warn off soldiers protecting the surveyors of the Northern Pacific Railroad line in the Yellowstone valley. To convince his warriors to quit the battle once it became obvious they had lost, Sitting Bull sat down in the midst of the fight to smoke. Several others joined him, and all were unharmed. This display of his bravery and power encouraged all but Crazy Horse and White Bull, who made one last run at the soldiers. Crazy Horse's horse was shot from under him, and he had to return to camp riding with another warrior.

Sees vision and unites tribes with Sun Dance

After the discovery of gold in the Black Hills in 1874, white miners and settlers increased pressure on the government in Washington to clear the land of Indians. In 1875 the government ordered all Sioux to come to agencies on the White River. Busy negotiating a truce with the Assiniboin and fighting the Canadian mixed bloods, Sitting Bull ignored the demand. In 1876 the government launched a military campaign to capture the rebel bands of plains Indians, placing General George Crook in charge.

Crook—assisted by Sitting Bull's former friend Grouard—attacked a Northern Cheyenne village on the Powder River. The victims from the village joined Crazy Horse and retreated to Sitting Bull's village; Sitting Bull and Crazy Horse began planning strategies for the combined bands gathered there. Of the Lakota people, there were gathered more than 10,000 Hunkpapa, Oglala, Sans Arc, Minniconjou, Blackfeet, and Brulé Indians. Other bands included Cheyenne, some Dakota refugees, and some Yanktonais. The groups moved gradually toward the Rosebud and Little Bighorn rivers.

Sitting Bull experienced a series of visions which were interpreted as signs of a great Indian victory. At a sun dance, known as "Sitting Bull's Sun Dance," Sitting Bull gave 100 pieces of skin from his arms as sacrifice and had another vision of hundreds of soldiers coming toward an Indian village, and all the soldiers were upside down. Again interpreted as a victory image, the vision gave new force to the feelings of outrage and strength in the camps.

Helps lead Battle of the Little Bighorn

On June 17, 1876, Crazy Horse and Sitting Bull led warriors against the soldiers at the Battle of the Rosebud. Still recovering from his sun dance sacrifice, Sitting Bull dropped out of the battle. Sensing victory, the village relocated in the valley of the Greasy Grass (the Little Bighorn) river and celebrated for six days. Although Rosebud was a great victory, it did not fulfill the sun dance vision of white soldiers falling upside down into their camp. On June 25, the prophecy was fulfilled when Custer's cavalry engaged them in the famous Battle of the Little Bighorn, a massive and historic defeat for U.S. troops in which Custer and his troops were killed.

Crook's troops routed the Indians in an ensuing battle; the white retaliation for Custer's loss pressured many of Sitting Bull's allies to abandon him and surrender. In October Sitting Bull and General Nelson A. Miles attempted to negotiate, but misunderstanding and lack of patience caused another battle to break out. Throughout the winter, continual military pressure forced the surrender of **Dull Knife**'s Northern Cheyenne, Lame Deer's Minniconjou and finally Crazy Horse's Oglalas.

Escapes to wander in Canada

In early May 1877, Sitting Bull crossed the international boundary into Canada, the land of the "Great Mother"—so-called because it was part of the British Empire of Queen Victoria. After Crazy Horse was killed while resisting incarceration, several of his followers escaped to join Sitting Bull. Delegations met with the Hunkpapa leader to convince him to return to the United States, but he refused. In 1879, he followed the buffalo south of the border to obtain food and supplies for his people, but General Miles drove him back into Canada.

Canadian officials gradually wore down the support of several of Sitting Bull's followers. Some of them left him in 1880. In July 1881, because of scarce food and lack of support from the Canadian government, Sitting Bull allowed the trader Jean Louis Legare to escort him to Fort Buford. He was confined at Fort Randall for the next two years while his followers were placed at the Standing Rock reservation. Once he himself arrived at the reservation, Sitting Bull began a feud with agent James McLaughlin, who almost immediately sent Sitting Bull on exhibition tours. For almost two years, Sitting Bull was a feature attraction in Buffalo Bill's Wild West show.

Throughout the 1880s, the government policy became one of "civilization," meaning that Indians were pressured in various ways to adapt to the white lifestyle. The tribal economy disappeared. Vanishing buffalo herds also meant the collapse of Indian social structure and cultural life. Red Cloud, Spotted Tail, and Sitting Bull held on to the institutions of chief and tribal council. Agents were encouraged to strip "nonpro-

Sitting Bull photographed in full war regalia

gressive" or uncooperative chiefs of their power and to break up tribal relationships. At the same time, they rewarded "progressive" chiefs with nice houses and more power than they would have had traditionally. Government-approved Indian police forces replaced the traditional *akicita* societies. Christianity was to replace traditional religion, and children were sent to day schools and off-reservation boarding schools to become educated in the white traditions. By the end of the decade, the Sioux verged on total despair.

To make things worse, the government took away more land in the Sioux Act of 1889. This left only three sections of land from the original Great Sioux Reservation, and this remaining land was divided into six reservations. Each one would contain only enough land to allow for individual allotments, which were basically family farms. The government would sell the remainder to white settlers as part of the General Allotment Act of 1887. Sitting Bull was part of a group of leaders taken to Washington, D.C., in October 1888 to negotiate a compromise.

Although Sitting Bull held fast, General Crook took advantage of division among the Sioux to get the necessary signatures of three-fourths of the adult males, in spite of overwhelming opposition to the agreement. After the harsh winter of 1889-90 led to starvation and mass sickness, the Sioux had lost hope. About that time, word spread to them of a new Messiah, and their hope was revived. A Paiute prophet called **Wovoka** (see entry) declared that by embracing his new religion and dancing the Ghost Dance, Indians would find eternal peace. The buffalo would return, as would the old life of the Plains, and the white man would disappear from the continent forever.

Tribes attempt to unite through Ghost Dance ritual

First at Pine Ridge, then at the Rosebud and Cheyenne River reservations, ghost dancers gathered. Sitting Bull invited Kicking Bear, a witness of the dance's power, to bring the message to Standing Rock. Kicking Bear arrived and began teaching the Ghost Dance, along with the message that wearing a Ghost Dance shirt would make warriors invulnerable to injury. The Lakota misinterpreted the message of Wovoka, to wait passively and patiently for divine intervention. By the time McLaughlin had Kicking Bear escorted off the reservation, Sitting Bull was already a supporter of the new religion as presented by Kicking Bear. It remains unclear whether he actually believed the Wovoka's message or just saw the religion as a new weapon in his ongoing war with McLaughlin. Fearing an uprising from the Paiute prophet's influence, the agent urged Sitting Bull's removal from Standing Rock reservation.

General Miles also believed that Sitting Bull should be removed, but he and McLaughlin disagreed about the best method for achieving this. Miles hired his old friend Buffalo Bill Cody to arrest the Sioux leader, but McLaughlin prevented this and instead sent the Hunkpapa police force, who entered Sitting Bull's cabin at daybreak, December 15, 1890. Sitting Bull submitted without a fight until his followers gathered around his cabin and encouraged him not to surrender. Sitting Bull was killed in the ensuing fight, along with his son,

Crow Foot, and several other supporters and policemen.

Two weeks later, Minneconjou leader Big Foot and a group of Ghost Dancers had traveled to a site known as Wounded Knee, where Kicking Bear and other militant Sioux were camped. Big Foot was, in fact, asked to the reservation in order to persuade the militants to surrender. The Seventh Cavalry, under Colonel James Forsyth, did not know this, and pursued the religious group. On the morning of December 28, 1890, 500 soldiers surrounded Big Foot's camp. When a rifle discharged, the soldiers began firing on the Sioux, killing more than 300 Indian men, women, and children.

Sitting Bull was originally buried without ceremony in the post cemetery at Fort Yates, but the Hunkpapa band requested his removal to the Grand River. In 1953, to keep the burial site from being flooded by the construction of dams on the Missouri River, Sitting Bull's nephew Clarence Gray Eagle may have taken the warrior's bones to a site on the Grand River, where a memorial was constructed. A marker that remains at the Fort Yates burial site states only: "He was buried here but his grave has been vandalized many times." The precise location of Sitting Bull's remains is unknown. In 1892, his cabin was moved to Chicago to become part of North Dakota's exhibit at the World's Columbian Exhibition, and his gray circus horse was purchased by Buffalo Bill and used to lead his grand procession at the fair.

By his two wives of 1872, Sitting Bull was known to have twin sons born just before the Battle at the Little Bighorn in 1876, a daughter born in 1878, twin boys (including Crow Foot) born in Canada in 1880, a son in 1887, and a daughter in 1888. Sitting Bull's memory has been an inspiration to generations of Sioux, and while sometimes he has been romanticized, there is no question that he was a great Hunkpapa patriot, true to the values and institutions of his culture, and one who remained adamantly opposed to white influence.

Further Reading

Native North American Almanac, edited by Duane Champagne, Detroit: Gale, 1994.

Paulson, T. Emogene, and Lloyd R. Moses, *Who's Who Among the Sioux,* Vermillion: Institute of Indian Studies, University of South Dakota, 1988.

Utley, Robert M., *The Lance and the Shield; The Life and Times of Sitting Bull,* New York: Henry Holt, 1993.

Utley, Robert M., *The Last Days of the Sioux Nation,* New Haven: Yale University Press, 1963.

Vestal, Stanley, *Sitting Bull, Champion of the Sioux; a Biography,* Norman: University of Oklahoma Press, 1957.

Smohalla

Wanapam spiritual leader
Born c. 1815, on the Columbia River
    (now Wallula, Washington)
Died 1895
Also known as Yuyunipitqana
    ("The Shouting Mountain" or
    "Big Talk on Four Mountains")

"You ask me to cut grass and make hay and sell it, and be rich like white men, but how dare I cut off my mother's hair?"

Smohalla was the Wanapam dreamer-prophet and spiritual leader who gave new life to the traditional Washani religion of the Pacific Northwest. He lived along the Columbia River in present-day Washington State during the middle to late nineteenth century and spoke out for a return to the Wanapams' ancient ways and values. Smohalla's teachings combined traditional Native beliefs with elements of Christianity. He also taught that the coming of the white man had put the world on a course of self-destruction and the only way to save the world was for Indians to restore the balance of nature by returning to traditional ways.

Smohalla opposed the U.S. government's attempts to put Indians on reservations and was against farming and ranching. He urged peaceful resistance to the U.S. government and missionaries. With his followers he remained on ancestral lands along the Columbia River, continuing to live a traditional life of fishing, hunting, and gathering. A version of Smohalla's teachings, the Washat, or Seven Drums, religion, is still being practiced by Indians along the river and on the Yakima (Tappenish, Washington), Nez Percé, and Warm Springs (Warm Springs, Oregon) reservations.

Smohalla was born sometime between 1815 and 1820 on the Columbia River in what is today Wallula, Washington. At Wallula ("Many Streams"), the area's tribes and bands gathered to fish, trade, and spend time together on the Columbia River. Like most Native Americans, Smohalla had several names; he did not receive the name Smohalla until he was an adult and recognized as a spiritual leader. From the Shahaptian language, *Smohalla* has been translated as "dreamer," although some sources claim it meant "preacher." At birth he was named *Wak-wei,* or *Kuk-kia* ("Arising from the Dust of the Earth Mother"); he was later named *Yuyunipitqana* ("The Shouting Mountain"), because of a revelation he had during a dream. This vision of a mountain speaking inside his soul was translated into English as "Big Talk on Four Mountains." Another of his names was *Waipshwa* ("Rock Carrier").

Becomes a spiritual leader

The Wanapams were peaceful people with a tradition of placing emphasis on their spiritual leaders, prophets (people who foretell future events), and shamans (priests who use magic to cure sickness and control events). Before Smohalla, another dreamer-prophet, Shuwapsa, had predicted the coming of the Europeans, warning his people that the newcomers would destroy them. Smohalla, who came from a family of shamans and prophets, began his spiritual training with the traditional vision quest, a sacred ceremony in which a person goes off alone and fasts, living without food or water for a period of days. During that time the quester seeks insight into his spiritual nature and hopes to experience a vision of a guardian spirit who will give him help and strength. Eventually Smohalla became what his people called a *yantcha,* a leader with strong spiritual qualities.

Smohalla's rise to leadership was challenged by the arrival of white missionaries, soldiers, and settlers. The diseases the Europeans brought to the Plateau ravaged many tribes, while at the same time the newcomers were exerting political power over the original inhabitants, encroaching upon their lands, and pressing to concentrate Indians on reservations. Traditional shamans seemed powerless against the threats posed by whites; the old ways didn't work against the white man's diseases. The Indians of the Columbia Plateau needed special leaders who could offer them hope and a new spiritual power. These spiritual leaders had to give their people a vision of a future in which the Indians not only survived but prospered. Smohalla was such a spiritual leader.

Smohalla was a small man with a hunched back and an unusually large head. Neither a great warrior nor a hunter, Smohalla's power arose from his charisma—the force of his personality—and his spiritual teachings. He had perhaps as many as ten wives and numerous children, and all of his children and grandchildren, except his son Yo-Yonan, died before he did. Smohalla's failure to save a beloved adolescent daughter's life, combined with the deaths of other Indian children, influenced him to become a dreamer-prophet.

Contacts with fur traders, Christian Indians, and missionaries exposed Smohalla to Christian ideas. Resurrection—Christ's return from the dead—was one of the ideas that influenced his teachings, and it became an important part of the Dreamer religion. In fact, Smohalla claimed to have been resurrected from the dead himself. Both he and his followers reported that he had died twice, each time returning to life. During these two temporary death-states, the dreamer-prophet received revelations from the Great Spirit. Smohalla said that he received the revelations from a small bird and had received as many as 120 power songs and numerous rituals during trances.

The idea that wisdom came to one in dreams was an ancient Wanapam belief and a fundamental teaching of the dreamer-prophets. Smohalla's creed, based on his dreams, included two essential teachings: all Indians were to return to their traditional rituals and religious practices, abandoning all aspects of "civilization" (modern life), and a supernatural force was going to destroy the whites. On a "Millennial Day" all of the dead Indians would return to life to carry on the old ways with their living relatives.

Opposes farming and ranching

Smohalla strongly opposed farming and ranching, stressing the importance of the Indians' traditional way of life. He preached that hunting, fishing, gathering berries, digging roots, and maintaining "first foods" and other traditional ceremonies would save the people. To him, farming was an act of violence against the earth. "You ask me to plough the ground!" says one of his most famous quotes. "Shall I take a knife and tear my mother's bosom? ... You ask me to dig for stone! Shall I dig under her skin for bones? ... You ask me to cut grass and make hay and sell it, and be rich like white men, but how dare I cut off my mother's hair?"

Smohalla's teachings not only led to conflicts with whites; they antagonized other Indian leaders. Chief Moses of the Columbia Sinkiuses offered the greatest challenge to Smohalla. According to one story, Moses nearly killed Smohalla in a fight. Smohalla then fled the country; he later returned after wandering as far south as Mexico. Whether or not the story is true, a rivalry certainly existed between these two influential leaders. Another conflict existed between Smohalla and the Wallawalla chief Homily, who tended to be more open to European-based ideas. Smohalla's rise to leadership also challenged the powerful Wallawalla chief Peopeomoxmox.

Desiring to be free of whites and Indian leaders who opposed him, Smohalla left Wallula and moved north with his followers to P'na Village on the Priest Rapids of the Columbia River. The Wanapams, who never signed a treaty, had been lumped in with the Yakima Nation during treaty negotiations in 1855. This was an uncomfortable arrangement since, when the Yakima War broke out shortly after the treaty was signed, Smohalla and his Wanapams had alienated the Yakima war chiefs by refusing to take up arms against the whites.

Influential dance

The Washat dance or Pom Pom ("drums beating like hearts") was the most important religious ceremony performed by the dreamer-prophet's followers. Other dreamer-prophets also conducted Washat dances, aiding in the revival of the older Washani religion among the Indians of the Northwest. The dreamer-prophets had followers among the Columbia Plateau's Umatillas, Yakimas, Wascos, Nez Percé, and the Modocs of southern Oregon and northern California.

Smohalla's teachings emphasized nonviolence, but most whites did not realize that. Rumors of war dances at Priest Rapids and of an Indian uprising led by Smohalla were common in the Northwest's white communities. Smohalla's reputation and his refusal to move onto a reservation labeled him a renegade (an individual who rejects lawful or conventional behavior) and troublemaker. Government officials and most other whites could not comprehend the Dreamers' beliefs; to them the Dreamer religion was nothing more than superstition and its followers "fanatics."

One exception to the Northwest's anti-Smohalla rhetoric was an article that appeared in the July 1886 issue of a local publication, the *North Yakima Farmer*. A writer recommended that the name Smohalla be adopted for the proposed state of Washington. In 1886 the suggestion found no support. A century later, in 1989 during Washington State's centennial celebrations, Smohalla was selected for the state's Hall of Honor as one of the 100 persons whose contributions influenced both the state and the nation.

Government applies pressure

By 1890 the government's efforts to round up Indians living off the Northwest's reservations increased. As access to their root grounds and fishing sites became more difficult and pressure from authorities to give up their traditional beliefs and practices continued, the Indians had few options. Although some stayed on lands along the Columbia River, most moved to reservations. By 1895, at the time of his death, even Smohalla had left Priest Rapids for the Yakima Indian Reservation.

When he left his village on the Columbia River, Smohalla passed on the leadership of the Washat religion to his son Yo-Yonan. After his son's death during a hunting expedition in the winter of 1917, Smohalla's nephew Puck Hyah Toot ("Birds Feeding in a Flock") took over as the leading Priest Rapids prophet. He conducted Washat ceremonies in the Priest Rapids longhouse (command residence) until his death in 1956. Another Wanapam, Rex Buck, took over after Puck Hyah Toot's death. Buck's son, Rex, Jr., succeeded him in 1975.

Smohalla's impact on the Indians of the Columbia Plateau was crucial. It gave them hope for the future and pride in their traditions. One hundred years after his death, Indians in the Northwest continue to practice a variant of his teachings. The Pom Pom, or Seven Drums, religion and its ceremonies, such as the first-foods feasts, are still being practiced on reservations and in Indian communities in the Northwest.

Further Reading

Native North American Almanac, edited by Duane Champagne, Detroit: Gale, 1994.

Relander, Click, *Drummers and Dreamers,* Seattle: Pacific Northwest National Parks and Forests Association, and Caxton Printers, Ltd., 1986.

Ruby, Robert H., and John A. Brown, *Dreamer-Prophets of the Columbia Plateau: Smohalla and Skolaskin,* Norman: University of Oklahoma Press, 1989.

David Sohappy, Sr.

Yakima fisherman and activist
Born April 25, 1925, Yakima Indian Reservation, Washington
Died May 7, 1991, Hood River, Washington

"They says, 'David, you can only stay here temporary.' I says, 'I'm only here temporary to begin with. I'm not here forever. Nothing is.'"

David Sohappy, Sr., was a leading figure in the battle for Northwest Coast Indian fishing rights. He strongly defended the rights of the region's Native Americans to live on and fish freely from the Columbia River, as was their traditional way of life. Sohappy followed the Washat or Seven Drums religion, also known as the Dreamer religion, which is practiced by members of the Yakima, Nez Percé, and Warm Springs reservations in the northwest coastal region of the United States. Dreamers believe in the sacredness (holiness) of traditional values and in the need for the Indian people to return to their ancient ways. A basic belief of the Washat religion is that Mother Earth provides all sustenance (food and other necessities of life), the salmon being the foremost.

Following the teachings of his great-granduncle **Smohalla** (see entry), the Wanapam prophet who revived the Dreamer religion in the 1800s, Sohappy was arrested and harassed for more than 25 years because of his beliefs. His continued resistance brought the issue of Indian fishing rights to

David Sohappy, Sr.

the forefront of a budding cross-cultural debate in the late 1960s, when his pioneering case, *Sohappy* vs. *Washington State,* led to the Boldt decision, a U.S. district court ruling that upheld Indian fishing rights. His belief in his right to live and fish along the Columbia River were repeatedly tested until his death in 1991.

Sohappy was born in 1925 on the Yakima Indian Reservation, near Harrah, Washington. He met Myra, the girl he would eventually marry, when they were children; both were raised in strict, traditional families. Sohappy only attended school through the fourth grade. His family believed that the only things worth learning in the white man's schools were reading and writing. Beyond that, they felt that the European influence might damage a young Indian child's ties to traditional culture and beliefs. Sohappy and Myra eventually married and had nine children: Steve, David, Jr., Andy, Sam, Aleta, Barbara, Donna, Dean, and Alfred.

After serving in the U.S. Army during World War II, Sohappy lived and worked with his family on the reservation for many years. He worked in a sawmill until the early 1960s, when he was laid off. The Sohappys then moved to Cook's Landing, Washington, on the north bank of the Columbia River, in order to live and fish as their ancestors had for thousands of years.

A number of Indian families still live in communities along the Che Wana (Columbia River), such as Celilo Village and Little White Salmon Indian Settlement, refusing to relocate to nearby reservations. Cook's Landing was a temporary fishing camp allotted to the Yakima, Nez Percé, and Warm Springs Indians after the 1957 flooding of the Indian village of Celilo and the destruction of the Celilo Falls fishing site, one of the nation's last remaining traditional Indian fishing spots. The flood was caused by the construction of a government-sponsored dam in the area. The village of Celilo had been part of the land accorded to the Indians in the Yakima Nation's Treaty of 1855, which granted them the right to fish in their "usual and accustomed times and places."

Challenged treaty rights in court

In 1968 Sohappy was arrested for fishing out of season on the Columbia River. He held an uncompromising belief that he was protected by the Treaty of 1855 and wanted to test Native American treaty and religious rights in U.S. courts. His landmark (marking a turning point) case against Washington State led to a federal court ruling that the state could regulate Indian fishing only when necessary for conservation (protection of natural resources) purposes.

Judge Robert C. Belloni, who presided over the case, also ruled that the region's Native American fishermen were entitled to a "fair and equitable" share of the fish caught in Washington waters. Later rulings further defined the meaning of "fair and equitable." The Boldt decision of 1970 established that the treaties gave the Columbia River Indians the right to 50 percent of the harvestable salmon from the river. The ruling, handed down by U.S. District Court Judge George Boldt, angered non-Indian commercial and sports fishermen.

Over the course of two and a half decades, the Sohappy family lived and fished along the banks of the Columbia River, but found themselves facing opposition from federal and state officials. During that time, Washington State confiscated about 230 fishing nets from Sohappy. The family also had to fight the federal government's attempt to evict them from their home. Nonetheless, Sohappy stayed firm in his beliefs and continued to live and fish as his ancestors and his religion dictated. In an interview for the documentary *River People—Behind the Case of David Sohappy,* Myra Sohappy declared: "The white man says I'm breaking his laws. But what about my laws? The laws we got, unwritten laws—our laws come from the Creator. That's the way you gotta live. Is it a crime to try to survive and eat in this country?"

Imprisonment captured national attention

In 1983, as a result of "Salmonscam," an undercover operation by the federal government, Sohappy and his son, David, Jr., were arrested and convicted of selling more than 300 fish out of season. They were sent to Geiger Federal Prison in Spokane, Washington, to serve a five-year sentence. The Yakima Tribal Council, Democratic senators Brock Adams of Washington and Daniel K. Inouye of Hawaii, and Sohappy's lawyer, Thomas Keefe, Jr., protested that the sentence was ridiculously harsh. This chorus of voices, combined with Sohappy's failing health, led to his release on May 17, 1988; he had served about 20 months of the sentence. Sohappy then returned to Cook's Landing to live with his family. During his time in prison, he had suffered a series of strokes and endured transfers to facilities in three other states.

Sohappy fished only occasionally after his release from prison but continued to fight for his right to remain on the land. During the late 1980s and early 1990s, the Columbia River became known as some of the best waters for windsurfing in the United States, second only to those of Hawaii. Land prices increased, and so did the government's attempts to evict Sohappy. In August 1990, the eviction case against the Sohappys was thrown out by the Ninth Circuit Court of Appeals. In a statement made for the *River People* video, Sohappy offered his thoughts on the continued efforts by the U.S. government to remove the family from their home: "They says, 'David, you can only stay here temporary.' I says, 'I'm only here temporary to begin with. I'm not here forever. Nothing is.'" David Sohappy, Sr., died in a nursing home in Hood River, Washington, on May 7, 1991, at the age of 66.

Further Reading

Geranios, Nicholas K., "Sohappy Battles on for Indian Fishing Rights," *Oregonian,* November 12, 1990.

Native North American Almanac, edited by Duane Champagne, Detroit: Gale, 1994.

Schuster, Helen H., *The Yakima,* New York: Chelsea House Publishers, 1990.

Senior, Jeanie, "Indian Activist Sohappy Dies," *Oregonian,* May 9, 1991.

Squanto

Wampanoag translator and guide
Born c. 1600
Died 1623
Also known as Tisquantum

The dying Squanto expressed his wish to "go to the Englishmen's God in Heaven."

Tisquantum, more commonly known as Squanto, is best remembered for living among the Pilgrim settlers of Plymouth Colony and instructing them about farming, hunting, fishing, and geography in their new home. Squanto was reported to have done more than anyone else to aid the survival of the settlement through its difficult early existence in the New World, even helping the Pilgrims maintain friendly relations with neighboring tribes. In recent history, the story of Squanto and the Pilgrims has become an oft-repeated and frequently distorted tale for young people as an example of friendly relations between Indians and the early colonists.

A member of the Patuxet band of the Wampanoag tribe, which dominated the area in which the colonists eventually settled, Squanto first appeared in written history in 1614 as one of 20 Patuxet Indians kidnapped by the English explorer Thomas Hunt. Hunt carried his captives to Spain, where he sold them into slavery. Squanto, however, was one of a number who were rescued by Spanish friars (members of a religious order) and he eventually made his way to England, where he worked for a man named John Slaney.

Slaney was interested in exploring the New World. He sent Squanto along on an expedition to Newfoundland in 1617. There the Indian met the explorer Thomas Dermer, with whom he returned to England the following year. Squanto may have been an indentured servant—paying off a debt by working for a limited time—to Slaney and Dermer. He may have hoped in this way to earn his passage home. In any event, he traveled once again to the New World with Dermer in 1619, returning to the Patuxet region of his birth.

In 1617, during Squanto's absence, a great epidemic that may have been the plague swept the Indian populations in the Massachusetts Bay region. The Patuxet band was virtually wiped out. Squanto returned to find the village of his youth abandoned. He left Captain Dermer to go in search of survivors but returned to his aid when Dermer met hostile Indians. Squanto remained with Dermer until the Englishman was killed in a skirmish with the Pokanoket Wampanoag. Squanto was then taken prisoner.

Some historians think that when Squanto was sent to meet the English settlers at Plymouth in 1621, he may have still been living with the Wampanoag as their captive. There were reports of hostility between him and **Massasoit** (see entry), who had become *sagamore,* or civil chief, of the Wampanoag confederation (alliance of tribes) after the epidemic. It was Massasoit who sent Squanto—who spoke English—to the newcomers at Plymouth (in present-day Massachusetts), where, in November 1620, they had settled on the former lands of the Patuxet.

The English—weakened from their journey, hungry, and ill—kept their distance from the Indians during the first winter of their residence; half of them died before spring. The Wampanoag, who had had mixed experiences with Europeans, watched the newcomers suspiciously. In March, Massasoit felt the time was right to approach the English and sent Squanto and a companion to reassure them of the friendly intentions of the Indians. The two arranged for a conference between the English leaders and Massasoit. That meeting resulted in the historic treaty in which the Wampanoag and the English pledged mutual peace and friendship.

"Sent of God"

Squanto was sent to live with the English settlers. His guidance proved so vital to them that the Plymouth governor, William Bradford, declared him an "instrument sent of God for [their] good." Squanto played an especially crucial role in introducing the English to neighboring tribes. His travels had made him a perfect intermediary between the cultures. The colonists were able to establish vital trade relationships with Native groups, giving them access to seeds and other supplies necessary to life in New England, as well as animal pelts (skins bearing fur) which they sent to England to repay investments and buy English goods. The Pilgrims were grateful to Squanto, Massasoit, and all the Wampanoags who helped

Squanto teaches the Pilgrims how to plant corn; illustration by C. W. Jefferys

them. In the autumn of 1621 they invited Massasoit to a feast to give thanks. Massasoit arrived with 90 people and the Pilgrims were not prepared to feed so many, so the Wampanoag provided food as well. This was the beginning of the traditional Thanksgiving holiday.

Tradition has it that Squanto taught the English, most of whom had not been farmers in their native country, to plant Indian corn and other local vegetables, and to ensure the success of the crop by the use of fish fertilizer. The English believed the practice of fertilizing with fish was traditional among the Indians. In recent years, however, this idea has come into question among historians. Some believe that Squanto learned the practice in Europe or in Newfoundland.

Life of conflict

Squanto's career was not without controversy. There are reports that he sought to raise his standing among the Indians by exaggerating his influence with the English. He has also been accused of alarming neighboring Native American groups with reports that colonists kept a plague (he may have meant gunpowder) buried underground that could be released at any time.

There is also evidence that he tried to undermine Massasoit's relationship with the English. In 1622 Squanto evidently tried to convince the English that Massasoit was plotting with the hostile Narragansett tribe to destroy the Plymouth Colony and that an attack would occur soon. The deception was quickly discovered, but Massasoit was angry enough to demand Squanto's life. The Plymouth settlers were furious with Squanto because of this deceit. Even Governor Bradford agreed with Massasoit that Squanto deserved death for his act of betrayal. The fact that the colonists protected him from Massasoit's vengeance shows how much they needed him.

In November 1623, with the arrival of additional English settlers who were unprepared for the approaching New England winter, Squanto guided an expedition from Plymouth to trade with Cape Cod Indians for corn. He fell ill with what William Bradford, who was in charge of the trip, described as an "Indian fever" and died within a few days. According to Bradford, as cited in *New England Quarterly,* the dying Squanto expressed his wish to "go to the Englishmen's God in Heaven" and "bequeathed his little property to his English friends, as remembrances of his love."

Some historians feel that Squanto's legendary role as the Pilgrims' savior has been largely exaggerated. They insist that he wanted power badly enough to endanger the peace between Indians and whites. However, Squanto remains a key figure in American folklore—and a symbol of Thanksgiving.

Further Reading

Ceci, Lynn, "Squanto and the Pilgrims," *Society,* 27, May/June 1990, pp. 40-44.

Humins, John H., "Squanto and Massasoit: A Struggle for Power," *New England Quarterly,* March 1987, pp. 54-70.

Salisbury, Neal, *Manitou and Providence: Indians, Europeans, and the Making of New England, 1500-1643,* New York: Oxford University Press, 1982.

Vaughan, Alden T., *New England Frontier: Puritans and Indians, 1620-1675,* Boston: Little, Brown, 1965.

Maria Tallchief

Osage ballerina
Born 1925

"What I do for the company is teach, and what I teach is what Balanchine taught me."

Maria Tallchief is an internationally renowned ballerina. She has achieved a number of firsts, including being the first American to dance at the Paris Opera; in the process she overcame the arrogant European belief that no foreigner could be a major ballet star. Soon, however, the leading people in ballet recognized her great ability and she became one of the premiere dancers of the twentieth century.

Tallchief was raised in a wealthy family; its resources were the result of her grandfather's participation in negotiating the Osage treaty, an agreement that led to the establishment of the Osage Tribe of Oklahoma Reservation. Later the reservation was found to contain large quantities of oil, which produced vast sums of money for some Indians. Tallchief's family was one of those who gained financially through alliances with the federal government and the discovery of oil on reservation land.

Tallchief began studying ballet and taking music lessons at age four. By the time she was eight, she had gone beyond the level of training offered in her native state of Oklahoma, and her family relocated to Beverly Hills, California. She was trained by the noted ballet specialists Bronislava Nijinska, David Lichine—a student of the great Maria Pavlova—and, later, George Balanchine.

When Tallchief was 15, she performed her first solo at the Hollywood Bowl in a piece choreographed by Madame Nijinska. Instead of attending college, she began her formal career as a member of the Ballet Russe. As a dancer with this prestigious Russian troupe, she met with prejudice and skepticism about her talent. Yet, when Balanchine took over as head of the troupe, he had no difficulty recognizing her worth and appointed her as understudy (substitute in case of illness) for the leading role in *The Song of Norway.* Creator of such ballet works as *Orpheus, Swan Lake,* and *The Four Temperaments* and a contemporary of the trailblazing modern composer Igor Stravinsky, Balanchine himself was an unrecognized talent at the time. As his technique developed, he helped shape Tallchief's abilities, and her reputation as a ballerina grew rapidly.

Achieved several ballet "firsts"

Tallchief married Balanchine in 1942, and they moved to France, where she became the first American dancer to perform at the Paris Opera. Though she encountered some resistance as a Native American, she won audiences over with her performances. After returning to the United States, she became the ranking soloist—and the first American prima ballerina (leading dancer) —in the Balanchine Ballet Society (later known as the New York City Ballet). In 1949 Tallchief danced the leading role in *Firebird,* a part Balanchine choreographed (designed the dance steps) especially for her and remembered as one of her finest performances. A decade later she retired from performance and began directing her own ballet troupe. In later years she painstakingly revisited the leading role she created for *Firebird* for her students.

Tallchief's dream of creating a Chicago-based resident ballet company first began to take form in 1974, when she was asked to develop a small troupe that would meet the needs of the Chicago Lyric Opera. In addition, she was invited to direct the Opera Ballet School. During her work there from 1974 to 1979, she established the same high standards for her students that she was given in her own training. An organizational split took place in January 1980. The Chicago City Ballet was formed when the Lyric Opera Ballet separated from the Lyric Opera.

Maria Tallchief in New York City Ballet production of *Firebird*

Tallchief noted in an interview with John Gruen for *Dance* magazine that Balanchine–whom she divorced in 1952—"was forging a whole new technique—a whole new system of dancing. He literally created a new style of classical dancing—and that's what we mustn't lose. It's what I'm promulgating [putting forward] at the Chicago City Ballet because I know it's right." Tallchief and the dancer/choreographer Paul Mejia seek to carry on Balanchine's style and artistic vision at the Chicago City Ballet. Mejia, too, is a student of Balanchine's, and he and Tallchief share a strong commitment to the late choreographer's creative ideals.

Although Tallchief officially retired from dancing in 1966, she is remembered as a ballerina with energy and style and a unique presence. In her interview with Gruen, Tallchief showed that the intensity of her youth burned on when she discussed working with her troupe: "What's important is that I'm working with very talented young people. Yes, we're in the process of growth, but I feel that if you have a choreographer like Paul Mejia and a syllabus based on Balanchine, you really can't go wrong. What I do for the company is teach, and what I teach is what Balanchine taught me." According to Gruen, Maria Tallchief "retains the dynamics that made her America's prima ballerina for over two decades" and described her as "a figure still capable of making temperatures rise."

Further Reading

Bird of Fire, the Story of Maria Tallchief, New York: Dodd, Mead, 1961.

Gruen, John, "Tallchief and the Chicago City Ballet," *Dance,* 58, December 1984, p. HC25–27.

Tecumseh

Shawnee warrior and tribal leader
Born 1768, Old Piqua (present-day Ohio)
Died 1813
Also known as"The Panther Passing Across," "Moves From One Place to Another," and "Shooting Star"

Tecumseh was "one of those uncommon geniuses, which spring up occasionally to produce revolutions and overturn the established order of things"
—William Henry Harrison

Tecumseh was a Shawnee war chief and one of the most influential Indian leaders of his time. He envisioned a confederacy comprised of many Indian tribes that would give his people a chance to stand united against the tide of white settlement. Much of his career was spent campaigning among the tribes of the Old Northwest; despite obstacles, he won many recruits for his cause. In the end, however, the superior numbers and technology of the whites, combined with differences of opinion among the Indians themselves, put an end to Tecumseh's great plan.

Tecumseh has become equally famous for his strong moral character. He stood out, according to historians, because of his special concern for others; he freely shared game and other provisions with the less fortunate. He was known for his humane treatment of prisoners in warfare as well, and influenced many of his people to abandon practices of burning and torturing their cap-

Tecumseh

translated as "Moves from One Place to Another," or "Shooting Star"). His father was Puckeshinwa, a respected Shawnee war chief, and his mother, Methoataske, was of Creek or possibly Cherokee origin. Although the exact number of children in the family is uncertain, Tecumseh had several siblings.

His childhood was passed during a time of crisis for the Shawnee people. From prehistoric times they had inhabited the Ohio valley, living in villages along the river, the women farming and the men hunting, fishing and, from time to time, warring with neighboring tribes. They had long been accustomed to contact with the Long Knives, as they called the white frontiersmen, trading with them and generally maintaining good relations.

Throughout the 1760s and 1770s, however, whites arrived in increasing numbers. Following their surveyors, who scouted out the land, they set up permanent settlements, clearing and fencing the land and driving away the game on which the Indians depended. The Indians objected to the intrusion, and by 1774 there was war between the Shawnee and the settlers. Puckeshinwa was a casualty of this war, and Tecumseh's older brother Chicksika reportedly promised the dying man that he would never make peace with the Long Knives.

After the death of Puckeshinwa, it fell to Chicksika to teach his younger brother the skills of the hunter and warrior that were so necessary for success in the tribe. Chicksika, an able hunter and warrior himself, was an excellent teacher, and there was a close bond between the two. Tecumseh learned quickly; several historians believe he displayed leadership qualities at an early age, organizing

tives. Although little is known for certain about his personal life, he married at least twice. The name of his first wife is unknown; they apparently separated after a disagreement. His second wife, Mamate, died young, leaving him with a young son, Pachetha, who was raised by Tecumseh's sister, Tecumpease. He may have had another son and perhaps a daughter with a Cherokee woman.

Early life

Tecumseh (probably originally pronounced "Tekamtha") was born at Old Piqua, a Shawnee village on the Mad River in what is now western Ohio. According to legend, a large meteor or comet passed through the sky at the moment of his birth, suggesting his name (which can also be and leading hunting parties of youngsters and always bringing home more game than anyone else.

When the colonies fought the American Revolution with England in 1776, the Shawnee remained neutral. When their principal chief, Cornstalk (Hokolesqua), was seized and murdered by settlers while on a peace mission in 1777, however, the Shawnee retaliated with a vengeance, attacking white settlements and killing many settlers. In 1779, the Long Knives responded in kind with an attack on Chillicothe, principal village of the Shawnee and residence of Tecumseh's family. The Shawnee fought off the attack easily, but this incident disturbed them deeply. War had come into their homes.

The tribe couldn't agree about how to respond to this aggression; before the year was out, the tribe had splintered. Nearly 1,000 Shawnee, including Tecumseh's mother Methoataske, migrated to southeastern Missouri. Tecumseh was 11 years old when his mother left the village, leaving her younger sons to the care of Chicksika and their recently married sister Tecumpease, who had decided to stay and resist the Long Knives.

Young warrior

Tecumseh's first brush with battle seems to have been in 1782. At the age of 14 he accompanied Chicksika, now a war chief in his own right, in an attack against a party of invading Kentuckians. Chicksika was slightly wounded and Tecumseh fled into the forest. He soon returned, however, and was forgiven for running off, which he never did again. After that, Tecumseh routinely accompanied Chicksika's war parties and made a name for himself as a brave and skillful fighter. And even when warfare between whites and Indians was extremely cruel, he became known for his compassion, always insisting on the humane treatment of prisoners. He is said to have objected strongly to the burning of a prisoner following a raid, speaking so persuasively that his fellow warriors promised to abandon such practices in the future.

During the years that followed the American Revolution, the new government set about acquiring more Indian land to satisfy settlers and make up for financial losses from the war. "Government chiefs," as the Indians called those among them who had dealings with the Americans, sold off huge tracts of land that they did not own. Tecumseh's people tried to avoid these arrangements and never saw them as legitimate. It may well have been during these years that Tecumseh developed his philosophy that the land belonged to all the Indians in common, and that therefore no one tribe or group had the right to sell it.

Tensions between the Shawnee and the Long Knives continued to build, and the years 1787 and 1788 found Chicksika's war party, including Tecumseh, roaming the South, raiding white settlements. In the summer of 1788, Chicksika was killed in an unsuccessful attack in Tennessee. Most of the party returned home following the loss of their leader. Tecumseh, however, remained in the South for another two years, hunting and raiding white settlements with a small party. He did not return home until 1790.

While Tecumseh was away, the U.S. government had created the Northwest Territory from his homeland, taking control of many of the disputed Indian lands. They opened the lands to white settlement by meeting Indian resistance with military action. Tecumseh returned in time to play an important role in his people's defense. Following several defeats at the hands of the Indians, the Americans took strong measures. Mounting a carefully planned, well supplied expedition, they clashed with the Indians in August 1794 at a place called Fallen Timbers. The Indians, badly outnumbered, suffered a crushing defeat, made worse by the failure of promised aid from the British. Tecumseh was in the forefront of the fighting at Fallen Timbers, and his brother, Sauwauseekau, was among those killed.

Tecumseh took no part in the negotiations that followed in the wake of this battle. These proceedings resulted in the Treaty of Greenville, which forced the Indians to give up their claims to lands in southern, central, and eastern Ohio. Grieved by his brother's death and disappointed at the failure of British support, Tecumseh headed for northern Ohio, where he spent the winter hunting with a small party of family and friends.

Influential among the Long Knives

The years following Fallen Timbers were relatively peaceful for Tecumseh. He lived with his followers for a time at Deer Creek in western Ohio, and then moved west to Indiana, where he remained for several years. During the periods between hostile encounters with the Long Knives, several attempts were made to re-establish friendship. Thanks to his strong personality, Tecumseh played an important part in these efforts. Government officials often asked him to negotiate for them, and he frequently agreed.

On one such occasion, following a panic by white settlers who had abandoned their farms in the wake of Indian attacks, he spoke calmly and eloquently to assembled whites, assuring them that the Indians intended to obey the Treaty of Greenville and wished to live in peace. The settlers were reassured and returned to their homes. Whites who heard Tecumseh speak were deeply impressed, in spite of the fact that he always spoke in the Shawnee language and had his words translated by an interpreter.

The Indian Movement

In 1805 Tecumseh's younger brother, Lalawethika, started a religious revival that became known as the Indian Movement. He attracted large numbers of followers from various tribes to a community he established at Greenville, Ohio. Preaching a return to traditional Indian values and a rejection of the ways of the white man, Lalawethika insisted that the whites had no right to the lands they had taken. In honor of his newfound status, Lalawethika changed his name to Tenskwatawa, the Open Door. He was also known as the Shawnee Prophet.

Tecumseh joined his brother at Greenville, where he helped shift the focus of the movement from religious to political matters. Tecumseh had two major goals: the common ownership of all remaining Indian lands by the tribes, and a political and military confederacy to unite the tribes under his own leadership. Soon government officials became alarmed at the growing number of warriors arriving at Greenville. From his headquarters at Vincennes, William Henry Harrison, governor of the Indiana Territory, watched the Greenville community closely, often sending messages to the Indians, asking them what they meant to do. Tecumseh and Tenskwatawa responded with reassurances of their peaceful intentions.

Tippecanoe

By 1808, the game and other resources at Greenville were depleted, and the community struggled to support its growing population. The brothers moved their supporters to a location on the Tippecanoe River, where game and fish were more plentiful and the Long Knives further away. The establishment of this new village, called Tippecanoe or Prophetstown, with its growing number of warriors, further unnerved the whites. Governor Harrison kept a careful eye on the settlement.

Meanwhile, Tecumseh worked to support his confederacy. In the fall of 1808, he made a trip to Canada and established political links with the English. During the next three years, he traveled widely among the tribes of the Northwest and the South in search of recruits, meeting with mixed success. Older leaders, particularly the "government chiefs," felt threatened by Tecumseh's leadership and warned their followers against him. It was also difficult for some of the more traditionally-minded to imagine joining a confederacy that united them, in some cases, with ancient enemies.

However, Tecumseh's following increased in the next year with the unwitting help of Governor Harrison. In September 1809 Harrison entered into new land negotiations with government chiefs. The result was the Treaty of Fort Wayne, which netted for the government about two and a half million acres of Indian lands. As word of this loss spread among the northwestern tribes, a flood of warriors—disgusted with the leaders who had thus betrayed them—joined Tecumseh's cause.

In 1810 Governor Harrison, convinced of the Tippecanoe community's hostility, made a final effort to subdue the Indians without warfare. He suggested that Tenskwatawa, Tecumseh's younger brother, visit Washington to meet the president. American whites often used this method, hoping to overwhelm the Indians with the power of the federal government.

Tecumseh himself travelled to meet Harrison at Vincennes in July to deliver a reply to this invitation. He was accompanied by several hundred warriors. The progress of the party was recorded by the commander of Fort Knox, who halted the Indians' canoes briefly. The commander wrote home: "They were all painted in the most terrific manner.... They were headed by the brother of the Prophet (Tecumseh) who, perhaps, is one of the finest looking men I ever saw—about six feet high, straight, with large, fine features, and altogether a daring, bold looking fellow."

At Vincennes, Tecumseh and Harrison met for the first time. A council was held at which Tecumseh spoke at length, reciting the long list of injustices that had been committed against the Indians, emphasizing his opposition to the Treaty of Fort Wayne, and admitting that he headed a confederacy dedicated to preventing further invasion of Indian lands. He concluded by saying that he was not at that time able to accept the invitation to Washington. Harrison came away from the meeting convinced that it was Tecumseh, not his brother, who was the real power at the Tippecanoe community.

By 1811 Harrison had become openly hostile toward the community at Tippecanoe.

Death of Tecumseh

Tecumseh was away from the village that autumn, recruiting among the tribes of the South, and Harrison took advantage of the opportunity. He marched his army out of Vincennes and proceeded toward Tippecanoe. Tenskwatawa, tracking Harrison's progress, also prepared for war but took no action until Harrison's forces crossed the river and camped within a mile of the village.

During the night, the Indians surrounded Harrison's camp and attacked before dawn. The Battle of Tippecanoe lasted just over two hours. At that time the Indians began to disengage, even though they had inflicted heavy losses on Harrison's troops. They abandoned their village and scattered. Harrison's troops burned Tippecanoe. Although the battle may not have been the glorious victory for the Long Knives that Harrison later claimed, it was a serious defeat for the absent Tecumseh, and also to Tenskwatawa, who had taken no active role in the fighting. It ended his career as a prophet.

To the Thames

Following the Battle of Tippecanoe, Tecumseh established a temporary village on nearby Wildcat Creek and set about rebuilding his confederacy, planning for the time being to appease the Americans. He assured Harrison that he would reconsider visiting Washington. As War of 1812 between the British and Americans approached, both sides courted the support of the northwest Indians.

For Tecumseh, the choice was not difficult. In June 1812, he headed for Canada, where he offered his support to the British. As American troops advanced toward Detroit, Tecumseh campaigned among the Indians of the region, seeking support for the British cause. Many of the tribes in the region made no distinction between the British and the Americans, but Tecumseh—mainly through his personality—won many converts. He participated in a number of battles in Canada and the Detroit area during the summer, as the British gained the advantage. At the Battle of Brownstown, he turned back an army of over 150 American troops with only 24 warriors. Shortly afterward, he was slightly wounded at the Battle of Monguagon, which the Americans claimed as a victory.

Tecumseh was pleased when General Isaac Brock took command of the British base of operations at Fort Malden in August. Brock's forceful manner won his immediate approval, and the general had similar confidence in Tecumseh. He informed the Shawnee leader of his plans to march on Detroit and placed him in command of all the Indian forces. Tecumseh played a vital role in the British conquest of Detroit on August 15, 1812.

But losses soon followed. Brock was killed in October and was succeeded by Colonel Henry Procter. Although he had less confidence in Colonel Procter's abilities, Tecumseh remained with and supported the combined forces. When Procter announced his intention to abandon Fort Malden after the British naval defeat at the Battle of Lake Erie, Tecumseh made such an inspiring speech before the assembled British and Indian troops that Procter reconsidered his position. Instead, he agreed that—after a strategic withdrawal—he would make a stand against the approaching American forces led by William Henry Harrison.

Procter retreated to Moraviantown as Tecumseh's forces guarded the rear. The colonel finally made a stand at the Thames River, but the British positions quickly collapsed under pressure from the Americans. Tecumseh's warriors fought until they were overwhelmed by superior numbers; he himself was killed by a bullet to the chest. The Indians gradually withdrew, and the Battle of the Thames ended in an American victory. With the death of Tecumseh, the Indian Movement ended.

Tecumseh is still one of history's more mysterious figures. In a letter to the secretary of war, William Henry Harrison described the war chief as "one of those uncommon geniuses, which spring up occasionally to produce revolutions and overturn the established order of things." Yet no known transcript exists of any of Tecumseh's speeches, nor do we have accounts from any of his Indian followers. His story is told through the eyes of his opponents, who respected him even in the heat of battle.

Further Reading

Drake, Benjamin, *Life of Tecumseh,* Anderson, Gates & Wright, 1858; reprinted, Ayer Company Publishers, 1988.

Eckert, Allan W., *A Sorrow in Our Heart,* New York: Bantam, 1992.

Edmunds, R. David, *Tecumseh and the Quest for Indian Leadership,* Boston: Little, Brown, 1984.

Gilbert, Bill, *God Gave Us This Country: Tekamthi and the First American Civil War,* New York: Anchor/Doubleday, 1989.

Sugden, John, *Tecumseh's Last Stand,* Norman: University of Oklahoma Press, 1985.

Kateri Tekakwitha

Mohawk Catholic nun and candidate
    for sainthood
Born 1656, Ossernenon (Auriesville), New York
Died 1680
Also known as Catherine Tekakwitha, "Lily of the
    Mohawks," La Sainte Sauvagesse

As a result of the miraculous cures that have been attributed to Kateri Tekakwitha since her death, the Jesuits submitted a petition in 1884 for her canonization, or sainthood.

Kateri Tekakwitha was the first Native American convert to Roman Catholic Christianity to be venerated—a high honor that is the first step to being named a saint—by the church. She was born in 1656 in Ossernenon (Auriesville), New York, to a Mohawk father and a Christianized Algonquin mother who had been captured by Mohawks in around 1653. This capture took place amid a great deal of fighting among Native factions (rival groups) and Europeans attempting to move deeper into the New World. Tribal warfare, as well as cultural and religious battles with Europeans, set the stage for Kateri's life.

Although the French Jesuits (a Roman Catholic order of priests) were making some headway in their attempts to Christianize and colonize New France (the territory in the New World claimed by France), Native hostilities remained. The 16-year interval between 1632 and 1648 was reportedly the worst period for the Jesuit Mission. Eight Jesuits were brutally murdered between 1642 and 1649, three by the Mohawks of Tekakwitha's village. After the slayings a constant state of war prevailed in the region until finally, in 1667, the French government sent a military expedition to avenge the killings. As a result of extensive destruction, the Mohawks, who were known for their violence among the Five Nations of the Iroquois Confederacy (an alliance of the Mohawk, Seneca, Cayuga, Oneida, and Onondaga tribes formed in about the year 1570), were forced to request missionaries from the French.

Eleven years prior to the capture of Kateri's mother, a Jesuit missionary, Isaac Jogues, had been captured by a band of warriors in 1642 and taken to Ossernenon. He, like other missionaries, received a good deal of pressure from French officials to convert the Natives and to bring them under French rule. Jogues encouraged the tribe to believe that the articles used in the Catholic mass, including the altar, were powerful tools of sorcery and magic and apparently threatened to use his powers to rain death upon them if they didn't accept his religion.

Some years after his capture, Jogues left for France, and on his return he found that a smallpox epidemic had swept the village during his absence. He was killed by a war ax when he reappeared in the village after what appeared to be the fulfillment of his prophecy to bring death to the village. The smallpox epidemic took the lives of Kateri's mother, father, and younger brother. At the age of four, Tekakwitha was orphaned and left facially disfigured as well as visually impaired by a bout with the disease. Kateri's

Kateri Tekakwitha

uncle, who was a village chief of some reputation and the husband of her mother's sister, took her in to live with his family.

Resists marriage

Kateri's uncle was violently opposed to Christianity. However, he was obliged to host the three missionaries sent to Ossernenon at the Mohawks' request. In 1667, when she was 11, Kateri was given the task of looking after them during their short stay. The young girl was reportedly impressed by the gentle, courteous behavior of the Jesuits. Later, two of the three missionaries returned to the area to settle and continue their work.

During these years, Kateri reached puberty and, according to missionary reports, refused all romantic advances made to her as well as every attempt to marry her off. Her family responded to her resistance with violence and extreme deprivation. Meals were withheld from her and her life was threatened. It is suspected that some of the Christian Algonquins and Hurons, who now made up about two-thirds of the village population, had told Kateri about the unwed Ursuline nuns of Québec, influencing her resistance to the idea of marriage.

The Mohawks were not traditionally opposed to the idea of perpetual virginity and chastity; in fact they believed that the practice could bestow great powers. Members of special virgin groups in the community followed specific codes of behavior expected of those of their stature. However, some evidence suggests that the Mohawks had been greatly shamed in the past when the virgins broke their vows. Europeans contributed to the process when they arrived with alcohol. Women unaccustomed to the influence of spirits sometimes embarrassed themselves and their village by violating the expected behavioral code. The elders disbanded the group. This incident undoubtedly had an effect on surrounding villages, including Ossernenon.

Conversion and subsequent personal trials

In his writings, Jesuit missionary Lamberville reported finding a teenage Kateri in her dwelling, unable to work because of a foot injury. By all accounts, she was ordinarily a very industrious, generous worker. "I conversed with her about Christianity and I found her so docile that I exhorted her to be instructed and to frequent the chapel, which she did," he noted. Observing "that she had none of the vices of the girls of her age, that encouraged me to teach her henceforth." Kateri then attended his catechism class (instruction in the Catholic religion) through the summer and winter.

Lamberville was so impressed with her learning that he baptized her the following Easter, in 1676, earlier than usual for new converts. Tekakwitha was 20 years old. She then received the name Kateri. For six months she remained in her village, enduring ridicule and scorn for her open practice of Christianity. She was accused of sorcery, repeatedly confronted on her trips to and from the village chapel, and deprived of food on Sundays and Christian holidays when she chose not to work. Her life was once threatened on her way to chapel by a Mohawk warrior who held a war ax above her head, and she was accused by her maternal aunt of enticing her uncle to engage in sex.

Lamberville dismissed the charges and advised her to leave the village to join the Jesuit mission of Saint Francis Xavier, at Kanawake, Québec, at the straits of Sault Saint Louis. Kanawake was a village known for the discipline of its inhabitants. It was formed in 1667 in reaction to the bad effects of alcohol on the Iroquois. When three Native convert members of the mission were recruiting in Ossernenon, Kateri left with them. One of them was the husband of her half-sister, her uncle's adopted daughter, who resided at the mission. Her uncle was gone from the village during her departure, but on learning of her absence, he vowed to have her and the three others killed. He pursued them, but they eluded him.

When she arrived at the mission, Kateri was entrusted to the spiritual care of Anastasie Tegonhatsiongo, a former friend of her mother. She received intensive Christian training and proved a gifted student. She was allowed to receive communion within months of her arrival. Anastasie, like many other inhabitants of the mission, was opposed to Kateri's desire to remain a virgin. She and others attempted to dissuade Kateri from this and pressured her to marry, reminding her that to do so would secure her a life free from poverty. But Kateri had formed close friendships with two other women at the mission.

After visiting the nuns of Hotel-Dieu hospital in Ville-Marie (Montréal) and learning of their ascetic, or strictly self-denying, practices, Kateri and her two friends wanted to form their own cloister (home for nuns). As a final resort, Anastasie asked one of the three head priests, Father Cholenic, to help them in their pursuit. Although Cholenic and the Catholic authorities considered the idea of establishing a Native American cloister premature, Kateri was allowed to take a vow of chastity on the Feast of Annunciation in 1679.

Kateri's life at the mission was not without difficulties. Her half-sister later charged her with having sexual relations with her husband during an annual winter hunting expedition. After the incident, Kateri no longer participated in the hunt. Instead, she is said to have remained at the nearly deserted mission, where she increased her religious activities.

Iroquois spiritual beliefs and Catholicism

According to observers at the mission, one of the most noticeable features of Kateri's Catholicism was her strict observance of frequent, regimented penances, or self-punishments. She consumed very little. What she did eat was often mixed with ashes. Kateri was known to stand barefoot for hours in the snow at the foot of a cross, saying the rosary (prayers). She once spent three continuous nights on a bed of thorns, secured an agreement to have a companion regularly flagellate (whip) her, and spent many hours on her bare knees in an unheated chapel during severe winter weather. Onlookers were amazed at the severity of her practices, and mission priests attributed such extreme behavior to virtue, godly reverence, and holy dedication.

However, Kateri's dedication also had significant roots in Iroquois spirituality, which placed great value on dreams and dreaming. Dreams were considered by the Iroquois to be the language of the soul and to be extremely important for a healthy, functioning society. Dreams were ritualized, interpreted, and acted upon by all members of the community. It was believed that depriving the soul of dreaming would cause sickness. If people did not or could not dream, Iroquois culture provided ritual (ceremonial) means for encouraging a trance state. Taking a sweat-bath, fasting, singing, chanting, performing self-mutilations, and practicing various types of sensory deprivation were all used to put the individual in touch with the soul. Food was sometimes mixed with ashes. Alcohol was sometimes used as well, after its introduction by the Europeans.

Her death and miracles

Kateri's devotion to these practices probably cut her life short. At age 24, in frail health, she died during Holy Week (the week before Easter Sunday). The Last Sacraments (religious observance for the dying) were administered to her at her bedside, rather than in the chapel. Kateri is said to have promised intercession to, or prayer on the behalf of, those present at her death. It is also said that shortly after her death, her badly scarred face became radiant with beauty and all scarring completely disappeared.

Since her death, miraculous cures have been credited to her. As a result of these, as well as the view of her life as one of extreme devotion and piety, the Jesuits submitted a petition in 1884 for her canonization, or sainthood. In 1932 her name was formally presented to the Vatican, and in 1943 she was venerated, receiving the first of three degrees of holiness. In 1980, Kateri was beatified (declared blessed), thus achieving the second degree.

Fifty biographies have been written about Kateri Tekakwitha, as well as numerous pamphlets and tracts. More than 100 articles have been dedicated to her life and influence. Kateri's life stories draw mostly on the accounts of two of the priests at Kanawake: Fathers Cholenic and Chauchetiere. Only one year after her death, Chauchetiere drew a portrait of her inspired by a visitation he received. He also compiled a short biography at that time. At least one modern scholar, meanwhile, has cast doubts on Kateri's actual existence, arguing that the Jesuits not only created Kateri Tekakwitha, but fashioned her to promote Christian missionary efforts.

Many other people accept her existence and her holiness on faith. Two American quarterly magazines are devoted to Kateri, keeping a record of the favors granted through her help. One of these, *Kateri,* is published by the Kateri Tekakwitha Guild; the other, *The Lily of the Mohawks,* is published by the Tekakwitha League. More than 10,000 Americans are associated with these organizations to build support for her canonization. Radio broadcasts and television and film dramatizations, two operas, and several plays draw on her story. In addition, more than 84 organizations, including camps, clubs, and missions, have been dedicated to her or named in her honor. An international Kateri Tekakwitha movement is dedicated to constructing a unique form of Native American Catholicism built on her influence.

Further Reading

"American Indian Group Finds New Catholic Path," *New York Times,* August 9, 1992, p. 18.

Koppedrayer, K. I., "The Making of the First Iroquois Virgin: Early Jesuit Biographies of the Blessed Kateri Tekakwitha," *Ethnohistory,* spring 1993, pp. 277-306.

Mathes, Valerie Sherer, "American Indian Women and the Catholic Church," *North Dakota History,* 47, 1980, pp. 20-25.

Peterson, Jacqueline, and Mary Druke, "American Indian Women and Religion," in *Women and Religion in America,* Harper & Row, 1981, pp. 1-11.

Jim Thorpe

Sauk and Fox athlete and Olympic champion
Born May 22, 1887, Oklahoma
Died March 29, 1953, Lomita, California
Also known as Wa-tho-huck ("Bright Path")

In 1950, sportswriters and broadcasters named Jim Thorpe the "greatest American football player" and the "greatest overall male athlete" in the first half of the twentieth century.

Even in 1912, with 17 years left in his professional career, James Francis Thorpe was recognized as "the world's greatest all-around athlete," according to the *New York Times*. He was already famous as a three-time all-American football player when he went to the Summer Olympics in Stockholm that year, where he won both the pentathlon and the decathlon. Six months after his return to the United States, however, officials learned that he had played semi-professional baseball. Since the Olympics then allowed only amateur athletes to participate, he was stripped of his medals and his name and performances were removed from the record books. Thorpe then played professional baseball and football, and later held a series of jobs until his death in 1953. He was adept in every sport he attempted: swimming, boxing, wrestling, lacrosse, golf, tennis, and others. An Associated Press poll in 1950, more than 20 years after he had quit professional sports, selected him as the greatest male athlete of the first half of the twentieth century, as well as the greatest American football player for the same period. In 1982,

the International Olympic Committee (IOC) restored Thorpe's amateur status, his medals, and his place in Olympic history.

Thorpe was born near Prague, Oklahoma, on May 22, 1887, the son of Hiram Thorpe, a farmer, and Charlotte Vieux, a Potawatomi Indian fluent in Potawatomi, French, and English, who raised her children as Catholics. Thorpe was a twin, but his twin brother, Charlie, died at age nine. There had been one child born in the family before the twins, and three more siblings were born afterward. The Thorpe children had the typical upbringing of the time: a smattering of school and much time spent out of doors, hunting, fishing, and playing. Thorpe attended the Sauk and Fox Mission School at age 6, and then went to Haskell Institute at Lawrence, Kansas, for three years, ending his term there in the summer of 1901.

Thorpe's mother was a descendant of the last great Sauk and Fox chief, **Black Hawk** (see entry), renowned not only as a warrior but as an outstanding athlete as well, strong and fast afoot. "Many believe that much of Thorpe's athletic prowess traces back to Black Hawk," notes Robert L. Whitman in his book *Jim Thorpe and the Oorang Indians,* "particularly his mother who was convinced that in Thorpe was the living reincarnation of the great chief." Thorpe was very proud of his Sauk and Fox heritage and, in later life, always had a likeness of Black Hawk in his home. Thorpe also had Potawatomi, Kickapoo, and perhaps Menominee blood, although it was as a Sauk and Fox that his parents registered him and that he participated in the land allotment—or parcelling out of tribal lands to individuals—of 1891.

Jim Thorpe

Begins football career at Carlisle

Beginning in 1904, Thorpe attended Carlisle Industrial Indian School in Pennsylvania, the first off-reservation school for American Indians to be established in the United States. By 1912, Thorpe's last full year at Carlisle, the students represented 87 different tribes, speaking 75 different languages. This diversity was not appreciated, however, since uniforms were required and students were forbidden to speak their native languages.

Thorpe played football and began to run track at Carlisle. He was selected as a third-team All-American in 1908, and returned from a two-year leave to make first team in 1911 and 1912, as a halfback. His coach at Carlisle was the legendary Glenn S. "Pop" Warner, whose teams regularly defeated some of the mightiest schools in the nation. The Carlisle Indians played almost all their games away from home, lacking a stadium of their own.

It was generally acknowledged that the team would have been severely limited without Thorpe. Highlights of his 1911 season included the Harvard game, when he scored all of Carlisle's 18 points—including field goals of 23, 43, 37, and 43 yards—to defeat the home team by three points. He also scored 17 points in 17 minutes against Dickinson and punted better than 70 yards against Lafayette. In 1912, he scored 22 of Carlisle's 27 points against Army, including returning two Army kickoffs for touchdowns on consecutive plays, the first having been called back due to a Carlisle penalty. One of the hapless Army defenders was a cadet named Dwight D. Eisenhower. The same superlatives applied to the Pittsburgh game; he scored 28 of 34 points and again punted more than 70 yards. At the end of the season, he had scored a record 198 points.

Dominates 1912 Stockholm Olympics

Thorpe was 24 when he departed New York for Stockholm with the American Olympic team aboard the S.S. *Finland* on June 14, 1912. The team had been groomed to represent the best of American athletics. Starting in 1906, with the encouragement of President Theodore Roosevelt, the American Olympic Committee had solicited private funds for the training and development of a world-class selection of Olympians. The 1912 team was the finest to date and was the best for many years to come. Tryouts were truly national, having been conducted at Stanford University in California, at Chicago's Marshall Field, and at Harvard University in Cambridge, Massachusetts.

Thorpe trained aboard ship and was ready to compete when the group reached Sweden. Twenty-eight nations had sent teams. Thorpe's events were the pentathlon and the decathlon. The pentathlon, held on July 7, consisted of five track and field events. Thorpe won the long jump and discus throw, and placed third in the javelin throw. He also won the 200-meter dash, as well as the 1,500-meter race. Five days later, Thorpe took on the decathlon, which consisted of ten track and field events. He won the shot put, the 110-meter hurdles, and the 1,500-meter run. He placed second in the running broad jump and discus throw, and took third place in the 100-meter dash, pole vault, and javelin throw.

Thorpe's worst finish was fourth place in the 400-meter run. His total for the decathlon was 8,412 points out of a possible 10,000—almost 700 points ahead of the Swedish second-place finisher. Thorpe's performance in the decathlon was not eclipsed for 36 years, and his truly amazing records in both the pentathlon and decathlon may never be repeated. The classic pentathlon was discontinued after the 1924 Paris Olympics.

To a thunderous ovation, King Gustav V presented Thorpe with the medal for winning the pentathlon and, later in the same ceremony, presented him with the prize for the decathlon. "Before Thorpe could walk away," writes Bob Berontas in *Jim Thorpe, Sac and Fox Athlete,* "the king grabbed his hand and uttered the sentence that was to follow Thorpe for the rest of his life. 'Sir,' he declared, 'you are the greatest athlete in the world.' Thorpe, never a man to stand on ceremony, answered simply and honestly, 'Thanks, King.'"

Glory is tarnished

Unfortunately, Thorpe's glory lasted only about six months, enough time to tour parts of the United States as a national hero. In late November 1912, he told the *New York Times* that he wanted to leave Carlisle after the Brown game on Thanksgiving Day, citing an "absolute dislike of notoriety and utter abhorrence of the public gaze, which his athletic prowess has brought him." Soon, however, the public gaze was to become intense. On January 22, 1913, a reporter interviewed Thorpe's former baseball coach, Charles Clancey, and broke the story that Thorpe had played minor league baseball for money in the summers of 1909 and 1910, between his years at Carlisle.

Thorpe acknowledged the two semi-professional seasons in a letter to James E. Sullivan of the Amateur Athletic Union (AAU), published in the *New York Times,* but he stated that he did not play for the money, but rather "because I liked to play ball. I was not very wise in the ways of the world." Later in the letter he said, "I hope I will be partly excused by the fact that I was simply an Indian schoolboy and did not know all about such things." Although Thorpe was unaware that his minor league experience might compromise his amateur status in track and field, the International Olympic Committee stripped him of his medals and removed his name from the record books—thus tarnishing his image as a national hero.

Makes impact in professional sports

Soon thereafter, Thorpe left Carlisle and signed up to play baseball with the New York Giants, his choice among the six teams courting him. With his limited playing experience, he spent much time under option to Milwaukee in the minor leagues, but played outfield with the Giants for three seasons. His batting averages were low, as were the numbers of games in which he appeared each season. He did not play in the majors in 1916, but rather was sent again to Milwaukee, with predictions that he would never again play in the majors. He proved these predictions wrong when he opened the 1917 season on loan to the Cincinnati Reds, playing 77 games before returning to the Giants. His team reached the 1917 World Series and he played in one game, though the Giants lost the series to Chicago, four games to two.

Thorpe stayed with the Giants through the 1918 season and two games of the 1919 season, and then went to the Boston Braves to complete his final and best year in major league baseball, posting a .327 batting average. He was used at both first base and in the outfield while in Boston. It was said that his weakness was an inability to hit a curve ball, but there is evidence that his easygoing demeanor did not sit well with the Giants' fiery manager, John J. McGraw. Thorpe last played professional baseball in 1928 for Akron in the minor leagues; he was 40 years old.

During his major league baseball years, Thorpe was also playing professional football. From 1915 to 1920, he was with the Canton (Ohio) Bulldogs, and in 1921 he played with the Cleveland Indians pro football team. The next two years he organized, coached, and played with the Oorang Indians, a promotional vehicle of Walter Lingo, owner of the Oorang Airedale kennels. This pro football team was composed entirely of American Indians. They played their two 1922 home games in Marion, Ohio, at Lincoln Park.

From 1924 through 1929, Thorpe played with six different teams, including a return to the Canton Bulldogs. He finished his pro football career with the Chicago Cardinals in 1929. In 1919, Thorpe was instrumental in forming the American Professional Football Association, and served as its first president. That group later became the National Football League. Besides being an outstanding halfback, Thorpe was a leader off the field and helped to increase football's popularity.

Retires from professional sports

After Thorpe's retirement from football, a series of jobs and situations came his way. He traveled to California in 1930 to be master of ceremonies for the cross-country marathon staged by C. C. Pyle, known as "the bunion derby," which was won by the Cherokee Andy Payne. He settled in the California town of Hawthorne and worked as an extra in motion pictures, but was never very successful. He also served as superintendent of recreation in the Chicago Park System and, in the late 1930s, lived in Oklahoma and became active in Indian affairs.

Thorpe's work in the midwest led to a national tour as a popular lecturer in the early 1940s on the subjects of sports and Indian affairs. In November 1951, he had an operation for lip cancer. By the time he was reduced to leading an all-Indian song and dance troupe, "The Jim Thorpe Show," it became clear that Thorpe was impoverished. Various groups throughout the United States, recognizing his plight and remembering his Olympic performance, raised funds for his medical care and welfare.

In 1945, at age 58, Thorpe joined the Merchant Marine, since he was past the age where the other services would accept him. His ship, the U.S.S. *Southwest Victory,* sailed to India loaded with ammunition for the American and British war effort in World War II. When his identity became known, he made a series of personal appearances and hospital visits to bolster troop morale. In 1949, his life story was made into the film *Jim Thorpe: All American,* with Burt Lancaster in the title role. Thorpe served as an adviser on the film, having sold his rights to the story some years earlier.

In 1950, two unprecedented honors came Thorpe's way. First, the Associated Press asked sportswriters and broadcasters to review the athletes of the first half of the twentieth century in a variety of categories. In late January, Thorpe was named "the greatest American football player" and the "greatest overall male athlete" in the first half of the century. Interestingly enough, Jesse Owens, the hero of the 1936 Berlin Olympics, was named first among track athletes with 201 votes to Thorpe's 74.

His death

Jim Thorpe died in his trailer home in Lomita, California, a suburb of Los Angeles, on March 28, 1953, at age 64. He was stricken with a heart attack—his third—while eating dinner with his wife. Initial efforts to revive him were successful, but after a short period of consciousness he passed away. His death was front page news in the *New York Times,* which asserted that he "was a magnificent performer. He had all the strength, speed and coordination of the finest players, plus an incredible stamina. The tragedy of the loss of his Stockholm medals because of thoughtless and unimportant professionalism darkened much of his career and should have been rectified long ago. His memory should be kept for what it deserves—that of the greatest all-round athlete of our time."

The call to restore Thorpe's Olympic medals was first sounded in 1943, when the Oklahoma legislature adopted a resolution to petition the Amateur Athletic Union to reinstate the records, but no action was taken. In 1952, a group in Congress made another unsuccessful attempt to have the medals restored. It was not until 1973 that the AAU restored his amateur status, and it took another nine years for the International Olympic Committee to follow suit. The IOC not only restored his amateur status but, more importantly to his family, put the name of Jim Thorpe back in the 1912 records.

Thorpe had married three times and had eight children. In 1913, he married Iva Miller. Their first son, James Jr., died at the age of three from an influenza epidemic during World War I, but their three daughters, Gail, Charlotte, and Grace, lived into the 1990s. In 1926, he married Freeda Kirkpatrick, and they had four sons, Carl Phillip (deceased), William, Richard, and John (Jack). Jack Thorpe, the youngest, became principal chief of the Sauk and Fox in the 1980s. At the time of his death, Thorpe had been married to Patricia Askew for almost eight years.

Town adopts his name

Thorpe's body lay in state in Los Angeles wearing a beaded buckskin jacket and moccasins—garments he wore in lecture appearances in his last years. Both Oklahoma and Pennsylvania asked for the right to bury him. The family held a Roman Catholic funeral service in Shawnee, Oklahoma, as well as secret rites with Thorpe's Thunderbird clan at the farm of Mrs. Ed Mack, the last descendant of Chief Black Hawk. After the funding for several memorial proposals fell through, Thorpe was buried in February 1954 in Mauch Chunk, Pennsylvania. The townspeople voted to change the town's name to "Jim Thorpe, Pennsylvania" and erect a suitable monument to him in exchange for the honor of burying Thorpe there.

After Thorpe's death in 1953, the National Football League renamed its "Most Valuable Player" award the "Jim Thorpe Trophy." In 1961, Thorpe was named to the Pennsylvania Hall of Fame, reflecting his many successes at Carlisle. In 1963, he was placed in the Professional Football Hall of Fame and in 1975 in the National Track and Field Hall of Fame. (He had joined the National College Football Hall of Fame in 1951.) In 1977, *Sport* magazine conducted a national poll and declared Jim Thorpe the "Greatest American Football Player in History."

In 1973, the Yale, Oklahoma, house in which Thorpe's family lived from 1917 to 1923 was opened as an historic site by the Oklahoma Historical Society. In addition, a portrait of the athlete by noted Oklahoma artist Charles Banks Wilson was unveiled in the Oklahoma State Capitol in 1966. It hangs alongside three other noted Oklahomans: U.S. Senator Robert S. Kerr, and the Cherokee **Sequoyah** and **Will Rogers** (see entries). In December 1975, the portion of Oklahoma Highway 51 running from State Highway 18 east of Yale to Tulsa was renamed "The Jim Thorpe Memorial Highway." Finally, in May 1984, a postage stamp bearing the likeness of Thorpe was issued by the U.S. government.

Further Reading

Berontas, Bob, *Jim Thorpe: Sac and Fox Athlete,* New York: Chelsea House, 1992.

Newcombe, Jack, *The Best of the Athletic Boys: The White Man's Impact on Jim Thorpe,* Garden City, NY: Doubleday, 1975.

Strickland, Rennard, *The Indians in Oklahoma,* Norman: University of Oklahoma Press, 1981.

Wheeler, Robert W., *Pathway to Glory,* New York: Carlton Press, 1975.

Whitman, Robert L., *Jim Thorpe and the Oorang Indians: The NFL's Most Colorful Franchise,* Defiance, OH: Hubbard, 1984.

John Trudell

Santee Sioux activist, actor, and musician
Born 1947

John Trudell reports that in one jail another inmate told him that unless he stopped his activist efforts, his family might be harmed.

The name of John Trudell is associated with Indian rights and activism, whether through his work with the American Indian Movement (AIM), his acting roles, or his music. An early organizer of political activities, he has worked both in the forefront and behind the scenes for the interests of indigenous (original inhabitants of a region) Americans.

The son of Thurman Clifford Trudell, a Dakota (Santee) Sioux, and an unidentified mother, Trudell is a native of Niobrara, Nebraska. Little is known of his early years before he began actively organizing Native Americans for political action in California in the 1960s. He came into public view in 1969, when he and his first wife, Lou, along with their children, Maurie and Tara, went to the San Francisco Bay area to join the group occupying the abandoned Alcatraz Prison. The family landed on the island on November 30, just over a week after the organization Indians of All Tribes, Inc. (IAT) had "seized" it under the terms of the Fort Laramie Treaty of 1868. That treaty included the provision that unused federal land could be taken by Native people; IAT took the island in order to set up a cultural and educational facility.

Wovoka Trudell, Lou and John's son, was born on Alcatraz, as was John's future as a spokesperson. During the occupation of the island, he hosted a daily radio program called *Radio Free Alcatraz,* in which he called for the founding of a Native studies center, archives, and a religious retreat, and interviewed some notable Natives, including the activist Grace Thorpe, daughter of the athlete **Jim Thorpe** (see entry). The Trudells stayed on Alcatraz until the end of the occupation in June 1971.

National spokesperson for AIM

By the time they returned to the mainland, Trudell was a member of the American Indian Movement; he went on to become its national spokesperson. He took part in the 1972 Trail of Broken Treaties, a mass march of Natives coming from across the country, which converged on the Bureau of Indian Affairs (BIA) headquarters in Washington, D.C. The event was intended to focus public awareness on Native rights and abuses of them, but things changed when the government seemed to be ignoring both the grievances the protestors presented and the immediate needs of the group while they stayed in the city. The demonstrators ended up occupying BIA building and inflicting substantial property damage.

Trudell's effectiveness as a speaker throughout the turbulent event attracted the attention of the Federal Bureau of Investigation (FBI). When he was elected cochair of AIM the next year, that interest intensified. In 1973, AIM and its supporters took over the small settlement of Wounded Knee, South Dakota, on the Pine Ridge Reservation, and

John Trudell

John Trudell took part in the occupation. When two FBI agents and one Indian were killed in a shoot-out at the Jumping Bull Compound at Pine Ridge in 1975, the AIM members "Dino" Butler, Rob Robideaux, and **Leonard Peltier** (see entry) were arrested for the murders of the FBI agents. Trudell parried with the press about the illegality of the government's presence on the reservation.

The well-spoken and sharp-tongued Trudell continued to make enemies of government officials with his public statements concerning Peltier, AIM, Native rights, and federal policy. In Owhyee, Nevada, in 1975, Trudell fired a pistol into the ceiling of a trading post to protest alleged overpricing of goods by the non-Indian owner. Though this incident did not discredit him as much as his enemies had hoped, Trudell did serve short jail sentences on several occasions. Trudell reports that in one jail another inmate told him that unless he stopped his activist efforts, his family might be harmed. At the time, such a threat seemed to be all in a day's work for a political organizer, and Trudell let the matter drop.

Years of absences from home for various causes contributed to the marriage of Lou and John Trudell to coming to a "friendly" end. John remarried, this time to a Duck Valley Reservation Shoshone and Paiute activist, Tina Manning. They lived on the Nevada reservation, working for AIM and other Indian rights groups. They had three children, Ricarda Star, Sunshine Karma, and Eli Changing Sun.

Mysterious fire

On February 11, 1979, Trudell was away from home speaking in Washington, D.C., on the abuse of Native rights by the federal government. To attract more attention to the Peltier case, Trudell burned an upside-down American flag and was arrested. Within 12 hours, the Manning-Trudell house on the Duck Valley Reservation was set afire. Tina Manning-Trudell, who was pregnant at the time, her mother, Leah Manning, and all three of Trudell's and Manning's children were burned to death. Later investigation proved the cause was arson; Trudell has repeatedly asserted that he suspects that the government was involved in the fire and the murders that resulted from it.

In the 1980s, Trudell began to shift his focus from AIM. He continued to speak on Indian rights, lobby for Leonard Peltier, and talk about his personal loss as an object lesson. He also tested some other fields. He played a cameo role in the Hand Made Films production *Powwow Highway.* In 1992, he appeared in the film *Thunderheart,* playing a character based on Peltier. That same year, he released his first album, *AKA Graffiti Man,* on the independent label Rykodisc. *Johnny Damas and Me,* his second effort, was released in 1994, and he has played numerous concerts on behalf of Native rights groups.

Further Reading

Matthiessen, Peter, *In the Spirit of Crazy Horse,* New York: Viking, 1983.

Native Americans in the Twentieth Century, edited by James Olson and Raymond Wilson, Urbana: University of Illinois Press, 1984.

Native North American Almanac, edited by Duane Champagne, Detroit: Gale, 1994.

Weyler, Rex, *Blood of the Land: The Government and Corporate War against the American Indian Movement,* New York: Everest House, 1982.

Nancy Ward

Cherokee warrior and tribal leader
Born c. 1738, Chota, Cherokee Nation
    (now Monroe County, Tennessee)
Died 1824, Chota
Also known as Nan'yehi ("One Who Goes
    About"), Tsistunagiska ("Wild Rose"),
    and Ghigau ("Beloved Woman")

Nancy Ward was spared the sight of her people's exile to Indian Territory in 1838, but because her spirit was present at Chota, they knew she had preserved that connection to their eastern home.

The role of Ghighua, or Beloved Woman, among the Cherokee was an influential one indeed. The most noted of the Cherokee Beloved Women was Nancy Ward, or Nan'yehi. Closely related to such leaders as Old Hop, the emperor of the Cherokee nation in the 1750s, Attakullakulla, the Wise Councillor of the Cherokee, and Osconostato, the Great Warrior of the Cherokee Nation, Ward won the honored title of Ghighua and her own leadership position after displaying great bravery in battle. But Ward was not merely a warrior. She spoke on behalf of her people with U.S. representatives and wisely counseled the tribe against signing away their land rights through treaties. Although she did not live to see it, her warnings became reality when the Cherokee were removed from their eastern lands in the early nineteenth century.

Earns title Beloved Woman

Born about 1738 at Chota, a "Peace Town" or "Mother Town" in the Overhill region of the Cherokee Nation, Ward came into the world at the beginning of a crucial era in Cherokee history. Raised by her mother, Tame Deer, and her father, Fivekiller (who was also part Delaware or Lenni Lenapé), Nan'yehi realized at a young age that her people were in turmoil. Missionaries, Moravians (Christians who seek to persuade others to accept their religion and follow the Bible as their rule of faith and morals) in particular, were trying to gain access to the Cherokee people in order to convert them. Still very conservative (resistant to change), preserving their traditional customs and religion, the Cherokee had a mixed reaction to the missionaries. Many regarded them as a threat, while others saw them as a blessing.

One of those who straddled this fence was Nan'yehi's very powerful maternal uncle, Attakullakulla ("Little Carpenter"). He eventually struck a deal allowing Moravians into Cherokee territory, but only if they would build schools to instruct Cherokee youth in English and the ways of the white man. Later critics would see this as evidence of Attakullakulla's desire for the Cherokee to accept European ways; others saw this as a tactic to teach the tribe more about their enemy. Like her uncle, Nan'yehi too would try to find the middle ground between tradition and innovation.

Ward married a Cherokee man named Kingfisher while in her early teens. Kingfisher was a great warrior in the battles between tribes, and Nan'yehi was at his side in battle, helping prepare his firearms and rallying Cherokee warriors when their spir-
its flagged. In 1755, the Cherokee fought the Creek at the Battle of Taliwa. During the fighting, Kingfisher was killed. Nan'yehi, about 18 years old at this time, took up her slain husband's gun and, singing a war song, led the Cherokees in a rout of the enemy. Out of her loss was born a decisive victory for her people and a title of honor for her: "Beloved Woman."

The Cherokee were a matrilineal (tracing family relations through the mother) society, and thus their fields had always been controlled by women. Women of great influence became known as Beloved Women, often working behind the scenes in shaping decisions. The role of Ghigau or Beloved Woman was the highest one to which a Cherokee woman could aspire. It was unusual for one as young as Nan'yehi to be so named, but since the name also translates as "War Woman" and was usually awarded to women warriors (or warriors' mothers or widows), Nan'yehi had duly earned it. Much responsibility went with the many privileges of the rank, and, although young, Nan'yehi showed herself capable.

Among the privileges accorded Nan'yehi as a Beloved Woman were voice and vote in General Council, leadership of the Women's Council, the honor of preparing the Black Drink—a tea used in ceremonies to purify—and giving it to warriors before battle, and the right to save a prisoner already condemned to execution. Nan'yehi would exercise all these rights and would serve as her people's sage (wise person) and guide.

Another of the Beloved Woman's duties was as ambassador, or peace negotiator. It is through this role that Ward became a figure in non-Cherokee history. Ward, who had been "apprenticed" as a diplomat at her uncle's side, was a shrewd negotiator who took a realistic view of how to help the Cherokee people survive. She had grown up during a time when continued white settlement on Cherokee lands—in violation of the Royal Proclamation of 1763, in which the British Empire had recognized the rights of Native people—created constant tension in Indian-white relations.

When militant Cherokees prepared to attack illegal white communities on the Watauga River, Ward disapproved of intentionally taking civilian lives. She was able to warn several of the Watauga settlements in time for them to defend themselves or flee. One of the settlers unfortunate enough to be taken alive by the Cherokee warriors was a woman named Mrs. Bean. The captive was sentenced to execution and was actually being tied to a stake when Ward exercised her right to spare condemned captives. Taking the injured Mrs. Bean into her own home to nurse her back to health, Ward learned two skills from her which would have far-reaching consequences for her people.

A time of change

Mrs. Bean, like most "settler women," wove her own cloth. At this time, the Cherokee were wearing a combination of traditional hide (animal skin) clothing and woven cloth purchased from traders. Cherokee people had rough-woven hemp clothing, but it was not as comfortable as clothing made from linen, cotton, or wool. Mrs. Bean taught Ward how to set up a loom, spin thread or yarn, and weave cloth. This skill would make the Cherokee people less dependent on traders, but it also Euro-

peanized the Cherokee in terms of gender roles. Women came to be expected to do the weaving and house chores; as men became farmers in the changing society, women became "housewives."

Another aspect of Cherokee life that changed when Ward saved the life of Mrs. Bean was that of raising animals. The white woman owned dairy cattle, which she took to Ward's house. Ward learned to prepare and use dairy foods, which provided some nourishment even when hunting was bad. However, because of Ward's introduction of dairy farming to the Cherokee, they would begin to amass large herds and farms, which required even more manual labor. This would soon lead the Cherokee into using slave labor. In fact, Ward herself had been "awarded" the black slave of a felled Creek warrior after her victory at the Battle of Taliwa and thus became the first Cherokee slaveowner.

From these accommodations to European-based ways of life, one might get the idea that Ward was selling out the Cherokee people. But her political efforts proved the contrary. She did not seek war, but neither did she counsel peace when she felt compromise would hurt her tribe. Nor was she thoroughly taken in with the ways of European-based society. In 1781 Ward entered into peace talks with Tennessee politician and soldier John Sevier at the Little Pigeon River in present-day Tennessee. She called for peace but warned Sevier to take the treaty back to "his women" for them to ratify. It did not occur to Ward that women did not decide matters of war and peace in the white man's world, as they did in many southeastern tribes. Ward was also a negotiator for the Cherokee at the 1785 signing of the Treaty of Hopewell, the first treaty the Cherokee made with the "new" United States.

By the turn of the nineteenth century, it was already becoming apparent to the Cherokee that the Americans intended to get as much Cherokee land as possible and that the day might come when the Natives would be forced off their homelands. Ward, by now called "Nancy" by the many non-Indians she had befriended, feared that each time the Cherokee voluntarily handed over land, they were encouraging the settlers' appetite for it. She feared that someday their hunger for land would destroy her people. In 1808, the Women's Council, with Ward at its head, made a statement to the Cherokee people urging them to sell no more land. Again, in 1817, when Ward took her seat in council, her desperation was ill concealed. She told the younger people to refuse any more requests for land or to take up arms against the "Americans" if necessary.

The road back to Chota

When she became too aged to make the effort to attend further General Council meetings, Ward sent her walking stick in her place thereafter. Some contemporary sources say she "resigned" her position as Beloved Woman with this action, but the mere absence from council did not indicate the end of her term. Ward was well aware that Cherokee "removal" west of the Mississippi River was almost a foregone conclusion. Rather than face the sorrow of leaving her homeland, she decided to find a way to adapt to the white world.

Nan'yehi had become Nancy Ward when she married the Irish (or Scots-Irish) trader Bryant Ward. By now, her three children were grown, so she was accorded the indulgence of "modern conveniences" because of her advanced age and the great integrity with which she had long discharged her duty to her people. Therefore, when she and Ward took to the innkeeping trade, there was no disrespect voiced toward the Beloved Woman. Their inn was situated near the Mother Town of Chota, on Womankiller Ford of the Ocowee River, in eastern Tennessee.

Ward returned to Chota, her birthplace, in 1824. She was cared for by her son, Fivekiller, who reported seeing a white light leave her body as she died. The light was said to have entered the most sacred mound in the Mother Town. Ward was spared the sight of her people's exile to Indian Territory in 1838, but because her spirit was present at Chota, they knew she had preserved that connection to their eastern home. The last woman to be given the title of Beloved Woman until the late 1980s, Ward remains a powerful symbol for Cherokee women. She is often referred to by feminist scholars as an inspiration and is revered by the Cherokee people of Oklahoma as well as the Eastern Band Cherokees of North Carolina.

Further Reading

Allen, Paula Gunn, *The Sacred Hoop*, Boston: Beacon Press, 1992.

American Indian Women: A Research Guide, edited by Gretchen Bataille and Kathleen Sands, New York: Garland Publishing, 1991.

Green, Rayna, *Women in American Indian Society,* New York: Chelsea House, 1992.

Native American Women, edited by Gretchen M. Bataille, New York: Garland Publishing, 1993.

Sarah Winnemucca

Northern Paiute interpreter, lecturer,
   and diplomat
Born c. 1844, near Humboldt Lake, Utah Territory
   (now Nevada)
Died October 16, 1891, Henry's Lake, Idaho
Also known as Thocmetony or "Shell Flower"

"Oh, can any one imagine my feelings, buried alive, thinking every minute that I was to be unburied and eaten up by the people that my grandfather loved so much?"

Sarah Winnemucca was a skilled interpreter, an army scout, a well-known lecturer, a teacher, and the first American Indian woman to publish a book. The homelands of her people, the Northern Paiutes, extended over parts of present-day Idaho, Nevada, and Oregon. On those lands, the Paiutes hunted, gathered seeds (especially pine nuts), and fished in the rivers and lakes. During Sarah's lifetime, however, they were crowded onto reservations and deprived of much of their land. Winnemucca became nationally known for her fight for her people's rights and for her struggle to keep the peace between her people and the new settlers in the West.

Winnemucca was born near Humboldt Lake in about 1844 in the part of Utah Territory that later became Nevada, the fourth child of Chief Winnemucca (also called Old Winnemucca) and Tuboitonie. They named her Thocmetony, meaning Shell Flower. Later she took the name Sarah and kept it for the rest of her life. Winnemucca's later friendship with white people may have been influenced by her maternal grandfather, the leader of the tribe. He was known as Truckee, from a Paiute word meaning "good" or "all right." The name was given to him by the U.S. army officer, explorer, and politician Captain John Charles Frémont soon after Sarah was born. Truckee and 11 Paiutes went with Frémont to California to help fight Mexican influence there. They returned full of stories of the ways of white people. Truckee, impressed by Frémont and the culture he had seen in California, told his people to welcome the "white brothers."

Buried alive

As more settlers moved west, however, the Paiutes heard horrible stories about the killing of Indians. They apparently also heard a garbled account of the Donner party, who survived a winter trapped in the Sierra Nevada mountains by eating their dead. These stories terrified Sarah. Her fears were intensified by an incident she later described in her book *Life among the Piutes*. It happened while Truckee was in California, and Old Winnemucca had become chief. One morning, hearing that white men were coming, the entire tribe fled in terror. Tuboitonie, who was carrying a baby on her back and pulling Sarah by the hand, found that she couldn't keep up. She and another mother decided to hide their older children by partially burying them in the ground and arranging branches to shade their faces. Winnemucca wrote, "Oh, can any one imagine my feelings, *buried alive,* thinking every minute that I was to be unburied and eaten up by the people that my grandfather loved so much?"

Sarah Winnemucca

At nightfall, the mothers returned and dug up the girls; it was an experience Winnemucca never forgot. It was a long time before she would look at white people or forgive her grandfather for loving them. Finding that the white men had set fire to the tribe's stores of food and that all their winter supply was gone, Chief Winnemucca could no longer agree with his father-in-law that the white men were his "brothers."

Winnemucca's distrust of white folk lasted for some time. In the spring of 1850, Truckee traveled again to California, taking 50 people, including Tuboitonie and her children. Carrying a letter of commendation given him by Frémont, Truckee was able to get a friendly reception and occasional gifts of food or clothing from the settlers they met. Winnemucca herself hid from the strangers, refusing to speak to or to look at them. Her attitude changed, however, after she fell sick with poison oak and was nursed back to health by a white woman. Although she never came to believe as strongly as her grandfather in the goodness of the "white brothers," she did try to understand them and to learn about their customs, without losing touch with her own traditions.

Serves as interpreter and scout as the wars begin

During the time she spent in California, Winnemucca showed quite an ability for languages, learning English, Spanish, and several Indian tongues. She also came in close contact with white people when she, her mother, and her sisters started to work in the houses of white families. When Sarah was 13, she lived with her younger sister Elma in the home of Major William M. Ormsby, a trader. Ormsby's wife, Margaret, and their daughter taught the girls to sew and cook. They became quite proficient at English and began learning to read and write.

As contacts between whites and Indians increased, Winnemucca often served as interpreter for her father when he met with Indian agents and army officers and in intertribal councils. In 1875, she was hired as interpreter for the Indian agent S. B. (Sam) Parrish at

Malheur Reservation in Washington, which had been established three years earlier. In 1868 Winnemucca served as interpreter at Camp McDermit while her father and almost 500 of his followers lived there under the protection of Captain Jerome and the U.S. Army. Winnemucca trusted Parrish and Jerome, believing they treated her people fairly.

Winnemucca, along with her brother Natchez, served as a scout at Camp McDermit. During the Bannock War in 1878 she met her greatest challenge as a scout. On her way to Washington, D.C., where she hoped to get help for her people, she learned that the Bannock tribe was warring with the whites and that some Paiutes, her father among them, were being held by the Bannocks.

On the morning of June 13, Winnemucca and two other Paiutes left Camp McDermit for the Bannock camp, arriving at nightfall of the second day. Wrapped in a blanket, her hair unbraided so she wouldn't be recognized, she crept into the camp. There she found her father, her brother Lee, and his wife, Mattie, among those held captive. They escaped during the night but were soon pursued by the Bannocks. Sarah and her sister-in-law raced their horses to get help, arriving back at Sheep Ranch at 5:30 on June 15. She rode a distance of 223 miles. "It was," Winnemucca said, "the hardest work I ever did for the army."

Winnemucca was poorly rewarded for her hard work on the U.S. Army's behalf. Both she and Mattie served as scouts during the Bannock War, after which the Paiutes were to be returned to Malheur Reservation in Toppenish, Washington. To Winnemucca's distress, however, they were ordered to be taken to Yakima Reservation on the other side of the Columbia River, a distance of about 350 miles. It was winter, and the Paiutes did not have adequate clothing. Many people died during the terrible trip, and others, including her sister-in-law Mattie, died soon after.

Writes and speaks out for her people

Over the years the situation worsened. Winnemucca sent messages, complaints, and entreaties to anyone she thought might help. She traveled to San Francisco and spoke in great halls, telling of the mistreatment of her people by the Indian agents and by the government. She was labeled "The Princess Sarah" in the *San Francisco Chronicle* and her lecture was described as "unlike anything ever before heard in the civilized world—eloquent, pathetic, tragical at times; at others her quaint anecdotes, sarcasms and wonderful mimicry surprised the audience again and again into bursts of laughter and rounds of applause."

News of her lectures reached Washington, and in 1880 she was invited to meet with the president. Together with Chief Winnemucca and her brother Natchez, she met with Secretary of the Interior Carl Schurz and, very briefly, with President Rutherford B. Hayes, nineteenth president of the United States. However, Sarah was not allowed to lecture or talk to reporters in Washington, and the small group were given promises that were not kept.

American educator Elizabeth Palmer Peabody and her sister, Mary Peabody Mann, the widow of the educator Horace Mann, helped arrange speaking engagements for Winnemucca in Boston and many other cities in the East. With their encouragement, she wrote many letters, at least one magazine article, and a book. Her friends also supported Winnemucca's dream of establishing an all-Indian school; she had been an assistant teacher on the Malheur Reservation, though her formal education was limited to three weeks at a California Catholic school. In 1884, she founded the Peabody School for Indian Children near Lovelock, Nevada, on land that had been given to Natchez. It was to be a model school where Indian children would be taught their own language and culture and learn English as well. Unable to get government funding or approval, however, she had to close the school after four years.

Her death

After brief marriages to First Lieutenant Edward Bartlett and to Joseph Satwaller, Winnemucca married Lewis H. Hopkins in 1881. He accompanied her on her eastern lecture tours. Hopkins died of tuberculosis at their ranch at Lovelock on October 18, 1887. Winnemucca's own life was cut short a few years later. On October 16, 1891, she died at the home of her sister Elma at Henry's Lake, Idaho, probably of tuberculosis as well.

Although Winnemucca died believing that she had failed to make the changes she worked for, she has not been forgotten. Many books have been written about her life and accomplishments, several especially for young people. The book she wrote in 1883, with the encouragement and editorial assistance of Mary Peabody Mann, *Life among the Piutes: Their Wrongs and Claims,* was republished in 1969 and remains an important source book on the history and culture of the Paiutes.

In Nevada, on the McDermit Indian Reservation, there is a historical marker, erected in 1971, honoring Winnemucca with the words "she was a believer in the brotherhood of mankind." General Oliver Otis Howard wrote that she "did our government great service, and if I could tell you but a tenth part of all she willingly did to help the white settlers and her own people to live peaceably together, I am sure you would think, as I do, that the name of Thocmetony should have a place beside the name of Pocahontas in the history of our country." The name of Sarah Winnemucca, as General Howard hoped, stands high among those Native Americans who have fought for the rights of their people.

Further Reading

Canfield, Gae Whitney, *Sarah Winnemucca of the Northern Paiutes,* Norman: University of Oklahoma Press, 1983.

Gehm, Katherine, *Sarah Winnemucca: Most Extraordinary Woman of the Paiute Nation,* O'Sullivan Woodside & Co., 1975.

Gridley, Marion E., *American Indian Women,* Hawthorn, 1974.

Scordato, Ellen, *Sarah Winnemucca: Northern Paiute Writer and Diplomat,* New York: Chelsea House, 1992.

Winnemucca, Sarah, *Life among the Piutes: Their Wrongs and Claims,* edited by Mrs. Horace Mann, privately printed, 1883; reprinted, Chalfant Press, 1969.

Winnemucca, Sarah, "The Way Agents Get Rich," in *Native American Testimony: A Chronicle of Indian-White Relations from Prophecy to the Present, 1492-1992,* edited by Peter Nabokov, with a foreword by Vine Deloria, Jr., New York: Penguin Books, 1992.

Wovoka

Numu (Northern Paiute) spiritual leader
Born c. 1856, Pyramid Lake, Nevada
Died September 29, 1932
Also known as Jack Wilson

God, he insisted, told him of a transformation that would occur by the spring of 1891, when the deceased would again be alive, the game would flourish once more, and the European settlers would vanish from the earth.

Inspired by a personal vision—and adapting the visions of others—Wovoka created the Ghost Dance religious movement of the late 1880s. A distorted interpretation of his beliefs and teachings contributed to the events leading to the Wounded Knee Massacre in late December 1890. Wovoka's impact on the local Paiute people and Native Americans throughout the West continued beyond his death in 1932. Until 1990 information about Wovoka's life was scattered, and for a century he has been the subject of both speculation and misrepresentation. According to biographer Michael Hittman, Wovoka was both "a great man and a fake."

Wovoka was born about 1856 and grew up in Smith Valley or Mason Valley, Nevada, one of four sons of Tavid, also known as Numo-tibo's, a well-known medicine man who was a "weather doctor," or controller of the climate. Like his father, Wovoka learned this skill and also became a leader of traditional dances. At about the age of 14, he was sent to live with and work for the Scotch-English family of David Wilson. During this period he acquired the names Jack Wilson and Wovoka, meaning "Wood Cutter." Both Wovoka's birth parents survived into the twentieth century.

Wovoka grew up in a region where travelling preachers were common and Mormonism prevailed, and he was influenced by a variety of religions. The pious Presbyterian values of the Wilson family clearly affected him: Mr. Wilson read the Bible each day before work. There is also a possibility that Wovoka travelled to California and the Pacific Northwest, where he may have had contact with Wanapam prophet **Smohalla** (see entry) and Coast Salish spiritual leader John Slocum. At about the age of 20 he married Tumm, also known as Mary Wilson. They raised three daughters; at least two other children died.

The Ghost Dance religion

Wovoka was recognized as having some of his father's qualities as a mystic. A long-time acquaintance described the young Paiute as "a tall, well proportioned man with piercing eyes, regular features, a deep voice and a calm and dignified mien [manner]"; a local census agent referred to him as "intelligent." Wovoka was known to be a temperate man during his entire life—meaning he abstained from alcohol and other drugs.

The turning point in Wovoka's life came in the late 1880s. In December 1888, suffering from illness that may have been scarlet fever, he went into a coma for two days. Observer Ed Dyer said, "His body was as stiff as a board." Because Wovoka's recovery had corresponded with the total eclipse

Wovoka

of the sun on January 1, 1889, he was credited by some for the sun's return, and thereby became—in their eyes—the savior of the universe.

After this apparent near death experience, Wovoka proclaimed that he had a spiritual vision in which God gave him specific instructions for the living. God, he insisted, told him of a transformation that would occur by the spring of 1891, when the deceased would again be alive, the game would flourish once more, and the European settlers would vanish from the earth. He had also been instructed to share power with the president of the East, Benjamin Harrison.

Until the future time when the apocalypse would occur, Wovoka counselled the living to work for their people and attempt to live a morally pure life. The plan for the future could only be assured if believers followed the special patterns and messages of the Ghost Dance, which Wovoka taught his fol-

lowers. The dance involved special costumes—ghost shirts—as well as ghost songs. The dancer typically entered, or at least seemed to enter, a trance state; this state represented a "death" that supposedly gave the dancer access to the spiritual realm. He would return with word of the dead ancestors and predictions of the world to come after the whites were swept away.

Another Paiute prophet, Wodziwob ("White Hair"), had reported a vision in the 1870s that prefigured Wovoka's. In Wodziwob's vision, a huge train would carry home all the dead ancestors of the Native people, wiping out the United States and heralding the return of the Great Spirit and the Indians' old way of life. This was the basis for the first wave of the Ghost Dance movement. Yet Wovoka brought new life to this flagging faith with his prophecies, and his familiarity with different religions added fire and versatility to his preaching.

Message begins to spread

While local believers already depended on Wovoka, in his capacity as a "weather doctor," to bring much-needed rain, his new message quickly spread throughout the western territory of North America. Before long, representatives of more than 30 tribes made a pilgrimage to visit Wovoka and learn the secrets of the Ghost Dance. Whites, on the other hand, generally didn't know what to make of him. A Pyramid Lake agent dismissed Wovoka in 1890 as "a peaceable, industrious, but lunatic Pah-Ute," who "proclaimed himself an aboriginal Jesus who was to redeem the Red Man." The first known formal interview with Wovoka was conducted by U.S. Army Indian Scout

Arthur I. Chapman, who had been sent to find the "Indian who impersonated Christ!" Chapman—who may have expected a crazy blasphemer—was evidently not disturbed by what he found.

The most powerful evidence of Wovoka's impact could be found near the Badlands of South Dakota. Regional Sioux delegates, including Short Bull and Kicking Bear, returned with the message that wearing a Ghost Dance shirt would make warriors invulnerable to injury. Among those who accepted the assurance was the famous chief, **Sitting Bull** (see entry). The conditions in the Badlands were desperate for the Sioux: the buffalo were vanishing; the Native residents were being pushed onto diminishing reservation lands as the designated area was opened to white settlement in 1889. The urgency of their circumstances probably caused the Lakota (Sioux) to misinterpret the teachings of Wovoka—which called for passivity and patiently awaiting divine intervention—as a call to rid the land of white settlers.

Fear spread among white settlers and the military in the region, who felt that the already uncertain future of the newly established states of North and South Dakota was further threatened by "the Ghost Dance craze." Memories of recent Indian uprisings—notably the 1862 attacks on white settlements by Minnesota Sioux and the 1876 defeat of U.S. troops at Little Bighorn by the Sioux and Cheyenne and other Indian warriors led by **Crazy Horse** (see entry)—were still strong.

Unsuccessful attempts to enforce a ban of the Ghost Dance among the Lakota led a government agent to order the arrest of **Sitting Bull** (see entry), a respected Lakota leader who supported the Ghost Dance movement. This set off a chain of events that resulted in the deaths of Sitting Bull and several others. Ghost Dance believers then headed for the Pine Ridge Reservation in South Dakota, hoping to find sanctuary. An overwhelming force of 470 soldiers confronted them at Wounded Knee Creek. Gunfire broke out, and over 200 Native Americans—many of them women and children—were killed. The next day, without ceremony, frozen bodies stripped of their Ghost Dance garments were tossed into a mass grave. For many this symbolized the end of resistance.

"He was riding a tiger"

There is certainly no evidence that Wovoka intentionally promoted the type of confrontation that occurred at Wounded Knee. He later referred to his idea of an impenetrable shirt as a "joke." His associate Ed Dyer evaluated the situation: "I was thoroughly convinced that Jack Wilson had at no time attempted deliberately to stir up trouble. He never advocated violence. Violence was contrary to his very nature. Others seized upon his prophecies and stunts, and made more of them than he intended ... in a way, once started, he was riding a tiger. It was difficult to dismount."

Within a few days of the atrocities at Wounded Knee, the local newspapers in Wovoka's region expressed concern about the presence of armed Paiutes, especially since these Indians had lost their land to whites and apparently expected to get it back. Government operatives also expressed concern, seeing in this Nevada-based "Messiah Craze" a pathetic source of hope to a people destined to lose their world to the tide of migrating whites. Their policy toward Wovoka—generally referred to by whites as Jack Wilson—was to ignore him; they felt confident that the "craze" would pass soon enough.

The middle years, 1890-1920

The role of Wovoka in the years after Wounded Knee has been generally overlooked. But it is clear that he did not fade into oblivion or hesitate to use his unusual fame and powers. An Indian Agent reported in June 1912 that "Jack Wilson is still held in reverence by Indians in various parts of the country, and he is still regarded by them as a great medicine man."

Although Wovoka had established a reputation as a strong, reliable worker as a young man, the fame he earned through the Ghost Dance phenomenon led him to other occupations during the balance of his life. Attempts to bring him to both the World's Columbian Exposition in Chicago in 1893 and the Midwinter Fair in San Francisco in 1904 apparently failed, but he made trips to reservations in Wyoming, Montana, and Kansas, as well as the former Indian territory of Oklahoma. Some trips lasted as long as six months. He was showered with gifts and as much as $1,200 in cash on a single trip. In 1924, historian-actor Tim McCoy delivered Wovoka by limousine to the set of a movie he was making in northern California. There he was treated with absolute reverence by Arapahos who had been hired for the film.

While at home Wovoka practiced another enterprise. With the aid of his friend Ed Dyer and others he replied to numerous letters and requests for everything from miracles to clothing he had worn. He charged for certain items; conveniently, Dyer, his frequent secretary, was also a supplier. One of the most popular items was a hat that had been worn by "the Prophet." The usual price to a correspondent was $20. Even Dyer admitted that what this supposed miracle worker charged for such souvenirs was outrageously high. Surprisingly, none of the response letters that Wovoka dictated have been found. Yet despite his relative notoriety and enterprise, Wovoka continued to live a simple life. As late as 1917, he was living in a two-room house built of rough boards.

Minor role in U.S. politics

Wovoka also had an interesting role in the "political" world. As early as November 1890, an ex-Bureau of Indian Affairs employee suggested that an official invitation to Washington, D.C., for Wovoka and some of his followers "might have a tendency to quiet this craze." Wovoka's early vision, of course, predicted that he would share national leadership with then President Benjamin Harrison.

In 1916, one newspaper reported that Wovoka was considering a visit to President Woodrow Wilson to help "terminate the murderous war in Europe." (Wovoka's grandson, following the prediction of his grandfather, became a pilot and died a hero in World War II.) In the 1920s, Wovoka was photographed at a Warren G. Harding rally. Perhaps the selection of **Charles Curtis** (see entry), a Sac and Fox from Kansas, as vice president of the United States appeared to Wovoka to be a sign of the predicted time when white people would disappear from the continent and Indians would once again rule their lands. Wovoka sent Curtis a message on March 3, 1929, stating, "We are glad that you are Vice President and we hope some day you will be President."

It is impossible to make an absolute judgement about the real talents of this Nevada mystic, to determine which of his activities were the product of true inspiration and which were merely a display of skill. Accounts of his accomplishments include claims that his prophesies came true, that he raised the dead, predicted weather, made rain, survived gunshot wounds, and produced ice in the middle of summer. Dyer reflected that it is "very human to believe what we want to believe."

Final years

It appears that Wovoka retained his faith in his visions and practices to the very end. His services as a medicine man were in demand until shortly before his death on September 29, 1932, from enlarged prostate cystitis. His wife of over 50 years had died just one month before. Yerington Paiute tribal member Irene Thompson expressed a local reaction: "When he died, many people thought Wovoka will come back again."

A Reno newspaper, although giving a lengthy account of his life, basically dismissed him as a fraud: "'Magic' worked with the aid of a bullet-proof vest; white men's pills and some good 'breaks' in the weather made him the most influential figure of his time among the Indians." But Scott Peterson, a modern scholar, argues that if Wovoka had not "set a date for the apocalypse ... the

Ghost Dance, with its vision of a brighter tomorrow, might still very well be a vital force in the world today."

In fact, elements of the Ghost Dance religion pervaded the practices of many tribes even after the tragedy of Wounded Knee. A form of the original dance is still performed by some Lakota today. Wovoka, meanwhile, remains an interesting, slightly mysterious figure. He has often been labeled a con artist and a religious fanatic, yet many remember him as a vital force in renewing the pride, energy, and hope of his people—and as a challenge to white settlement on tribal lands.

Further Reading

Brown, Dee, *Bury My Heart at Wounded Knee; An Indian History of the American West,* New York: Holt, Rinehart and Winston, 1970.

Hittman, Michael, *Wovoka and the Ghost Dance, a Source Book,* Carson City, NV: Grace Dangberg Foundation, 1990.

Murray, Earl, *Song of Wovoka,* New York: Tom Doherty Associates, 1992.

Peterson, Scott, *Native American Prophecies,* New York: Paragon House, 1990.

Rosebud Yellow Robe

Sioux storyteller, writer, and educator
Born February 26, 1907
Died October 5, 1992

"When I first lectured to public school classes in New York, many of the smaller children hid under their desks, for they knew from the movies what a blood-thirsty scalping Indian might do to them."

R osebud Yellow Robe was born February 26, 1907, the oldest of three daughters of the prominent family of Chauncey and Lily Yellow Robe. Throughout her life, she worked to introduce Native American culture and traditions to others. She was best known as a storyteller, repeating her father's stories to schoolchildren for over 20 years as the director of the Indian Village project at Jones Beach on Long Island, New York.

Chauncey Yellow Robe was the son of the Brulé Sioux leader Tasinagi (Yellow Robe) and Tahcawin (Female Deer), the niece of the great Sioux leader and warrior **Sitting Bull** (see entry). Yellow Robe's father was only six years old in June 1876, at the time of the Battle of the Little Bighorn, where the army led by General George Custer was defeated by Sioux and Cheyenne forces. Chauncey Yellow Robe often told the story of watching the warriors return from battle. He was also one of the first Sioux students to attend Carlisle Indian School in Pennsyl-

vania, and he spent his life educating other Indian students. At the time of Rosebud Yellow Robe's birth, her father was in charge of discipline at the United States Indian School at Rapid City, South Dakota; her mother was a nurse. Chauncey Yellow Robe instilled in his daughters a love of education, and each became successful in a career.

Rosebud wrote in a letter in 1975 that she and her sisters owed their success to their parents. "We were very fortunate in having parents who gave us great pride in and knowledge of our family background," she declared in the letter. "My father was very active in American Indian society. As in old times, he told us the folklore, legends and history of the tribe. He was anxious to keep alive the good of the old culture and combine it with the good of the new. He taught us that we could not isolate ourselves from people. He urged us to always seek knowledge from our own and from other friends we would meet."

"Beautiful Indian maiden"

Yellow Robe was educated in a one-room schoolhouse a mile from her home until she attended high school in Rapid City, South Dakota. As one of the first Indian students to attend the University of South Dakota in the late 1920s, she impressed the other students with her performances at "Strollers," the annual student stage production. Her first national recognition was in 1927 when the thirtieth president of the United States, Calvin Coolidge, visited the Black Hills of South Dakota for the summer. On August 4, during a special ceremony, Coolidge was named an honorary member of the Sioux tribe; Yellow Robe placed the Sioux warbonnet on the president's head and later led him and Mrs. Coolidge back to their seats. Rosebud's grace and beauty charmed reporters, who commented on the "beautiful Indian maiden." One of the newspapermen covering the event, A. E. Seymour, married Rosebud within a few years, and they moved to New York.

Yellow Robe's father also received attention after the ceremony and was given a role in the film *The Silent Enemy.* He resigned from the Indian School to research and work on the movie. In 1929, he returned briefly to Rapid City and was convinced to pose in his film costume for a photographer, Della B. Vik. He returned to New York with a severe cold which developed into pneumonia and died April 6, 1930.

Vik also photographed Rosebud on several occasions. Mildred Fielder quotes one of Vik's letters, describing Yellow Robe as "exceptionally beautiful. I photographed her many times. Chauncey was always present even when I photographed her atop Hangman's Hill, and another pose of her down on her knees by Rapid Creek looking at her reflection in the water. Rosebud had all the full blood Sioux looks and in a very refined way. She was exceedingly graceful and naturally gracious." The famed movie director Cecil B. de Mille was also struck by Rosebud, calling her "most beautiful."

Continues father's work in education

From the 1930s through the 1950s, Yellow Robe worked in the field of education, teaching schoolchildren about Indian life. A 1975 article in the *Rapid City Journal*

quoted her recollections: "When I first lectured to public school classes in New York, many of the smaller children hid under their desks, for they knew from the movies what a blood-thirsty scalping Indian might do to them." In the course of her long teaching career she met thousands of children, told them Indian stories, showed them her costumes, and played games with them. Many New Yorkers got their first impression of a real Indian from her work.

Becomes an author

Yellow Robe also educated Americans through radio, television, and writing. During the mid-1930s, she wrote and read her own scripts on CBS radio. According to an obituary in the *New York Times,* Yellow Robe and the radio and film innovator Orson Welles worked on several dramatic shows during the 1940s, and she may have inspired Wells to make "Rosebud" the last word uttered by the protagonist (main character) in his classic film *Citizen Kane.* In the 1950s Yellow Robe appeared regularly on an NBC program for children and other TV shows. Her first book, *Album of the American Indian,* was published in 1969. Ten years later *Tonweya and the Eagles,* which compiled the stories she had learned from her father, appeared. It was later published internationally in translation, and excerpts from it were included in textbooks.

John Milton of the University of South Dakota recommended Rosebud for an honorary doctorate degree. In his recommendation letter he praised her for doing justice to her oral (unwritten) sources in her writing. In May 1989, the university awarded the degree to Yellow Robe, honoring her as a gifted communicator "who, through her talents and native background, promotes an authentic view of Indian life and character and who is able through her techniques of cultural exchange to pass her scholarly knowledge on to mixed audiences of young and old which numbered many thousands throughout the years."

Rosebud Yellow Robe died of cancer on October 5, 1992. In 1993 the MacMillan/McGraw-Hill School Publishing Company released a textbook in her honor, *Write Idea.* The National Dance Institute's event of the following year, *Rosebud's Song,* was presented "in honor of and inspired by Rosebud Yellow Robe, a woman of the Lakota nation who devoted her life to teaching children through storytelling." Her collection of ethnographic materials has been donated to the W. H. Over State Museum in Vermillion, South Dakota.

Further Reading

Fielder, Mildred, *Sioux Indian Leaders,* Seattle: Superior Publishing Company, 1975.

Moses, George, "Rosebud's Talents Remembered," *Rapid City Journal,* November 22, 1992, p. D11.

Yellow Robe, Rosebud, *Album of the American Indian,* New York: Franklin Watts, 1969.

Yellow Robe, Rosebud, *Tonweya and the Eagles and Other Lakota Indian Tales,* New York: Dial Press, 1979.

Peterson Zah

Navajo leader
Born December 2, 1937, Low Mountain, Arizona

"Someday the coal, oil, and gas are going to be gone. What's going to happen to the Navajo children then?"

Peterson Zah has devoted his life to the service of the Navajo people. He has been active in education and law, in resolving conflicts between the Navajo and the Hopi, and in combatting the depletion of natural resources on the reservation. In 1990 he was elected as the first president of the Navajo Nation. He also received the Humanitarian Award from the city of Albuquerque, New Mexico, and an honorary doctorate from The College of Santa Fe in Santa Fe, New Mexico.

Traditional background

Zah was born in 1937 in Low Mountain, Arizona. His birthplace was part of the disputed joint-use area, which in 1882 had been assigned to both the Navajo and Hopi peoples by the U.S. government for their joint use and had been the cause of conflict between the two groups ever since. Henry and Mae Multine Zah raised their son to respect his heritage. In his addresses Zah often quotes his mother, whom he considers his greatest teacher. She speaks no English and is one of the 125,000 who are still fluent in the Navajo language. Zah recalls that his mother always told him to use his Navajo culture "as a canoe with which to stay afloat." The metaphor, so

Peterson Zah

out of place in a desert setting, is over six centuries old and comes from Athapaskan ancestors who migrated from the north to New Mexico perhaps 1,000 years ago. Zah, as an educator, is attempting to restore the ancient Navajo language on the reservation.

Zah attended Phoenix Indian School, in Phoenix, Arizona, until 1960, then went to Arizona State University in Tempe on a basketball scholarship; he graduated with a bachelor's degree in education in 1963. He then worked for the Arizona Vocational

Education Department in Phoenix as a journeyman (intermediate-level) carpenter, instructing adults in employable skills, and later joined in the domestic peace corps, Volunteers in Service to America (VISTA). Zah served as field coordinator of the training center at Arizona State University at Tempe from 1965 to 1967. In this assignment he used his considerable gifts of cultural mediation, helping people with different customs and beliefs to cooperate with each other. Part of his job was to teach cultural sensitivity to those volunteers who would work on Indian reservations.

From 1967 to 1981, Zah was executive director of the people's legal services at Window Rock, Arizona. This nonprofit organization, chartered by the state of Arizona, was called DNA: *Dinebeuna Nahiilna Be Agaditiahe,* or "Lawyers Who Contribute to the Economic Revitalization of the People." During his decade directing DNA, Zah was in charge of more than 100 employees at nine reservation offices, as well as 33 tribal court advocates and 34 attorneys. He saw several cases reach the U.S. Supreme Court, which helped establish Indian sovereignty (self-rule) and other important Native rights. This grass-roots (local level) legal aid system offered hope to impoverished Native Americans who would have otherwise had no access to the law courts.

Teaches Navajo language and culture

Misguided U.S. educational policies have hindered the Navajo for decades. In the years since the government's military conquest of the tribe, reservation agents have tried to send children away to Bureau of Indian Affairs (BIA) boarding schools to speed their assimilation, or blending into European American culture. Mission schools run by various religious denominations competed with public schools in towns neighboring the reservations for Indian students. By 1946, only one Navajo child out of four was enrolled in any of these schools. The Window Rock Public School District compiled evidence that led to significant changes: a more useful curriculum, or design of studies, and parental involvement increased enrollment.

Zah was elected in 1972 to the first all-Navajo school board at Window Rock and became its president in 1973. He hired more Navajo teachers, installed a Navajo curriculum, developed Navajo textbooks, renewed religious ceremonies, and restored knowledge of tribal history. Zah believed that to preserve the language, it must be taught in all classes, including science and math, before English was introduced, because the Navajo language conveys concepts that cannot be translated. The ecological wisdom of the elders, who sought to preserve the harmony of the natural world, is contained in their native vocabulary. For example, to live as a Navajo, one must "speak the language of the earth."

Materials were created in a Navajo spelling system devised by Oliver LaFarge and John Peabody Harrington; medicine men were invited into classrooms to lecture; students set up a local television station and published a Navajo newspaper. One of the Rock Point graduates, Rex Lee Jim, went on to Princeton University in New Jersey and then returned to the reservation to compose a libretto, or script, for the first Navajo opera and to try to found a school for the performing arts on the reservation. By the 1990s, there were twice as many applicants for college-level professional training as tribal scholarship funds could support.

In 1987 Zah began fund-raising for a group who solicited people in the private (nongovernment) sector for scholarships for Navajo students. The Navajo Education and Scholarship Foundation enabled many impoverished young people to attend school. In 1989, Zah founded the Native American Consulting Services to obtain congressional assistance for constructing new schools on the reservation. From 1989 to 1990, he was director of the western regional office of the Save the Children Federation.

Becomes tribal chair

From 1983 to 1987, Zah served as chair of the Navajo Tribal Council at Window Rock. The council meets in an eight-sided stone building modeled after the traditional dwelling known as a hogan. There, the elected delegates govern the largest reservation in the United States—about 24,000 square miles or close to 16 million acres in Arizona, New Mexico, and southeastern Utah. These badly eroded lands house over 200,000 Navajo, whose population is increasing at the rate of more than 2 percent per year. Zah invested his energies in reforming education as one way of coping with poverty.

Elected president of the Navajo Nation

From 1990 to 1994, Zah served as the first elected president in the history of the Navajo Nation. His childhood friend and classmate Ivan Sidney became the tribal leader of the Hopi; the two tried to work out the difficulties of government-imposed relocations that occurred in the dispute over land between the Hopi and Navajo. A film, *Broken Rainbow,* was made about this Hopi-Navajo conflict. Underneath the disputed land is coal, and each year the Peabody Coal Company extracts seven million tons from this area, ruining the landscape and polluting the air. The two longtime friends worked to resolve past hostilities by ordering a suspension of all lawsuits over land in April 1983 and by pledging cooperation in all areas of mutual concern, including negotiations of future contracts with mining companies.

Zah's administration has been grievously tested. Just as plans had been drawn up and sites approved for the construction of six sorely needed hospital facilities, the government announced a 30 percent cut in health services. While Zah was in Washington, D.C., attempting to reverse this policy, an outbreak of hanta virus afflicted his people. A mysterious rodent-carried disease, the hanta virus was responsible for the deaths of 16 people on and around the reservation, most of them Navajo. Epidemiologists (scientists and physicians who study disease epidemics) from the Centers for Disease Control worked frantically to find the causes of the mysterious deaths occurring on the reservation.

Also, an extraordinary number of miners who had worked for Kerr-McGee extracting uranium died of anaplastic cancer of the lungs. The Atomic Energy Commission, which bought the uranium ore, refused to clean up the radioactive waste that had begun to seep into the drinking water.

Drilling for petroleum and gas by Mobil, Standard Oil, and Exxon has poisoned the ground, desecrated (treated irreverently) sacred sites, and polluted the air. The strip mining of coal subjects the Navajo to a perpetual fallout of toxic fumes from the power plants. According to Stephen Trimble, Zah has tried to warn his people to think of the future when these nonrenewable energy sources have been depleted: "Someday the coal, oil, and gas are going to be gone. What's going to happen to the Navajo children then? Pete Zah won't be around then ... you have to think about the future."

Zah lives in Window Rock, Arizona, with his wife, Rosalind (Begay), and his children, Elaine, Eileen, and Keeyonnie.

Further Reading

Matthiessen, Peter, "Four Corners," in *Indian Country*, New York: Penguin, 1984.

"Navajo Education," in *Handbook of North American Indians; Southwest,* Volume 10, edited by Alfonso Ortiz, Washington, DC: Smithsonian Institution, 1983.

Trimble, Stephen, "The Navajo," in *The People,* Santa Fe, NM: School of American Research Press, 1993, pp. 121-94.

INDEX BY
FIELD OF ENDEAVOR

Volume number appears in **bold.**